Persons, Rights, and the Moral Community

Persons, Rights, and the Moral Community

LOREN E. LOMASKY

New York   *Oxford*
OXFORD UNIVERSITY PRESS

Oxford University Press

Oxford   New York   Toronto
Delhi   Bombay   Calcutta   Madras   Karachi
Petaling Jaya   Singapore   Hong Kong   Tokyo
Nairobi   Dar es Salaam   Cape Town
Melbourne   Auckland

and associated companies in
Berlin   Ibadan

First published in 1987 by Oxford University Press, Inc.,
200 Madison Avenue, New York, New York 10016

First issued as an Oxford University Press paperback, 1990

Oxford is a registered trademark of Oxford University Press

Library of Congress Cataloging-in-Publication Data

Lomasky, Loren E.
Persons, Rights and the Moral Community

Includes Index
1. Civil rights.   2. Liberalism.   I. Title.
JC571.L595   1987   323.4   86-18011
ISBN 0-19-504209-3
ISBN 0-19-506474-7 (PBK.)

2   4   6   8   10   9   7   5   3   1

Printed in the United States of America

To Louis, Elizabeth, Linda, Alexander—

members all of the moral community

Preface

Rights are valuable because they can be invoked. They become more valuable, though, if we understand them. Who are the rights holders, what rights do they have, and why? Those are the questions I set myself in this book. Surely they are questions appropriate for moral philosophers to examine. While philosophers are by no means barred from *first-order rights discourse,* the claiming of rights for themselves and others, they can and should do more. *Second-order rights discourse* involves development of the grounding theory on which first-order rights claims are ultimately based. This book is primarily an attempt to develop that grounding theory. To the extent that we come to hold a better grip on the provenance of rights, first-order rights discourse becomes more solid.

Rights without foundations are treacherous entities. How are we to adjudicate between contending rights—or "rights"? In the absence of a coherent second-order theory, the task is more than Herculean; it is Sisyphean. Contemporary practice both within and outside the academy bears out this diagnosis. Rights are so easy to claim, but so terribly difficult to justify. Naked appeals to intuition or moral insight too often supplant analysis, and, not surprisingly, one person's right is another's fantasy. The result can be pleasing only to the moral sceptic.

The first step toward making sense of rights is to understand how they can be possible. If some moral commodity—happiness, liberty, equality, or whatever—is valuable, then isn't more of it necessarily better than less? If so, then that moral commodity (or perhaps an appropriately weighted average of several) should, it might appear, be maximized. Maximization is the keystone of utilitarian ethics and its modern counterpart, cost-benefit analysis. These theories take as evident the "more is better than less" dictum.

viii PREFACE

Accordingly, they have no place for robust rights that stand athwart unconstrained maximization. At most, they allow rights to enter through the back
door as a concession to human moral frailty. Because we don't do a very
good job of dispassionately and accurately maximizing the good, acknowledgment of rights is accepted as a "second best" strategy. By pretending
that there are rights that must constrain conduct, we end up with better
conduct than if each person were free to maximize the good according to
his own lights. Or so the story goes.

Can rights be more than this? That is, can it be rational deliberately to
eschew maximization of an overall good? The question was brought to my
attention by Thomas Nagel, director of a 1977 National Endowment for the
Humanities Summer Seminar in Recent Ethical Theory that I was privileged
to attend. I have been chewing on responses ever since. The existence of
this book is a direct product of his insightful teaching and the generosity
of the Endowment. Along the way, I have been the fortunate beneficiary
of much additional support. Periods of uninterrupted reflection and writing
were provided by the Reason Foundation, the Institute for Humane Studies,
and the Graduate School of the University of Minnesota. The Liberty Fund
of Indianapolis, Indiana, has graciously included me within a cornucopia of
their activities. No other organization equals their commitment to the support of the study of the intellectual underpinnings of free societies. My debt
to each of these groups is profound.

No less significant are the debts I owe individuals. I have been enriched
by discussion with more people than I can here list individually. Henry
Veatch, though, is due special thanks. He read and commented at length on
an initial draft of the manuscript. Although he and I differ on some fundamental matters of ethical theory, his persistent challenges have sharpened
my thinking on innumerable points. A philosopher is fortunate indeed to
have so skilled an interlocutor, especially if he is someone personally gra-
cious but who never pulls a punch.

I was invited in 1982 by the Social Philosophy & Policy Center of Bowl-
ing Green State University to present my preliminary results at their Conference on Human Rights. The timing was fortuitous. The gathering provided
an incentive to crystallize my previously disorganized musings and to receive useful criticism from the other participants. That presentation subsequently was published as "Personal Projects as the Foundation for Basic
Rights," *Social Philosophy & Policy* 1 (Spring 1984), pp. 33–55.

References in the text only partially indicate those from whose writings I
have benefited. I have chosen not to burden the book with an intimidating
welter of footnotes. That is both because I want it to be readable by those
who are not aficionados of scholarly paraphernalia and because I am, at

best, an indifferent cataloger. So, those who wish to find a comprehensive bibliography of the relevant literature will have to look elsewhere. Instead, I have aimed to note only those sources from which I directly and substantially took my bearings. Even so, there are many. I hereby apologize to those other persons from whom I have learned but who are not otherwise acknowledged.

Moral philosophy is burgeoning. As I was writing, new and important discussions emerged. This book would have been delayed, perhaps forever, had I attempted to respond to each significant contribution. I have instead, for the most part, kept a discreet silence. One book in particular deserves special mention. Derek Parfit's *Reasons and Persons* (Oxford: The Clarendon Press, 1984) is an enormously rich and stimulating investigation that poses clear challenges to the sort of position I wish to advance. Although *Reasons and Persons* is not confronted in these pages, I have sketched out an initial response in a review essay that appeared in *Reason Papers* 11 (Spring 1986), pp. 73–85. Interested readers are invited to consult that piece.

An almost universal law: a teacher learns more from his students than they do from him. I am no exception, and this book is a reflection of that fact. I am, however, specifically indebted to several. Bruce Gardner and James Bonner provided valuable bibliographical assistance. Bonnie Parker painstakingly typed the final manuscript draft under conditions that were far from ideal and, with Daniel Ginsberg, checked it for accuracy. Wayne Hayes assisted in preparation of the index. They also proved to me that a diet of academic jargon is not needed for survival. Their readings pointed me toward the simple and direct. Were it not for their many textual suggestions, the prose would certainly be less scrutable.

My final acknowledgment is also the deepest and most personal. This book is the product of many years and of much teeth gnashing. Countless garbage pails have been filled with the detritus tossed off in its wake. Often I despaired of ever bringing it to a full stop. Priscilla did not. She sympathized when I was spinning in circles, gently pushed when I was stuck on dead center. There are, I'm sure, some authors easy to live with. This one is not. Could I have written without her unwavering support? I am glad I never had the chance to find out.

Duluth, Minn.   L.E.L.
August 1986

Contents

Persons, Rights, and
the Moral Community

1

The Use and Abuse of Basic Rights

Rights are not the whole of moral value, nor is respect for rights the highest of moral virtues. Unsophisticated generosity and compassion may take one a good bit higher on the ladder of moral worth than does a well-schooled punctiliousness in not overstepping the boundaries set by the rights of others. Concern for rights is a necessary cornerstone in the design of a social ethic, but it should not be confused for the completed edifice.

I offer these remarks so that what follows will not mislead. I have much to say in subsequent chapters about the foundations and applications of a theory of basic moral rights. A protracted argument will be offered concerning the conditions under which it makes sense to attribute basic rights to a being, the general nature of those rights, and to whom they extend. In the final chapter admittedly speculative reflections concerning the place of rights within the overall theory of value are offered. Then I shall stop. No illuminating picture will be drawn of the truly flourishing human life or the excellence that men can hope to attain through political means. Such illumination has characteristically been the goal of classical moral and political philosophy, and it is no less valuable today. Indeed, twentieth-century philosophical ethics passed through its most arid period while burdened with a methodology that found no room for investigations of the good human life. This book bristles with respect for those investigations even though it does not advance them. But if a clear basis for talk about moral rights can be set out, then it might serve as an accessory to subsequent acts of moral viewing with a synoptic eye. That is the immodest hope that stands behind a limited work.

The Welter of Rights

In another sense, though, a work of foundational analysis in the area of rights is necessarily ambitious. For it is the attempt to impose method and order upon a realm of discourse that has been exploding in all directions in recent times. Wherever one turns, one finds oneself awash in a sea of rights claims and rights claimants. The traditional triumvirate of rights to life, liberty, and the pursuit of happiness can still be discerned, but they have been joined by a host of less familiar figures claiming kinship status. Even casual inspection of issues that currently agitate public consciousness reveals that disputes over permissible conduct, just and unjust policies, resound with the language of rights.

The concern precedes birth. Fetuses are alleged to enjoy a right to life that guarantees them protection from abortion. Proponents of this antiabortion line are not satisfied to present their case as based on concerns of general decency or an overall assessment of what policy a reasonable and humane society should choose to follow. That would be to opt for a mode of discourse perceived as *understating* the gravity of issues at stake. Only a self-description as the *Right* to Life force is felt to be an adequately forceful characterization of the moral grounds undergirding the position. Entirely unsurprisingly, this movement begets an antagonist that also couches its claims in terms of rights: it is the *right* of privacy, of control over one's own body, of uncoerced choice—or some combination of these—that validates a woman's recourse to abortion. At this point I waive appraisal of these arguments;[1] they are noted only as a reminder of how deeply the language of rights has insinuated itself into our habitual manner of responding to policy issues. It requires an act of imaginative dexterity to conceive how the abortion issue might be recast in language that avoids all invocation of rights.

Little demonstration is required to reveal that subsequent stages of life are also graced with their appropriate rights claims. A child, once born, enjoys the right to be wanted. At the other end of its existence it has the right to die with dignity. Between these extremes its rights include provision of an education adequate to its special needs, an unpolluted environment, meaningful and appropriately remunerated work, due consideration for his or her affectional preference, social and economic welfare rights—and the list can be extended indefinitely. Or so we are told—repeatedly. It is difficult to discover any domain of human life concerning which claims of basic rights have not been earnestly and enthusiastically championed.

This heady proliferation of alleged rights is not the happiest of all possible states of affairs. There are real costs to be paid in public debate when the turn to rights is taken. If you and I have opposed preferences, then we find ourselves in a conflict situation, perhaps a bitter one. Yet certain strategies short of all-out combat may present themselves as offering reasonable bases for the pursuit of a solution. If we are not fanatics, we realize that one person's plans and projects can easily interfere with those of another and that accommodation will then have to be made. This involves my recognition of you as someone to whom his own goals matter as mine do to me, as a fellow moral agent deserving of consideration. I will try to persuade you to alter your plans on the basis of reasons which I hope will be as cogent to you as they are to me. Or perhaps you will persuade me to alter my plans. Even if neither of us is willing to give way entirely, the discussion process can suggest a workable compromise that safeguards what is most central to each. Alternatively, we might have recourse to a mutually acceptable second-order conflict resolution procedure: voting, binding arbitration, casting lots, or some other mechanism. Of course, things might not go so well; fair and reasonable persons might fail to discover, despite their best efforts, a fair and reasonable resolution. However, they have good reason to look in that direction.

Disputes of alleged right against right differ importantly from disputes of preference against preference. One who is convinced that nothing short of a right is in jeopardy will not be equally motivated to pursue a strategy of compromise. Rights stake out chunks of moral turf that others are forewarned not to trespass; they issue demands with which others *must* (the 'must' is moral, not causal or logical) comply. It is not for nothing that we tend naturally to speak of someone "standing" on his rights. One who is entitled as a matter of right to some outcome is under no obligation to move away from that result in his dealings with others. They must accede to his claim rather than open up a bargaining exchange in which each gives up something in order to secure something.

Admittedly this inherent structure of rights claims will not be played out in just this way on every occasion. One who has a right to some particular outcome may choose not to exercise the right or might waive it altogether. Not every occasion calls for a staunch defense of what rightfully belongs to one even if that defense could be successfully essayed. If concern for the well-being of others or my desire to be a moderate—and moderating—person is best served by a less than all-out defense of my rights, then I will stop short of issuing nonnegotiable demands. But note that even in such pacific cases, it is the rights holder who is the leading actor from whom others must take their cue. If I claim my right, that is my decision, and if I waive it, that is no less a case in which I am the prime determinant of the ultimate resolution. Whether I choose to be a jealous guardian of my prerogatives or to display *noblesse oblige,* the situation is one in which, so long as I conceive of myself as a genuine rights holder, I can regard myself as entirely free to act in accord with *my* best lights.

Nor is it even the case that one is always at liberty not to press a rights claim to its utmost. The discretion one has concerning one's own due is typically not present where one is legally or morally empowered to act on the behalf of someone else. B may relinquish that to which he has rightful title, but C, acting in a fiduciary or guardianship capacity for B, may not have the option to relinquish B's claim. When alleged rights enter into public policy disputes, they are frequently of the sort that no one is in a position to waive. If a class of persons, for example, those who have been victims of past discrimination, are owed compensation for their injuries, then no one person is entitled to waive for that class the right to compensation, not even someone who himself is a member of the class of those discriminated against. (He might of course relinquish his own share of the settlement, but that is a different issue.) Also, rights claimed for fetuses, children, or the mentally incompetent (or animals or inanimate beings; see Chapter 8) must necessarily be urged on their behalf by others if they are to be pressed at all. While such a rights advocate might decide to apply his energies elsewhere, he is not at liberty to ease the debate by offering a complete or partial waiver of the right heretofore claimed. (Imagine a spokesperson for the Right to Life Movement offering the following "statesmanlike" proposal: "On behalf of all fetuses, I hereby waive the right to life of those within the first trimester provided that no abortion be performed at a later stage of development." Is it possible to conceive of any circumstance such that this makes sense?)

There is, then, a significant difference between debates carried out simply in terms of opposed and conflicting preferences and those in which rights are asserted. The dynamics of the former suggest the prospect of accommodative movement between the contending sides, while the latter bespeaks the readiness (or commitment) to take a stand and defend it against all comers. If, as has happened in recent years, more and more policy disputes take this latter form, there are apt to be severe consequences for civic harmony. Under the best of conditions it is a difficult matter to balance the interests of diverse groups within a large and varied community. To the extent that rights are recognized, the scope for permissible juggling is limited. In Robert Nozick's terminology, rights provide *side constraints* setting bounds within which policy may be formulated.[2] If side constraints are very many and permeate the range of activities carried out within a society, room for maneuver can shrink practically to zero.

Of course, not all proclaimed rights need be acknowledged as legitimate. Indeed, in those cases in which both sides to a dispute lay claim to rights which are necessarily and unalterably opposed, a consistent adjudicator will judge at least one claim to be ill-founded. (The adjudicator may judge both to be invalid, thus recapturing some measure of flexibility for the decision-making process. But, since the contending parties are at least agreed that the dispute does revolve around matters of rights, there is a tendency for that not to happen.) So, in practice, disputes at the level of rights can be and are settled. But even when institutions succeed in imposing such determinations, results are apt to be less acceptable to concerned parties than where rights have not been invoked. After the appropriate judicial or administrative body has spoken, it may be impractical or imprudent for the loser to press his rights claim further. In that case a sort of finality has been achieved. It is important to note, though, that this is not *moral finality;* a right slighted or ignored does not thereby forfeit its legitimacy. Indeed, adverse decisions may tend to magnify the importance of the disputed right. A right scorned casts accusing glances at the dispute resolution machinery itself, suggesting that the social order has become implicated in unjust policies. The unfortunate consequence is that what begins as a dispute between two private parties turns into a grievance against the polity.

Again, it is helpful to contrast this case with one in which the conflict is not couched in the language of rights. Each party will advocate a policy for which he believes there to be good reason, yet without maintaining that all others are morally required to concur. It is—or can be—recognized that opposition may be based on cogent considerations which also have moral standing. The adjudicator is thus conceived of not as one whose duty is to vindicate in toto the unimpeachability of one's own position, but rather as someone who will intelligently and dispassionately weigh competing arguments and then issue a judgment (possibly incorporating a compromise) which lies within the range of morally permissible outcomes. This task may be done well or ill. When bias, conflict of interest, or incompetence intrudes, the adjudicator's decision may justifiably be regarded as contestable. The important point to note, though, is that the frustration of one's preferences does not give rise to the same grounds for outraged complaint as does the disregarding of one's rights.

Are Rights Necessary?

There is ample reason to view with alarm a public discourse that increasingly ascends (descends?) to the level of rights-talk. Problems tractable if formulated in terms of contending *interests* or *preferences* become rigidified when transformed into disputes over basic *rights*. This unfortunate escalation of charge and countercharge can take on the appearance of inevitability; so long as rights are the heavy artillery within our moral arsenal, there exists a temptation to wield them in all conflicts where deep and important issues are at stake. The problem is to propose a strategy for resisting that temptation, a no-first-strike mechanism.

One possible solution is to eschew talk of moral rights altogether, to search elsewhere in the moral idiom for means to seek one's due. Robert Young writes:

> I frankly fail to see why a world lacking moral rights would be a morally impoverished world. . . . [T]here is some tactical advantage to be gained from appealing to one's rights, but this is not to say that there is significantly greater moral richness in doing so than if one simply relies on forming judgments based on (correct) moral principles.[3]

Although the suggestion that moral rights can be profitably abandoned swims against what has become a powerful tide, it is nonetheless appealing. (Indeed, the transformation of that tide into what looks like a tidal wave lends added charm to the proposal.) What would be lost by replacing the question of whether person P *has a moral right* to X with the question of whether it *is morally right* that P have X? Apparently nothing. If we are moved to judge that P has a right to X, then there exist moral principles which yield the truth of that judgment. Those same principles justify asserting the moral rightness of P having X. That is, whenever there exists a basis for ascribing a moral right to some person, and acting in accord with that right, those considerations can equally well be taken as defining a course of morally right conduct with respect to that person. The replaceability does not work in the opposite direction, however: it may be morally indicated that P be allowed X without it being the case that P has any right to X. If P enjoys chocolate cake and I do not, it is right for me to give my piece to him although he has no right to it. The language of what is morally right covers more ground than that of moral rights; this is one reason why it is constricting to phrase disputes in terms of the latter.

Moral rights are not emblazoned on the foreheads of those who enjoy them. If we have knowledge of their existence and nature, it must come from having derived them by means of antecedently held moral principles. (The universal rights to life, liberty, and the pursuit of happiness, proclaimed by the American Declaration of Independence to be "self-evident," are no exception. They were in fact the fruit of a protracted tradition of natural right theory culminating in the work of John Locke. Whatever self-evidence is, it can emerge posterior to involved analytic investigation.) If we are to know what is meant by affirmations of basic rights, it is to their underpinnings we must turn. Otherwise we may find that our proclamations have turned into platitudes, ritualistically carted out to excite a hoped-for emotional response, but bereft of substance. Appeals to rights that neglect discussion of their provenance are suspect. One may be forgiven for suspecting that there often obtains an inverse correlation between the grandiloquence of claims being urged and the degree of warrant proponents are prepared to offer. If so, the substitution of ethical analysis for pious invocations of rights will have a cleansing effect on normative discourse.

Philosophers have not stood aloof from the rush to embrace moral rights. Robert Nozick's *Anarchy, State, and Utopia* is this century's most ambitious attempt to define the limits of the politically permissible by reference to Lockean-type natural rights. Other works that have had major impact on contemporary academic philosophy have also accorded a central place to basic rights, even if not the absolute primacy Nozick claims for them. Alan Gewirth[4] purports to demonstrate the rational necessity of recognizing in oneself and all other agents rights to freedom and well-being. Ronald Dworkin[5] argues that the right of each person to be treated as an equal is a fundamental presupposition of any adequate social morality. Even John Rawls' *A Theory of Justice*,[6] though not primarily a development of moral rights theory, argues for a lexically primary first principle of justice that assigns to each person an equal right to the most extensive liberty compatible with a similar liberty for all others. This listing could be indefinitely extended.[7]

One might infer from the sheer bulk of work being done that rights theory is an especially healthy area within philosophical ethics. Unfortunately, a close look at the literature suggests otherwise. What one sees above all else is disarray—albeit exuberant disarray. Beyond a shared conviction among these authors that rights are crucial, all else is up for grabs. While Nozick concludes that the only legitimate, that is, rights-respecting, state is a minimal one confined essentially to protective and reparatory functions, Dworkin maintains that taking rights seriously is not only compatible with but, to a large extent, requires that governments undertake sweeping social welfare measures for purposes of wealth redistribution. Rawls argues for the recognition of rights because they would be agreed to by hypothetical contractors choosing fundamental social structures behind a veil of ignorance. Gewirth, however, rejects this rationale as question-begging and instead insists that a satisfactory account must strictly deduce rights from the concept of (purposive) agency. Nozick cuts the Gordian knot by declining to offer *any* systematic rationale for the vaguely specified collection of rights he takes to be basic.[8] Instead, he is content to offer a few suggestive remarks concerning what it is to treat another person as an end and not merely as a means, and to display the closeness of fit between Lockean rights and some carefully selected moral intuitions.

Even this brief synopsis understates the level of discord current within academic philosophy. A tolerable measure of agreement might be obtainable for very general and vaguely specified rights claims, for example, the assertion that all persons are entitled to an adequate degree of respect and consideration from others. But even this comity is quickly dissipated once one attempts to pin down its content. What is the extent of the consideration owed persons as a matter of right? Does it merely require that others forbear from harmful incursions, or does it additionally impose duties to render positive assistance? (And how can the avoidance of harm/provision of aid be conceptually distinguished from each other?) If the latter, what amount of assistance is mandatory, on whom does the duty fall, and to what extent may public agencies adopt coercive measures to ensure that such assistance is forthcoming? Responses by philosophers—and not only by philosophers—differ widely.

It is, of course, not uncommon for there to be sharp disagreements concerning important moral questions. However, the extent to which rights claims are wielded in such remarkably discrepant ways does indicate that those insisting on the importance of basic rights have vastly different things in mind. It follows that much confusion is likely to result from focusing attention on rights claims without simultaneously paying heed to their foundation in moral principles. No doubt it is an exhilarating release for academic philosophy to immerse itself in claim and counterclaim concerning basic rights after decades of being largely confined to metaethical analysis of the language and logic of moral discourse. We may now, however, be witnessing an overreaction. Perhaps it is time to play down *moral rights* in favor of less flashy but more solid reasoning about *moral rightness*.

The Need for Rights

Have the preceding reflections shown that basic rights are dispensable at the levels of both ethical theory and practical discourse? I think not. To be sure, the tendency to couch all moral disagreements in terms of rights is disruptive and obfuscatory. Nor can it be denied that normative analysis is better served by careful attention to the structure of ethically relevant considerations than by rights appeals that rest on air. Yet the very vigor and insistence of rights advocates may lead us to conjecture that the language of rights has an importance which would not survive a shift of idiom. In part this may be explained away as a residue of the emotional resonance affirmations of basic rights have evoked throughout the tradition that stretches back to Locke and beyond. That, though, is merely to push the question a step further back: what is it within the tradition that seems to respond so aptly to our most deeply prized convictions concerning the justified claims of individuals against their governments and against each other? To ask the question is to begin to answer it; affirmations of basic rights spring from a commitment to the *value of the individual* and in turn reflect that commitment into the moral arena.

Much more needs to be said to flesh out the nature of that value (and much more will be said), but the core of this notion is that each person possesses a kind of sovereignty over his own life and that such sovereignty entails that he be accorded a zone of protected activity within which he is to be free from encroachment by others. Since the nation-state has developed into the encroacher par excellence, there is a natural tendency to conceive of basic rights primarily as rights against the state. This parsing of basic rights is historically well grounded, but it should not lead one to overlook the wider rationale for rights: *all incursions* into the protected zone entail erosion of the sovereignty of the individual. I shall use the term 'individualism' to denote the conviction that great value attaches to the ability of persons to lead their own lives, and that within a wide and durable sphere of freedom from interference by others they ought to be able to develop and pursue their own ideals of the good. In Chapter 2 I shall develop an argument attempting to spell out *necessary conditions* for it to be reasonable to recognize individualism as a significant value. In subsequent chapters I shall try to augment these with conditions *sufficient* for it to be the case that a being possesses the basic rights that the recognition of individualism entails. At this point I simply wish to note that basic rights rest on an individualistic foundation, and that it is the language of rights, more than any other component of our moral lexicon, that accents the special value of individualism.

Beings who look upon themselves and their fellows as bearers of rights evince a keen sense of their own worth and the comparable worth of others. Joel Feinberg observes:

> Having rights enables us to "stand up like men," to look others in the eye, and to feel in some fundamental way the equal of anyone. To think of oneself as the holder of rights is not to be unduly but properly proud, to have that minimal self-respect that is necessary to be worthy of the love and esteem of others. Indeed, respect for persons (this is an intriguing idea) may simply be respect for their rights, so that there cannot be the one without the other; and what is called "human dignity" may simply be the recognizable capacity to assert claims. To respect a person then, or to think of him as possessed of human dignity, simply *is* to think of him as a potential maker of claims. Not all of this can be

packed into a definition of "rights"; but these are *facts* about the possession of rights that argue well their supreme moral importance.[9]

What Feinberg labels an "intriguing idea" suggests that references to moral rights are not only convenient in practice but may also be ineliminable in theory; no reduction of rights claims to the moral principle which generate them can be successfully carried out. That is because the principles to which we wish to appeal may themselves include reference to the special dignity and hence inviolability of individuals. For example, consider the claim by B that he has a right to free speech that must be respected by C. This right can indeed be explained by citing moral considerations which provide reasons showing that C ought not impede B's exercise of free speech. But among those considerations—and very likely the one of greatest force—is that B is the type of being whose moral status makes it mandatory that he have control over his own utterances. If that is the case, our moral principles of greatest weight are already "infected" by the individualism that the language of rights expresses.

Of course, it is legitimate to ask for further explanation, to inquire why it is that individualism has such paramount importance, and to ask what characteristics beings must have such that they are to be regarded as bearers of rights. It may then be urged that the theory which satisfactorily answers these questions thereby offers the *deep justification* (to the extent that justification is forthcoming) of rights claims. It can then be maintained that rights are, after all, eliminable in favor of the moral theory that underlies them.

I do not intend to duck the challenge to display the deep theory within which rights emerge; its development is the main task of this book. Nor do I insist that the term 'rights' (or 'basic rights') could not be shelved. Word choice is not the central issue, even though it is the case that arbitrary redefinitions and substitutions cloud the intelligibility of discourse. I do, however, wish to suggest that the following two remarks show it inadvisable to insist on the eliminabilty of rights:

1. Even if a full-blown theory of rights that is massively supported by our best moral reasoning were conveniently at hand, it does not follow that we could thenceforth eschew talk of rights in favor of reference to the underlying theory. Tedium imposes costs too, and a severe one is that central concerns may drift out of focus when submerged under a mass of peripherally associated factors. An adequate theory of morality will have a place for well-entrenched moral intuitions, principles of conduct, an account of the good, reflections on moral experience, epistemological and metaphysical foundations, scientific hypotheses, logical links binding these various strands— and no doubt a good deal more. To insist that this cumbersome machinery

be hauled out in its entirety each time one ventures into normative analysis is as perverse as the insistence that all talk of "electrical charge" or "cold fronts" be accompanied by the respective physical or meteorological theories within which they function.

2. In fact, a *fully* adequate moral theory from which rights can be generated does not yet exist and possibly will never be produced. At least, as was previously noted, there is no consensus among moral philosophers as to the shape of that ideal theory. It follows that any *particular* reduction of rights claims will meet skepticism from other quarters. It does not follow, however, that the rights claims themselves are as suspect as the theory developed to generate them. Consider theories T, U, and V, each of which is inconsistent with the other two and each of which entails p. Though each of T, U, and V may have low warrant, it can be the case that p is highly warranted. In the limiting case where we know somehow that *either* T *or* U *or* V is correct but we do not know which, the warrant for p is 100%. Even in the more usual event where one does not know that some one of the theories already developed is correct, p can possess a high degree of rational acceptability. That is the case when p possesses evidentiary support independent of that which attaches to any theory from which p is a consequent. For example, prior to the development of biochemistry and Mendelian genetics, there was good reason to accept the proposition that the young of a species inherit characteristics from their parents. No credible theory then existed that could explain this result. Similarly, if T, U, and V are moral theories each of which entails rights claim p, p can be better warranted than any of those theories. If so, no theoretical reduction can be effected which preserves the degree of rational acceptability enjoyed by p. The result holds as well for the theory I am about to develop. Though naturally I judge it to be credible, I would not be so rash as to maintain that the status of basic rights rises or falls on the strength of my accounting for them.

I provisionally conclude that the recommendation to dispense with rights is ill-founded. Moral theory minus rights would be poorer for their absence.[10] One may suspect, though, that if there exists any strong move to set aside rights claims, its main impetus is not theoretical. Rather, because basic rights establish boundaries that others must respect, their recognition places severe constraints on the furtherance of social goals. Jeremy Bentham's impatience with basic rights, "nonsense on stilts," as he called them, is very much in keeping with his zeal for remaking society along utilitarian lines. If one is guided by some one luminous ideal for social improvement— whether it be the happiness principle, communism, vegetarianism, or whatever—then basic rights are, at best, a bothersome nuisance that needs to be skirted. At worst, they will be seen as a fount of the malignancies that infest society and that must be swept away for the Bright New Age to dawn.

A century that has witnessed the Holocaust and the Gulag is not one which can aptly be characterized as paying too much heed to basic rights. Normative debate that deemphasizes the importance of rights does not necessarily lead to such enormities, but by enlarging the boundaries of moral permissibility it tends to deemphasize individualism in favor of designs for large-scale social reconstruction. It follows, then, that reverberations from impatience with the language of rights are not confined to metaethics; to propose doing away with rights-talk is to adopt a normative stance. Typically, it amounts to endorsement of an ethic that is pluralistic in the sense of not recognizing one set of overriding conditions within which moral life must take its bearings. Correspondingly, insistence on the role of rights acknowledges the existence of such conditions. We shall have occasion subsequently to scrutinize the opposed alternatives; here it is simply noted that the choice of preferred language is not ethically neutral.

This brief excursion into the presuppositions of rights discourse helps to explain why recourse to rights claims is so popular both within and outside of the academy. Rights and the doctrine of individualism are intimately associated. Where concerns are perceived to have an important bearing on personal dignity, and where individuals' ability to conduct their own lives in a satisfying manner are at stake, the turn to rights is natural. That is not to deny the possibility of excess spotlighted in the early part of the chapter. As rights claims proliferate, two kinds of significant costs are imposed on the community. Because disputes pitting alleged right against right are less tractable than those waged on other terrain, they tend to lead to a decline of sociality. And the recognition of varieties of rights hitherto unsuspected increases the number of constraints imposed upon the actions of everyone. This cost is measured in terms of diminished flexibility within both private and public spheres.

Since, as I shall eventually argue, a rational and worthwhile individualism must incorporate both sociality and a wide degree of flexibility, an internal practical inconsistency disables accounts that scatter basic rights throughout the moral landscape. It does not follow that the recommended antidote is wholesale elimination. There is an Aristotelian mean between deficiency and excess of rights within a moral structure. If the extremes are avoided, neither individualism nor the possibility of harmonious social existence need be forfeited. There are two sides to the metaphor of "standing" on one's rights. It can connote a lack of forthcomingness, a refusal to ascribe any weight to claims pressed by others. But it can also connote a relaxed *assurance* of one's place (one's *standing*, to extend the metaphor) as a full and equal member of the moral community. From this vantage point, one can engage in dealings with others comfortable in the conviction that one does so not as an inferior begging favors or as a superior dispensing them, but as an equal who is thereby entitled to respect. A community of such rights holders, secure in their own status and prepared to recognize the comparable status of others, will be a community infrequently riven by divisive clashes. The common recognition of rights eliminates areas of potential conflict that will bedevil a society in which rights are less visible or altogether unrecognized. Not the least of the attractions of rights is that they function best when unobtrusive.

2

Persons and Projects

Concern for basic rights is concern for the individualism they express. We would not be inclined to recognize rights were it not for the conviction that individuals genuinely are owed some measure of sovereignty over their own lives, that a person's life is deficient unless it is directed by his own will. Self-direction as an essential component of human good is one postulate of an ethic with an individualistic core. It is not the only postulate, however; a person's path to perdition can be one he consciously and deliberately chooses for himself. Perhaps Socrates is persuasive in arguing that the person who so chooses must lack some element of knowledge concerning the badness of the condition toward which he guides himself, but lack of omniscience is the common human condition, not a myopia that blinds a wretched few. At any rate, there is no reason to think that self-direction is incompatible with ignorance, viciousness, bad luck, or any of the numerous other shortcomings that can debilitate a life. Not all goods come wrapped together in one package.

A doctrine of basic rights, then, need not and should not present individualism as the only value worth upholding. It is, however, committed to regarding individualism as of paramount importance such that other ends taken to be of value to particular individuals or to society may not be pursued in ways that violate rights. Because rights do constrain permissible action, a community that recognizes and respects basic rights is thereby signifying its willingness to sacrifice benefits that could otherwise be procured. Nor need these benefits be small; as was noted in Chapter 1, reformers and revolutionaries who espy the possibility of a vastly improved human condition tend to regard claims of basic rights as burdensome or nonsensical or both. It is therefore a crucial task of the rights theorist to explain how it can be reasonable to place such a premium on individualism that it is allowed to stymie the procurement of goods that are attainable only through rights-violating means.

A convincing response to this problem is not easy to produce. It is insufficient merely to allege that individualism ought to be assigned great weight within moral deliberation and to show in graphic detail the deficiencies of a society within which self-direction is largely absent. No matter how successfully such a demonstration were carried through, it would not suffice to provide a basis for rights as side constraints on action. Rather, it would argue for a maximizing procedure within which individualism would be one moral commodity to be dispensed along with others so as to yield the greatest attainable product. The calculations could be pursued along strict utilitarian lines, with individualism being assessed in terms of the utility of its various consequences. Individualism, education, health care facilities, the arts, clean air, commodious housing: each of these has certain expected utility payoffs, and one empowered to make social choices will strive for a balance that optimizes the sum of expected utility. Alternatively, the difficulties involved in estimating cardinal utilities for individuals and comparing utilities interpersonally may be taken as justifying recourse to a proxy function whose variables take as values items that can be conveniently measured and which intuitively seems to correspond to well-being. Real GNP provides a crude measure; an index of what John Rawls calls "primary social goods"[1] will allow for more discriminating welfare comparisons. But whatever function one settles on as providing the most finely honed proxy for well-being, the same choice procedure will apply: act so as to maximize the value of that function.

Suppose that the chosen calculus assigns a high disvalue to violations of rights. Then it will not often be the case that recommended actions incorporate violations of rights. Sometimes, though, when either many small benefits or some very weighty one conflicts with the upholding of rights, the decision procedure will sanction their violations.[2] There is thus an important difference between a maximization model, which sanctions violations of rights when the payoff is sufficiently great, and a side constraint account, which rules out from consideration all maneuvers incorporating rights violations. And it is the maximization model rather than the side constraint account which is the more intuitively plausible. If there are more goods than one to be considered, then it may seem that there *must* be some level at which it is rational to trade off between any two different goods, to accept a lesser amount of one to secure more of the other. It has been admitted that other things besides respect for rights are valuable; then surely there is a price in terms of those other goods which would make it reasonable to "buy" rights violations.

A heroic upholder of the supreme value of rights might wish to deny that *any amount* of other goods is adequate compensation for the violation of a right. The defense strains credulity. Yet even this strategem is not enough to rule out all violations of rights. It might prove to be the case that by violating the rights of one person, five equally grave rights violations will be averted. If so, then a "utilitarianism of rights"[3] will endorse the one rights-violating act while a side constraint account will reject it. But how can this rejection be presented as anything other than a single-minded fanaticism that devours its intended beneficiary in the cause of preserving it? "You maintain that the protection of rights is of great, even transcendent value. Very well; then more upholding of rights is better than less. If one violation is necessary to prevent many others, your own principles ought to lead you to prefer the former. Yet you obstinately resist." How is this criticism to be countered?

The problem that has been identified is that rights may prove to be inconvenient. They set up barriers which neither private individuals nor governmental bodies may breach at their pleasure. To be sure, that may often be advantageous in a morally unproblematic way. Human beings are notoriously susceptible to temptations to pursue their narrow self-interest at the expense of the well-being of others. Were sympathy and beneficence the strongest and most universally shared emotions, it might be feasible to do without barriers of any kind—moral rules, rights, legally enforceable obligations—and rely instead on the promptings of individuals' hearts to secure a decently livable life for all. Unfortunately, the animal that we are is much more recognizable in the Hobbesian caricature than in this idyllic alternative. So incursions must be prevented if we are to attain a tolerably decent measure of sociality. By recognizing each individual as a bearer of rights, all are afforded some protection against the predations that would otherwise ensue. Even when arguments for overriding rights are couched in the most high-minded terms, laced with references to the general welfare or the need for mutual sacrifice in a just cause, one may suspect that the rhetoric is meant to veil the quest for power or personal advancement. History is a textbook for cynics. Having read from it, we may be prompted to insist on undeviating respect for rights, no matter how beckoning are inducements to the contrary, because we have no confidence in people's ability to discriminate accurately and dispassionately between incursions that will maximize public good and those that will debase it. If we are to err either on the side of too much flexibility or excess rigidity, better—far better!—the latter.

This sort of advocacy of unbreachable rights bears marked affinities to some defenses of moral rules in the face of a relentless act utilitarianism. Rule utilitarianism in all its versions is reconciled to forfeiting some opportunities for incremented utility gains: those which would entail the violation of an optimifically utility-enhancing rule. And in some versions, stress on the place of rules is supported in part by considerations of human incompetence to maximize utility on a case-by-case basis. J. J. C. Smart has labeled this strategy "superstitious rule worship,"[4] and his strictures against rule utilitarianism apply *mutatis mutandis* to the above argument for inviolable rights. It will often be the case that respecting individualism is efficacious in advancing the general welfare, and it is also true that shortsightedness, haste, perceived self-interest, or unacknowledged malice may delude one into supposing incorrectly that a special circumstance justifying the overriding of rights has arisen. Therefore, it will be claimed, one ought to be chary about yielding to temptations to advance a cherished goal at the expense of someone's rights. Yet, in those situations where it is manifestly clear that maximization of the good requires that a right be violated (most simply when the good attained is the prevention of other, more serious rights violations), it is flatly irrational to stand unbudgingly on an undeviating fealty to rights. To do so is to accept a less desirable result when a more desirable one is at hand. Rights ascriptions, it may be said, are a generally reliable rule of thumb—at least when they are purged of rhetorical excrescences— but to rule out of court otherwise salutary actions merely because they involve rights violations is to transform a useful instrument into a fetish.

Prudential and Moral Reasons

The criticisms recounted above rest on the assumption that there is some general standard of moral value in terms of which actions are to be tested, and that one action is to be preferred to an alternative if it produces more of that which the standard of value endorses. Utilitarianism is one such theory, but it is possible to adopt as the regnant standard of value something other than overall utility. Survival of the fittest members of the species, fidelity to the Categorical Imperative, glimpses of the Form of the Good, obedience to Divine revelation: all of these can be and have been put forth as the inclusive end of action. And if more is always better than less, moral rationality involves a particular kind of maximization exercise. This assumption may go unstated because no alternative to rationality as maximization has been given any consideration. Once it is critically examined, it will be seen to be faulty. My suspicion is that its prevalence is due to the belief that moral rationality is very much like the rationality of prudence. It is that belief I now wish to examine.

One acts in order to attain some end that one values. It may be a remote consequence whose fruit will not be enjoyed for many years. The end also can be the performance of that very action and thus secured immediately. The two are not exclusive; the action may be chosen for its own sake, for the pleasure of doing that very thing, *and* it may be done for the sake of valued consequences that will flow from it. One who swims does so for the delight of slicing through clear, cold water, or for the health benefits that swimming provides, or both. Bodily movements like a twitch or a knee jerk reflex can occur without there being any purpose to them, but action is inherently purposive.

Although all action is to secure some end or other, not all ends are equally valued. They range from the satisfaction of transitory desires assigned little weight—pausing briefly on one's walk to sniff a rose—to the pursuit of momentous goods to which one is wholeheartedly devoted. Were we unable to evaluate ends differentially, then there would be no prospect of rationally deliberating among alternative possibilities. Also, if an agent could simultaneously pursue all the ends he values without one interfering with another, then again there would be no place for deliberation. (If all valued states could be attained sequentially but not simultaneously, it would not be entirely immaterial in which order they are enjoyed. The child wondering which birthday present to unwrap first is faced with the need to make a decision. This is perhaps the limiting case for deliberation to be conceivable.) Almost always, though, when a person pursues one good, it is at the expense of others that could have been secured in its place. One who stops on his way to smell the rose will arrive at his destination a little bit later. If an earlier arrival would have been more advantageous, then one end has been sacrificed for another. If you spent your money to buy this book, then you were unable to use those funds to purchase delicacies at the local supermarket. (Even if you borrowed the book from someone else, you expended effort in securing and reading it, effort that could have been applied elsewhere.) To appropriate a handy term from economics, the employment of a scarce resource, including one's own time, has an *opportunity cost,* which is represented as the next most highly valued use forgone. Only if a resource has no other uses valued by the agent is it free of cost.

It is because (1) action is purposive, (2) ends differ in assigned value, and (3) actions are costly in the opportunity sense that choice is a matter for rational appraisal. The rational chooser is one who, not being able to secure everything that he values, selects his actions in a way that gives precedence to more highly valued goals over those held in lesser regard. If lives were either infinitely long (so that all pleasures would eventually be enjoyed) or momentary happenings (so that causal connections could be disregarded), then the problem of rationality would be less involved. But since lives are neither of these, rational calculation involves both satisfaction *at a time* and satisfaction *over time*, with no assurance as to how much time that will be. Uncertainties abound, but they are the uncertainties that each human being meets on a continual basis. One weighs the disagreeability of going to the dentist today against the pleasure of playing tennis instead, but also against the misery of the toothache that might or might not eventuate in the future. Luck is involved—but also skill. The skill involved in juggling possibilities for action in the light of their opportunity costs and probabilities of future goods and ills is the virtue of *prudence*.

We may, if we wish, think of prudence in Aristotelian terms as a mean situated between the all-encompassing concern for present rewards and the miser's perpetual postponement of enjoyment into a future that is always advancing before him (although 'imprudent' is an adjective typically reserved only for the former behavioral trait). But it is also an extreme: it is the *maximization* of expected value over the course of a lifetime. The prudent man is, if not entirely indistinguishable from *Homo economicus*, then at least his twin. Prudence and economizing are both rational activities in the same sense: they involve the maximization of expected value over time. Or, to be more exact, prudence is the maximization of *one person's good.*

The qualification is suggestive. Each person has reason to make trade-offs within his own life of less valued states of affairs for more highly valued ones. This is true whatever standard of value he applies for determining the value of circumstances he can bring about. A hedonist will take as his all-encompassing end the enjoyment of pleasurable experiences. A somewhat different standard accords value to any achievement of satisfaction, whether or not it is productive of feelings that can be labeled "pleasurable." For example, someone might take as a component of his well-being an eventual burial at sea. This can be assigned some positive value by a preference satisfaction standard, though not by a hedonistic one.[5] And a religious person may take compliance with the word of God as his ultimate standard by which actions are to be appraised, augmented perhaps by a lexically subsidiary standard to be employed in those cases where God is not believed to have pronounced. Numerous alternative imputations of value could be discovered or invented, but in each case the person who subscribes to it will be acting rationally from the prudential standpoint if he evaluates all possible outcomes in terms of that standard and acts so as to achieve the greatest possible amount of good as measured by the standard. Conversely, he acts irrationally if he forgoes some amount of attainable good through responding to promptings external to that standard. In particular, to prefer some good *simply* because it will occur earlier than another is to behave irrationally. Suppose that person P opts for good G_1 at time t_1 rather than G_2 at t_2 although G_2 scores higher than G_1 on the scale to which P subscribes. This must be judged an incorrect exercise of practical reason. Reason for choosing G_1 is a function of G_1's worth, and its occurrence at t_1 is, by itself, an external factor that leaves G_1's worth unaffected. Likewise for the worth of G_2. Moreover, G_1 and G_2 are alike in being *goods for P*, because each is accorded whatever value it has on P's own standard. Therefore, P has reason to advance G_2 in preference to G_1, and if he does not do so, he is acting imprudently—or, to use what is here an equivalent expression, acting irrationally.[6]

Before Robinson Crusoe encountered Friday, he could proceed entirely on the basis of prudential calculation. But in a world with many persons, each of whom can act in ways that affect the well-being of others, more than one person's good has to be considered. Without denying that moral considerations can apply to self-regarding actions or that it is meaningful to speak of duties to oneself, it is appropriate to maintain that by far the largest part of morality is concerned with interpersonal transactions. Prudence concerns itself with the good for one person, but morality involves the good of many persons. Appraising actions from the standpoint of morality thus involves due consideration of the several goods of each of the parties who will be affected by what is done. A central question of moral theory then is: what is it to give due consideration to each affected party? The proffered answer will be the basis for a theory of moral rationality.

Prudence here invites its own extension. If it is rational to maximize good over the course of a lifetime, irrespective of *when* particular satisfactions occur, then is it not similarly rational to maximize satisfaction over all persons, irrespective of *to whom* particular satisfactions accrue? An affirmative answer yields one important version of the numerous related doctrines that have gone by the name 'utilitarianism.' Its great appeal is that it offers a decision procedure for choice in a social context that is plausible in the same way that the claim of prudence is plausible in the one-person context. This version of utilitarianism is not unique in providing such appeal, nor is the family of utilitarianisms privileged in this respect. In fact, a vast array of moral theories can be constructed on the model of prudence.[7] What is required is that there be some standard of value by means of which ends are appraised, that this standard apply to the ends of all persons (or, conceivably, to other beings regarded as having interests; animals are the most likely candidates), that it apply uniformly and indiscriminately to those ends, and that alternative achievable outcomes are quantitatively comparable by reference to that standard. If these conditions are met, then there exists a decision procedure—the *moral decision procedure*—for rational choice of action. More value is better than less, and if all ends are commensurable in terms of one standard, then right action is determined by a simple maximization procedure. This is to take the rationality of morality to be isomorphic to the rationality of prudence.

Both on the level of practice and of theory it is vastly appealing to view morality as modeling prudence. Since we already have some fairly serviceable conception of what prudent conduct entails, this prior familiarity enhances our understanding of why morality prescribes as it does. Occam's razor comes into play too; it is *prima facie* desirable that moral rationality have the same general form as rationality in the purely self-regarding realm. By thinking of morality as a kind of extended prudence, practical reasoning as a whole can share a common maximization core.

The parallels can be spelled out more fully. What is the moral analogue to the prudent man's temporal indifference? It is indifference or, better, *impartiality* concerning whose ends are being advanced. On this account, morality involves treating all persons alike, though of course not in the simpleminded sense of acting in precisely the same way toward everyone. Rather, impartiality involves weighing all ends by the same standard of value and striving to maximize the sum of this value irrespective of whose particular interests turn out to be favored. Impartiality is not indifferent *to* persons; it is indifference *among* persons.

If there were no conflicts among persons, there would be no need for an interpersonal morality. Because conflicts do occur, because the attainment of end E_1, desired by person B, may be incompatible with the realization of E_2, desired by C, there is need for an interpersonal morality. More specifically, such conflicts can be resolved if there is some rational basis for determining which of E_1 or E_2 ought to be preferred. This is provided by a standard of value that provides a measure for each. It is not B's standard—which would merely provide a ranking in terms of value-for-B—nor is it C's; rather, it must be one applicable to various persons' ends and must issue in a determination which is not value for some particular person but value *simpliciter*. A standard that ranges over persons and their ends in this way is what I shall call an *impersonal standard of value*.

If morality is to be a rational enterprise in the way that prudence is, there must be an impersonal standard of value that can be brought to bear on interpersonal conflicts. It can be relatively simple, such as a Benthamite pleasure principle that takes all differences in value as reducible to differences in quantities of pleasurable experience. Or it can be as complex as one needs to make it, involving a host of desiderata, each assigned its respective weight so as to be commensurable with any of the others. For example, one could supplement a pleasure principle with a distributional equality measure, define an index which incorporates each in the desired respective proportion, and then judge the merits of actions by reference to their scores as measured by this index. Not all standards of value are equally appealing, but each standard of value that is impersonal will satisfy the demand of impartiality.

Moral theorists who disagree among themselves as to which impersonal standard of value ought to be accepted may be entirely united in affirming the following proposition: morality is impartial among persons. It is not merely that impartiality is a valuable component of a moral theory or that the impartiality that some persons display is a commendable quality; rather, it is maintained that impartiality is understood as *constitutive* of morality. Adoption of "the moral point of view" is defined, in part, by it. This stricture is a crucial determinant of whether an agent's action springs from moral motivation or from some other source. It is morally based only if the principle guiding choice is neutral with respect to whose interests are advanced. If E_2 is judged to score above E_1 by impersonal criteria, then to favor E_1 because E_1 is B's end is to be motivated by a morally irrelevant consideration. Partiality for B may not, within the context of morality, be invoked as *any reason at all* for choosing to realize E_1, let alone as the decisive factor. From the moral point of view, partiality is flatly irrational. Of course, one may *feel disposed* to prefer B's well-being to C's, one's *empathy* may be more engaged by B than C, one may *delight* in B's good while being cold to C's; insofar, however, as the agent is endeavoring to choose morally, he must totally discount these emotional stirrings.

Suppose though that *I* am B and am to choose between advancing my end or deferring in favor of C's. Does this provide a morally relevant factor that could tip the scales in favor of pursuing E_1—my end—rather than bringing about E_2? The answer is no. The type of theory of moral rationality now being considered classifies temptations to favor oneself as yet further instances of impermissible partiality.

[We are required] to be impartial between our own and other people's preferences, not altruistic in its correct sense of giving *more* weight to the preferences of others. We have to treat everybody as one, including ourselves: to do unto others *as* we wish they should do to us (sc. in their situations with their preferences), and love our neighbors *as* (not more than) ourselves. We get no extra weight for our own preferences.[8]

A few qualifications are called for in order that this claim not be misunderstood. An agent may indeed have impersonally validated reasons to pursue his own ends rather than those of someone else. He may have more knowledge concerning his own ends than he does concerning the ends of anyone else. An impersonal standard certainly can regard knowledge as an objective factor bearing on one's likelihood of producing a desirable outcome. An agent may be in a position of being causally better situated to advance his own end. He is, after all, spatially closest to himself and can exercise more control over his own body than over any other body. So an impersonal standard can recognize causal efficacy as morally relevant. An obvious final point: the agent's own end might simply outweigh in impersonal value every other end that conflicts with it.

All these reasons for advancing one's own ends can be and are admitted. What is denied, however, is that the claim "E_1 is *my end;* it is *what I most of all care for*" provides a moral reason for B to choose E_1. Again, the analogy to prudence can be invoked: just as prudence rejects pure time preference, so does morality reject pure preference for persons—including the person that one is. It may be psychologically explicable why I am drawn toward advancing my end E_1, just as it may be psychologically explicable why the imprudent man irrationally prefers a lesser present satisfaction to a greater future satisfaction. But neither explanation is a *justification.* An agent aspiring to act morally must evaluate his own end by reference to the same impersonal standard of value he utilizes for the evaluation of any other individual's ends. If it is his that loses out, then so be it.

Projects

The foregoing analysis has been presented in order to erect a foil to the contrasting account of the place of reason in morality I shall now begin to develop. Although I shall argue that it is fundamentally deficient, it does, I believe, enjoy considerable acceptance within moral philosophy, past and present. For the sake of simplicity, I shall refer to it subsequently as "the Foil." I hope that I have succeeded in presenting it in a forceful and persuasive manner that accentuates its credibility so that what follows will not appear to be the pointless exercise of knocking down a straw man of one's own shoddy creation.

It will now be helpful to take a closer look at differences among the kinds of ends that motivate persons' actions. Most obviously they differ in respect of the intensity of the desire for their realization. Intensity of desire is, however, one but by no means the only indicator of an end's gravity. An infurating itch might produce in an agent a well-nigh irresistible temptation to scratch even though he simultaneously denies that scratching that itch at that time is a crucial component of his good. To come closer to a procedure for discriminating between relatively grave and relatively inconsequential ends, it is necessary also to consider how they differ in respect of their persistence and centrality within the life of an individual.

Some ends are not once-and-for-all acknowledged and then realized through the successful completion of one particular action. Rather, they persist throughout large stretches of an individual's life and continue to elicit actions that establish a pattern coherent in virtue of the ends subserved. Those which reach indefinitely into the future, play a central role within the ongoing endeavors of the individual, and provide a significant degree of structural stability to an individual's life I call *projects*.[9] Beyond the three characteristics of persistence, centrality, and structure, projects assume variant forms and are pursued by both saints and sinners. Among them are: raising one's children to be responsible adults, striving to bring about the dictatorship of the proletariat, serving God, serving Mammon, following the shifting fortunes of the New York Yankees come what may, bringing relief to starving persons in Africa, writing the Great American Novel, promoting White Supremacy, and doing philosophy. Nor are all projects expressly devoted to bringing about and maintaining a desired external state of affairs; some are directed at becoming and remaining a certain sort of person. One can commit oneself to carrying out one's promises and avoiding lies not simply because of consequential considerations establishing the generally optimific tendency of that practice, but because one wishes to be a man of one's word. Similarly, one can devote long-term efforts to developing a beautiful body, being a passionate and compassionate lover, facing testing situations courageously, overcoming shyness, becoming an accomplished disco dancer, staying sober, being able to kill in cold blood without a glimmer of remorse.

This is a sundry lot. No one person could subscribe to all or even more than a small fraction of these. Nonetheless, projects constitute a family within the wider community of ends. When we wish to understand or describe a person, to explicate what fundamentally characterizes him as being just the particular purposive being that he is, we will focus on his projects rather than on his more transitory ends. "This is someone who, three years ago, decided to plant tomatoes in his backyard garden" provides less substantial information about his purposive dimension than to say, "She is an ardent Zionist," or "He treasures Mozart." Projects explain more than an action; they help to explain a life.

Although a project can prompt various actions over the course of many years, projects are irreducible to these various episodes of desire satisfaction. Logical priority runs in the opposite direction: whether some specific achievable result is an item of value for the agent is frequently a function of the projects to which he stands committed. For example, whether an event of lying in an entirely convincing manner is valued or disvalued will largely depend on whether the agent is committed to fidelity or to being instead a shameless deceiver. (That is not to deny that yet *another* determinant of the value assigned to this act of lying can be the causal contingencies that happen to obtain on this particular occasion. Some, but certainly not all, valuation is derived from commitment to projects.) It is not possible to explain a project pursuer's various purposive actions without some prior understanding of what his projects are, and it is even more hopeless to try to discern an order supervenient upon a person's actions without recognizing the directive force that project pursuit affords to a life. It follows, then, that project pursuers are not Indiscriminate Evaluators. Not any and every attainable state of affairs can motivate one who defines himself by reference to ongoing activities directed by and toward a persistent end. One who undertakes projects has thereby ceased to be a tabula rasa. His volitions have become channeled, not in every respect and not in a rigid and unvarying way, but channeled nonetheless by the ends he has undertaken to serve. The fact that some action would conflict with pursuit of one's project is, by itself, reason to reject motivation from that direction. One who has identified himself with ends that constitute his own enduring reasons for leading a life of a certain sort is someone who has voluntarily assumed much of the burden of selecting what will or will not exert motivational force on him. For such a person, more than others, if indeed there be others, the model of a person as the passive locus at which passions collide is ill-suited. Project pursuers are passionate beings, but they have, in large measure, actively determined what will move them.

Projects and Partiality

Project pursuit is at odds with the Foil. It will be recalled that the Foil puts forth an account of moral rationality such that an agent is bidden to choose between conflicting ends on the basis of their conformity with an acknowledged impersonal standard of value. From the point of view of this standard, it is immaterial whether one, all, or none of the ends that conflict are those of the agent himself. The catchword that best characterizes the prescribed decision procedure is 'impartiality.'

Project pursuit, though, is partial. To be committed to a long-term design, to order one's activities in light of it, to judge one's success or failure as a person by reference to its fate: these are inconceivable apart from a frankly partial attachment to one's most cherished ends. An individual's projects provide him with a *personal*—an intimately personal—standard of value to choose his actions by. His central and enduring ends provide him reasons for action that are recognized as his own in the sense that no one who is uncommitted to those specific ends will share the reasons for action that he possesses. Practical reason is *essentially differentiated* among project pursuers, not merely contingently differentiated by the various causal constraints that each person faces from his own unique spatiotemporal location. That end E_1 can be advanced by B may provide B overwhelmingly good reason to act; that C could be equally effective in advancing E_1 may merit vanishingly little weight in C's deliberations concerning what to do.

The Foil offers a theory of rationality for making interpersonal trade-offs. (It also, and less controversially, prescribes intrapersonal trade-offs.) It is always rational, *ceteris paribus*, to trade off an end that scores lower on the impersonal standard of value for one that scores higher; it is always irrational, *ceteris paribus*, to accept a low-scoring end when a higher-scoring one could have been achieved instead. Morality is seen as a kind of skill— and the willingness to use that skill: it is the art of effecting trade-offs sanctioned by an impersonal standard. Project pursuit rejects this account of morality.[10] If E_1 is tightly bound up with B's self-conception of the type of person he is, then he cannot regard its promotion as subject to trade-offs with C's E_2 *simply on the grounds* that an impersonal standard of value ranks E_2 above E_1. That impersonal standard cannot be accepted by B as providing a comprehensive basis for choosing how to act, although it can merit attention as one factor entering into his deliberations. But, in addition, he will regard the assertion "E_1 is *my* deep concern" as a significant reason in itself for opting to advance E_1 rather than the end that conflicts with it.

Let me try to sharpen the contrast between the Foil and concern for project pursuit one step further. Those ends which issue in projects are, by definition, held to with distinctive tenacity. Though they need not be embraced come what may (in part because what comes may be a radical change of heart), they serve as a kind of shelter from the lure to abandon oneself to some whim or passing fancy. They truly involve a serious level of commitment, and one who is unable or unwilling to commit himself to anything is not a pursuer of projects. Instead, his ends may be likened to commodities he has bought on spec, to be kept if they happen to suit him but ready to be sent back if their attraction should pall or if some shinier item should catch his eye. The pursuer of projects is tenacious, his opposite number tentative.

The Foil implies that a moral person is tentative with respect to *all* his personal goals, *all* his plans, *all* that he would like to be. This is a consequence of the fact that any end to which he happens to subscribe might, at some point, conflict with the maximization requirement. When such a conflict does occur, it is his moral duty to abandon his own end for the sake of promoting the one that has ranked higher on the impersonal standard. He may be called upon to realize an outcome to which he had previously assigned some slight value, one which he had disvalued, or one to which he had never previously given the slightest bit of thought. It follows, then, that a person's commitment to any persistent end must be less than wholehearted. He will be prepared to divert his attention from it to whatever new opportunity presents itself as a means for increasing impersonal value. That which the project pursuer embraces, this other man holds at arm's length.

To the extent you the reader have bound yourself to the pursuit of projects that have captured your devotion, you may perhaps now have been persuaded to edge away, at least somewhat, from the Foil. But its attractive force is powerful, if for no other reason than its extraordinarily long history as a dominant paradigm within philosophical ethics.

Plato's Form of the Good is a union of the metaphysically and morally primary that holds up a dazzling standard—an impersonal standard—of that which is Ideally Rational and Ideally Pursuable. It is, of course, one and the same for all men, and the extent to which one falls short of ascendance to it is the extent to which one falls short of being maximally human with respect to both theoretical and practical reason. Aristotle, in spite of other divergencies from his great teacher, remains enough of a platonist also to espouse an impersonal standard of value. Pure *nous* is that which is highest in man, prior in the order of being and as an object of practical endeavor. To be sure, Aristotle hedges his discussion through recognition of a pluralistic array of goods for man, with an explicit statement that the virtue of any individual is a mean relative to his own personal endowments, and even with the crucial suggestion that there is something not altogether human ("more than human" expresses, in my interpretation, a deeply felt ambivalence in his thought) in the attachment to an entirely impersonal final cause. Yet he will not bring himself to reject Plato's understanding of that which is best for a man as something impersonal.

The two most influential molders of moral thought in our century, utilitarianism and Marxism, differ in many respects but are alike in imposing impersonal standards of value. For the former it is the achievement of maximum realizable utility; for the latter it is the furtherance of the historically conditioned class struggle that will reach fruition in the transcendence of class division. Because the Foil is so recognizable within the tradition of moral thought to which we are heir, it is discomfiting to consider seriously that it might be fundamentally flawed.

Nor is it the case that upholders of the Foil will be cowed into silence by the suggestion that they have habitually undervalued the significance of personal projects. One can imagine a response like the following:

It is true that morality as I perceive it entails that there are no absolutely untouchable projects. You take that to be a deficiency of my view; I regard it as a strength. There are many persons who inhabit this one world, and each can be importantly affected by the actions of others. In particular, the deeply cherished pursuits of one can, if unregulated, lead to intolerable results for others. None of your uplifting talk about the importance of projects can gainsay this evident fact. Since it is the case that the success of the life of one person depends on the actions of numerous others, it is irrational to espouse an ethic that would make the permissibility of an action hinge merely on the actor's own personal standard of value. "It's *my* end," is not a good enough reason when there exists a multitude of persons, each of whom can say the same. To suppose otherwise is to countenance an incessant Hobbesian war of all against all in the turmoil of which no one would stand a good chance of realizing those ends for which he cares. Your own concern for personal projects confutes you! If morality is to be good for anything, it must be to provide a rational basis for conflict adjudication. Personal standards of value cannot do this because they vary from person to person, yielding mutually inconsistent rankings that throw us all back again into the Hobbesian jungle. Only an impersonal standard of value, one that is impartial among persons, provides a means of egress. Ends will be valued by reference to a standard that confronts each person identically and that appraises all ends irrespective of whose ends they are. Yes, one who is a moral being may be called upon at times to sacrifice that which is nearest and dearest to him. It is a charade, though, to pretend that this will be the rule, that one will be precluded as, a matter of course from pursuing one's plan of life. The most efficient means of maximizing value is generally to allow people to develop and pursue their own personal attachments, subject only to constraints of minimally decent behavior toward others. Occasionally, but *only* occasionally, more will be demanded—perhaps even *very* much more—but acceptance of this condition for the rational settlement of conflict is the difference between rampant egoism and morality.

Variations on this theme, I suggest, lend to the Foil much of the power to convince that it enjoys. Yet the criticism rests on a mistaken dichotomy between what it takes to be the essence of morality and untrammeled self-servingness. For I have not claimed that project pursuit insulates one from all reason to consider the well-being of others and to take another person's good as providing reasons that bear on one's choice of conduct. Rather, what I have tried to cast doubt on is the claim that an impersonal standard of value is *by itself sufficient* to justify trading off ends toward which one has undertaken commitments. If it is the case that individuals' different projects provide them with personal standards of value that they have reason to employ in deciding what they are to do, then the insistence on through-and-through impersonality is irrational in the most profound sense. It is instead the case that an adequate account of moral reasoning is one that incorporates *both* impersonal and personal elements, the former applicable in the same way to everyone, the latter being as various as the projects to which persons commit themselves.

Furthermore, it has not been claimed that, in practice, one who espouses an impersonal morality will be hampered at every turn in the pursuit of his own ends. A consistent utilitarian may often be able to produce most utility right at home, working for the satisfaction of his own desires. Or so it is argued.[11] If this is correct, it is less a *vindication* of utilitarianism than an *indication* of why its theoretical antipathy toward project pursuit tends to remain hidden. If an agent is usually free to advance his own ends, it is not so noticeable that the theory bids him to evaluate those ends by reference to an impersonal standard that allows them no more primacy in his calculations than any other ends he is in a position efficiently to advance. The same may be said of nonutilitarian theories that are like it in insisting on parity within each individual's deliberations between those ends that he personally values and those whose source of value lies elsewhere. If these theories are deficient, it is not primarily because they typically result in agents being obligated to advance ends for which they care little. Rather, they are deficient in not being able to express correctly the relation that obtains between an agent and his own projects.

Projects and the Coherence of Persons

What is it that constitutes the identity of a person over time? This especially vexing question has been at the forefront of metaphysical debate since Locke's *Essay Concerning Human Understanding.* Memory retention, criteria of bodily continuity, some sort of transcendental unity inseparable from perception: each has had its champions. Each is also beset with problems. Rather than rashly attempting to adjudicate their respective merits, I shall instead suggest another factor that bears on the identity of an individual: it is the persistent attachment to ends that shape and continue to shape a person's life. In the absence of such ends—that is, in the absence of projects—bodies could continue to endure in the way that bodies do and memory might still exert cohesive force. What would be absent, though, is continued identity as the selfsame purposive being. One who was open to motivation from one source at time t_1 and then to motivation from a wildly disparate source at t_2—and so on, and so on—would be what I called above an *Indiscriminate Evaluator*. Various short stretches of his life, taken individually, would exhibit purposive activity, but the life as a whole would exhibit no coherence of practical activity. Such a person is difficult to imagine without venturing into the realm of extreme psychosis. Or, rather, perhaps we can regard an Indiscriminate Evaluator as a kind of exaggerated adolescent. Adolescents adopt first one mode of response and then another on the way to forging a more settled character. "I'm trying to find my real self!" is the adolescent's characteristic plaint. But of course the adolescent does eventually find out who he is; and he finds out by *making himself* into a certain kind of individual. Being an Indiscriminate Evaluator would be like a heightened and interminable adolescence. It could not terminate because one's unity as a purposive being is a function of the temporally extended projects that afford structure to one's activities and, by definition, an Indiscriminate Evaluator has no projects.

I claim, then, that one component of a person's identity over time is constituted by his commitment to projects. This is not put forth as a replacement for other criteria employed to establish identity but as an addition to them. For the kind of coherence through time that projects establish is different in at least two respects from the aspects of personal identity that are more often considered in the philosophical literature.

First, one's identity as a purposive project pursuer is not an innately given property that a being has simply through existing, in the way that *this rock* remains identical to itself so long as the rock continues to exist. Rather, it is an identity which one creates by the act of *identifying* oneself with some ends above others. It is not innate but acquired. Second, and indeed as a consequence of the former point, identity in this sense is not what Derek Parfit calls an "all or nothing" relation, that is, one which either simply obtains or does not obtain and admits of no difference in degree.[12] Rather, it is much closer to what he calls "psychological continuity" and "connectedness," relations which obtain between temporal stages of a person's life and of which there can be more or less. There is obviously a very wide degree of gradation possible between someone who embraces projects to which he then holds in an undeviating manner, never forswearing or acting inconsistently, and the Indiscriminate Evaluator whose purposive behavior is completely chaotic. Hence it is appropriate to compare persons in terms of the *degree* of identity their lives manifest. If it is strange for philosophers to be confronted with a notion of personal identity that incorporates more and less, such is not the case for developmental psychologists. I risk the possible confusion that may be associated with this usage because it is important to emphasize the persistence over time of a person as recognizably the same purposive being. "You're not the same person I once knew" need not be taken as a flagrant contradiction or even as thoroughly metaphorical. Rather, it expresses the conviction that a very basic component of a person's nature consists in the ends he adopts to become the being that he is.

The Foil, however, presupposes a radically different conception of the relation between an agent and his own ends. If it is rational for B to be motivated to advance E_1, then it is rational for any other person to be motivated by E_1 to the same extent and for the same reason. E_1 is acknowledged to provide reason for action because of whatever standing it possesses on the impersonal standard of value, a standard that is equally binding on all individuals. It follows, then, that whatever relation E_1 bears to B *as an end that thereby provides reason for its own advancement* it also bears to C, D, or any other being subject to the demands of morality. B has no reason to advance E_1 that they do not share and share equally. But if that is the case, we must review the manner in which we have been speaking all along. For if B has no reason to advance E_1 that everyone else does not share, how can it be correct to refer to E_1 as "B's end"?

Perhaps the end originated within the psychophysical organism that is B. For example, consider an annoying itch in B's left ear that would be relieved by scratching. This is sufficient grounds for maintaining both that there is an itch and that it is B's itch. But is that sufficient reason to say that the relief of the itch by scratching is an end that is B's end? Apparently not, for one must also invoke a standard of value that justifies scratching, presumably on the basis that positive value is assigned to any individual's relief from annoyance. If, as is reasonable to assume, the Foil assigns positive value to bringing about the relief of B's itch, then bringing about that relief is B's end. It is also, however, C's end and the end of every other moral agent. Each has the same reason for bringing about B's relief: that this will tend to enhance impersonal value. So, as a first approximation, B has no reason to scratch B's ear that C does not have to scratch B's ear.

As it stands, this is too crude. For it might be the case that the relief enjoyed by a person through scratching his own ear far exceeds that which any foreign fingernails can provide. Or, more realistically, the relief that one enjoys from having an ear scratched might be outweighed by the alarm occasioned by the intrusion of the would-be helper. So it turns out, after all, that the only state of affairs assigned positive value is B's scratching his own ear. Is this, then, an end which *as an end* (that is, as providing rational motivation for action) is unique to B? Again, the answer is no. The state of affairs, B scratching B's ear, is one that B has reason to bring about, but it is also one that C and every other agent has reason to bring about. True, it is probably more efficient for B to arrange for his own ear scratching than for anyone else to do so, but this merely tells us who is *best situated* to bring about an end that holds out equal value for all. To put it another way, the *value* that is achieved by the successful completion of B's ear scratching is not uniquely or even particularly value-for-B; it is impersonal value which each moral being has equal reason to prize.

The example chosen is trivial—by design. Because it barely deserves to be thought of as a situation calling for moral choice, it abstracts from the complications that surround any genuine moral dilemma. But the principle exemplified is general. Although the existence of some end may be due solely to causal antecedents localized within one person, once it has been created it provides reason for action to all. E_1 provides no guiding structure specific to B's life—nor does anything else. Rather, E_1 is a free-floating ground for action, to be promoted by whoever is in the most advantageous position to do so. The Foil renders ends perfectly socialized, the completely common property of all active beings. The price to be paid for this evaluational socialism is far more extreme, though, than that occasioned by economic socialism: it is the metaphysical breakdown of the person. The Foil endorses a view that entails the impossibility of individuating agents by reference to what each has reason to bring about. If all ends *qua* ends are impersonally determined and impinge on agents equally, then no agent is individuated as the particular purposive being with just those projects to pursue. Agents are dissociated from their ends because the ends are no longer, in any significant sense, theirs.

To be sure, one who pledges his allegiance to the Foil may, in practice, embrace personal projects and assign to their realization weight that is not legitimately derivable from the impersonal standard. He then tacitly acknowledges a unique connection to his own ends, one that does set him apart as an active, purposive being. "It is *my* end" is now admitted as offering a motivational impetus that is not common property. B can still acknowledge the impersonal value of E_1, but he additionally recognizes and responds to the value-of-E_1-for-B. However, that is to foresake the Foil and its entailments in favor of an ethic that has room for the recognition of an intimate and unique relation between the agent and his own ends. It is to acknowledge that personal projects too can provide reasons.

The Road to Rights

If the Foil in all its manifestations has been demonstrated to be inadequate, then an adequate ethic must find a place for personal as well as impersonal considerations. I say "as well as" because the preceding analysis should not be misunderstood as asserting the total supremacy of the personal. It has not been claimed that project pursuit insulates one from all reason to pay heed to ends that are not uniquely one's own. So, in particular, it would be entirely fallacious to conclude that persons enjoy carte blanche to engage in completely selfish behavior, mindless of the well-being of others. Concern for the personal dimension of morality is not equivalent to the endorsement of egoistic rapacity.

No attempt has yet been made to justify any particular allocation of moral cogency between personal and impersonal considerations. It will not come as a complete surprise to the reader, though, that when that allocative problem is confronted in Chapter 4, the ability of individuals to formulate and pursue their various projects with a substantial degree of freedom from interference will be prominent. To this point, though, the argument has been mostly negative in character; it was directed at showing that the initial plausibility of regarding morality as an unconstrained exercise in the maximization of some social value function should be questioned. It should be questioned because the maximization requirement rests on a presupposition that there does exist or can exist some impersonal standard of value to which all persons have reason to adhere throughout their self-regarding conduct and in their dealings with others. This no longer remains credible once the centrality of projects in giving coherence to fully human lives is acknowledged. Project pursuers have reason to reject trade-offs of their own ends for the ends of others. I reiterate that this is not an absolute shield from external impositions. It is instead the denial that morality enrolls us all as partners in *the human enterprise* to which all our efforts must be devoted. There is no such thing; there are only the various personal enterprises in which individuals enroll themselves and which provide them with irreducibly personal ends that they strive to realize.[13] That the ends are personal does not, of course, preclude their being directed toward the welfare of other persons. The relations of mother to child, lover to beloved, friend to friend generate projects that are as intensely personal as they are other-directed. Rejection of an omnivorous human endeavor does not entail commitment to a nakedly atomistic Hobbesian egoism. Indeed, as will be argued at some length in Chapter 7, a genuine moral community is possible only because projects typically, almost inescapably, involve essential reference to the well-being of others.

Morality will be correctly understood only if it is seen as supervenient upon the value-creation that individuals bring about through identifying themselves with ends that are their own. For that reason, a theory of basic rights as side constraints is *prima facie* plausible. Beings who are holders of rights are not properly subject to unlimited trade-offs of their own ends for the sake of other persons' ends. Rights holders are free within the boundaries established by their basic rights to direct their own lives according to their own lights. Individualism is deserving of protection even though individualism can be inconvenient. Respect for basic rights affords that protection.

These reflections indicate that to endorse an ethic built on basic rights is at least to move in the right direction; basic rights have the *shape* of an account sensitive to personal as well as impersonal demands. So this chapter serves as indirect support for the recognition of basic rights. But much more work needs to be done before anything that deserves to be called a *justification* of basic rights will emerge. An argument is needed to sketch out the range of concerns that can legitimately be said to be protected as a matter of right; the criteria that a being must satisfy in order to be afforded the status of a rights holder also must be examined. Most crucial because most basic is the need to answer the question, what reason can an individual have to regard *another's* interests as deserving of respect, as a constraint on his own conduct that he rationally should acknowledge? There is work to be done!

3

Projects and the Nature
of Ethics

It was argued in Chapter 2 that the standing of human beings as project pursuers is a fact so portentous that any account of morality that explicitly or implicitly denies that project pursuers have reason to be partial to their own abiding commitments is thereby disqualified as an adequate moral theory for beings like us. It follows, then, that a wide range of ethical theorizing, most notably utilitarianism in its various guises, but also numerous other incarnations of the Foil, is fundamentally deficient. The critique was negative, clearing away unqualified pretenders but not itself nominating an acceptable candidate. That latter task remains.

It may be objected, though, that ascribing a prominent role to project pursuit makes the business of *constructive* moral theorizing impossible. Two bases for that gloomy forecast suggest themselves:

1. Project pursuit may be a widespread characteristic of human beings, but it is far from universal. Very young children are conspicuous instances of beings who are not (yet, at any rate) project pursuers but who nonetheless possess moral weight—as do, at the other end of the developmental spectrum, senile individuals who are no longer project pursuers. Somewhat more arguably, fetuses, the incurably comatose, severely retarded persons, and animals impose moral claims on the rest of us that cannot be dismissed by noting that such beings are incapable of directing their lives in accord with long-range commitments they have autonomously undertaken.

A *friendly* critic might here suggest that an ethic centered on project pursuit is heir to precisely those ills endemic to any account that attempts to base moral status and obligation on "nature": on some characteristic that all and only those beings who are moral claimants possess and which is sufficient to justify their moral claims. Natural rights theories are a subclass of such nature-based theories. They routinely are embarrassed by the absence of any characteristic *universally* shared by those beings they wish to single out as rights holders, possessed *only* by them, shared *equally* by them (else rights possession would be an analog function admitting of degree rather than all-or-nothing), and which can credibly be taken as *justifying* the preferred moral status that is ascribed to rights holders. All such attempts to ground rights—or morality in general—in nature fail because the class of moral claimants does not coincide with the class possessing property Φ, where Φ is the alleged natural basis of rights. In particular, while *being a project pursuer* may be a property morally relevant for certain purposes, it is too restrictive a criterion for the grounding of rights.

An *unfriendly* critic will maintain that project pursuit is not merely less than universal but parochial. Personal projects may consume the attention of upper-middle-class, highly educated adults of contemporary Western liberal democracies: college professors, for example. But most individuals in most settings throughout human history have led lives of less rarified reflective delicacy than a model of project pursuit can comprehend. People concerned with humdrum matters like survival are not afforded the luxury of devoting their attention to framing and giving effect to a personal vision of the good. That may or may not be a misfortune for them, but it does not preclude their possession of full moral agency. One who argues for the centrality of project pursuit is thereby tacitly confining to the periphery those individuals whose lives fail to match some philosopher ideal. To be sure, this exclusionary strategy boasts distinguished ancestry. One is reminded of Aristotle's restriction of flourishing human activity to well-bred Greek males with the inclination and leisure to devote their lives to philosophical contemplation: in other words, to men like Aristotle himself. This idealization of one's own distinctive life situation as a norm for all men is not only myopic but also disreputable. It is a kind of intellectual imperialism by means of which a parochial conception of the good life is advanced under the banner of universalism. An ethic emphasizing project pursuit, it may be charged, is yet another addition to this sorry lot.

2. Ethics, whatever else it may be, is the investigation of rationally justifiable bases for resolving conflicts among persons with divergent aims who share a common world. Because resources and opportunities are not unlimited, the success of one person is often the failure of another. If morality is possible, then there must be some immanent standard, whether reason, moral sentiment, or another, that can acceptably adjudicate conflict. (A Nietzschean nihilistic critique of conventional morality maintains that, whatever the appearance, conflict can only be resolved through superior will or strength. Such *resolution* is not to be confused with *solution*.) Conversely, if there

does not exist some interpersonal standard by means of which claims can be scrutinized and compared, morality is impotent.

The argument of the preceding chapter, a critic may charge, is not genuinely a moral argument—one *within* morality—but one *about* morality, more specifically, about the bleak prospects for the successful generation of a comprehensive moral theory. For morality to weigh the competing claims of diverse individuals, it must be scrupulously neutral among them, that is, impersonal. However, if project pursuit necessarily entails recognition of personal standards of value to which agents commit themselves, then individuals cannot regard themselves as bound by any one scheme for conflict resolution. Morality breaks down into a sea of competing claims. The recognition of the primacy of project pursuit is then not a contribution to ethics but instead a line in its obituary.

These objections deserve to be taken seriously. They amount to a prediction of the futility of attempting to erect a theory of basic rights on the incommensurably distinct commitments that individuals undertake. The most satisfactory way to confute a prediction is, of course, to realize the result that was deemed unattainable. The remainder of this book is an attempt to disarm the critic in just that way, by developing a persuasive account of rights. Still, a few preliminary remarks in response to these objections may help clarify the direction of the argument that follows.

Project Pursuers and Other Persons

It is not being claimed that all beings who are rights holders or who merit some degree of moral attention are so in virtue of being project pursuers. Let us call an ethical theory *univalent* if it attempts to ground all ascriptions of moral status to beings on their possession of some one property; a theory that incorporates more avenues than one by way of which a being can be accorded moral status will be said to be *multivalent*.[1] For example, a theory maintaining that all and only rational beings have (equal) moral weight is univalent; one holding that both rationality and sentience convey moral status (of differing degrees) is multivalent.

A univalent theory of basic rights centered around project pursuit will hold that all and only those beings who are project pursuers are rights holders. A multivalent theory need not. It can recognize that project pursuers possess rights *and* that other beings who do not pursue projects are also rights holders. A univalent theory is tidier, but the costs of simplicity are high: characteristically, the inability to accommodate a range of moral phenomena not captured by the favored criterion yet the suppression of which

is strongly counterintuitive. The upshot may be a tortuous effort to assimilate untoward cases under the one criterion recognized by the univalent theory through strategies that forfeit the desired univalence. For example, if the
basis of rights is found in *personhood,* understood as the possession of some
elevated level of mentality, it may be noticed that the account denies to very
young children the status of persons. They then are not rights holders. The
result is uncomfortable; it seems *prima facie* dubious that infants merit no
further moral attention than need be paid to a piece of cheese or a puppy.
Some will bite the bullet here and dismiss the recalcitrant intuitions.[2] More
commonly though, an emendation will be offered: it is not only *actual* persons that possess rights but also *potential* persons.

I shall note, but not pause to examine, the conceptual difficulties inherent
in explicating what is to count as potential persons (Are zygotes potential
persons? Does any disjoined pair of sperm and egg constitute a potential
person?) or in extending the rights argument from actual to potential persons. (In general, claims that are justified in virtue of one's being an actual
Φ are not similarly justified by being a potential Φ. If I am a potential
president of the United States, I do not thereby have the right to veto
congressional legislation, although I would have that right were I actually
president.) Rather, the example has been cited as an instance of a univalent
theory responding to external pressures by turning itself into a multivalent
theory. Acorns are not (yet) oak trees, and potential persons are not actual
persons. If both actual personhood and potential personhood confer the status of rights holder, it follows that there are more ways than one in which a
being can merit acknowledgment as having rights. The alleged simplicity of
a univalent theory is lost once it is transformed into its multivalent offshoot
and, importantly, much confusion can result if that metamorphosis is not
openly avowed but instead disguised as, say, merely two different ways in
which one can be a person.

I shall offer an account of basic rights that is multivalent. By doing so I
hope to avoid the troubles that plague theories of rights purporting to find in
all rights holders some one essential property vouchsafed by nature (or Nature) such that it, and it alone, guarantees the possession of rights. Most,
but not all, adult human beings are project pursuers. Therefore, they have
reason to accord to themselves and to other project pursuers the status of
rights holder. Unless there were project pursuers, there could be no basic
rights. However, project pursuers are not the only holders of rights. Others,
young children for example, also enjoy that status. They do so in virtue of
the social relations to project pursuers in which they stand. They, as it were,
piggyback on project pursuers. The development of this argument is found
in Chapter 7.[3]

It might be maintained that *multivalent theories of ethics* are acceptable, but a *multivalent theory of rights* is not. The moral mansion may indeed contain many rooms such that human beings, animals, and even natural objects or artifacts merit moral consideration and respect. Each can have its own particular status by virtue of its distinctive properties, and the respective moral weights assigned can vary from the infinitesimal to the profound. But rights holders cannot be deployed in a stratified order of castes. A right is a claim with which others *must* comply; it is a *maximally weighty* moral consideration, and there cannot be degrees of maximal weightiness. While some rights holders can possess *more rights* than others, there is no such thing as being *more of a rights holder*. All and only those beings who issue maximally weighty claims are rights holders. Therefore, multivalence is an inadmissable basis for a theory of basic rights.

Even if it be granted that all rights are equally stringent, itself a debatable proposition and susceptible to various interpretations, it does not follow that a multivalent theory of rights must embrace invidious distinctions among those individuals accorded rights. It is a mistake to suppose that different bases for the acquisition of rights entail different degrees of stringency in the rights that have been acquired. If two unrelated properties, F_1 and F_2, each confer rights, they may do so to the same (maximal) degree. And even when one class of rights holders is primary in that unless it existed, there could be no rights holders at all, it still does not follow that these rights holders are preeminent in the weightiness of the rights they possess.

An analogy might help. Consider the following recursive definition of natural number:

1. 1 is a natural number.
2. If n is a natural number, then Successor (n) is a natural number.

Something, then, is a natural number if it is 1 or if it is the successor of a natural number. Although this is a multivalent account of natural numbers in which the property of *being 1* is primary, it does not follow that 1 is "more" of a natural number than, say, 7. No matter how something is introduced into the class of natural numbers, it is equally and fully a member of that class. By analogy, whatever may serve as the justification for someone being a holder of rights, one who is justifiably a rights holder is so equally and fully.

What of the complaint that project pursuit is too insular a condition to support a general theory of rights, that it is only a favored few human beings who enjoy the leisure to devote themselves to projects, while the mass of men must make do with responsibilities, necessities for survival, and occasional diversions? I do not believe this to be a significant objection. The forms that projects may take are so diverse that it cannot successfully be maintained that the image of man as the project-pursuing animal illegitimately presupposes as the norm for all some one favored philosophical conception of flourishing human life. One who pursues projects lives a life structured by abiding commitments that determine what will count as a motivation toward action for that person, but no particular motivational structure is presupposed. A project pursuer's life is coherent over time, but the values around which practical activity cohere are open-ended.

It is true that there is something of a middle class flavor that attaches to the term 'project.' It will come more easily to some lips than to others, and perhaps it is only a distinctive minority that will recognize what they do to be the pursuit of projects. Were some other term available that lacked the connotation of reflexive self-awareness and introspective scrutiny that 'project' conveys, one might elect to take advantage of its semantic neutrality. But not necessarily; the noun 'project' resonates through its association with the verb to 'to project.' Projects are precisely those motivated dispositions that *project themselves temporally* through various stages of a life and render it one connected life rather than a jumble of discrete episodes. They also *project at a time* across an individual's various inducements to act such that the person is more than an arena on which disconnected and warring impulses collide. To the extent that one is attached to certain persistent ends, not all of equal gravity but some central and others subsidiary, and that one expresses such attachment through appropriate action, then one is a project pursuer.

It follows that one who pursues a project need not have antecedently deliberated concerning toward which values to devote his efforts or has carefully compared the ends to which he is attached with sets of alternate possible ends in order to appraise their respective degrees of worthiness. The perpetually introspective and discriminating consciousness is indeed an artifact of a particular moment of civilizational development and class standing that cannot be extrapolated to all mankind. A person's commitments may be unarticulated and not at all the product of conscious deliberation culminating in a moment of supreme decision. They may rather be something that he has gradually and imperceptibly come to assume over time in much the same way that one takes on distinctive vocal inflections or the cast of one's face. To be committed to end E is not necessarily to know that one is committed to E, and it is certainly not to regard E as something one has chosen over alternatives for specifiable reasons.

During the two centuries since Kant, the norm for practical activity that has much attracted philosophers, Kantian and non-Kantian alike, as fitting for a human life is that of the *autonomous agent*. An autonomous life is not merely the Socratic examined life. One acts autonomously only if one decides on a course of action through rational consideration of the prospects before one, *and* if one is unconstrained by external influences that make one behave (heteronomously) in a manner that was not freely willed. J. S. Mill celebrates openness to endless possibility in *On Liberty*, where he writes:

> As it is useful that while mankind are imperfect there should be different opinions, so it is that there should be different experiments of living; that free scope should be given to varieties of character, short of injury to others; and that the worth of different modes of life should be proved practically, when anyone thinks fit to try them. It is desirable, in short, that in things which do not primarily concern others, individuality should assert itself. Where, not the person's own character, but the traditions or customs of other people are the rule of conduct, there is wanting one of the principal ingredients of human happiness, and quite the chief ingredient of individual and social progress.

*   *   *

> He who lets the world, or his own portion of it, choose his plan of life for him, has no need of any other faculty than the ape-like one of imitation. He who chooses his plan for himself, employs all his faculties. He must use observation to see, reasoning and judgment to foresee, activity to gather materials for decision, discrimination to decide, and when he has decided, firmness and self-control to hold to his deliberate decision. And these qualities he requires and exercises exactly in proportion as the part of his conduct which he determines according to his own judgment and feelings is a large one. It is possible that he might be guided in some good path, and kept out of harm's way, without any of these things. But what will be his comparative worth as a human being? It really is of importance not only what men do, but also what manner of men they are that do it.[4]

In this century autonomy has been apotheosized by numerous thinkers, including John Rawls in *A Theory of Justice*. Rawls' contractors, whose deliberations are to issue in the fundamental framework of a just society, are placed behind a veil of ignorance that shields them from any awareness of the particularities of their own lives. The veil is explicitly designed to filter out the distorting effects of bias and strategic bargaining. It thereby renders the contractors perfectly pure specimens of autonomy. None can be deflected from rational reflection by the force of any untoward inclination, because behind the veil one does not know what one's inclinations are. Choice cannot be bent to concern for one's own or to that which one has antecedently come to regard as fitting and proper, because these too are unknown. All one can do—one *must do*—is legislate absolutely *de novo*. In the Rawlsian original position one's autonomy is safeguarded not only from the encroachments of others but also from one's own preconceptions.

It may be satisfactory to deduce a theory of justice from a decision-theoretic model of perfectly autonomous deliberators.[5] It does not follow that actual lives are lived satisfactorily only to the extent that they are lived autonomously. How can one conceive of an individual who is reared to develop the capacity for rational deliberation yet for whom that developmental process does not inculcate unchosen affections and antipathies that condition the judgments he subsequently makes? Even if a person could dissociate himself from those attachments which have prerationally formed themselves and so could dispassionately and neutrally examine all possible manners of life, this ability may be less praiseworthy than the champions of autonomy would have it be. Consider the individual who has schooled himself to ask, "Do I really have good reason to carry around this baggage of commitment to friends and family that has hitherto shaped so much of my activity?" Or: "Perhaps I ought to work to overcome my visceral repugnance toward the torture of innocent persons if I could thereby improve my score on the utilitarian calculus." One who has come to entertain these reflections may be a person whose capacity for autonomous choice has expanded wonderfully; he may also have become morally corrupted.[6]

It is important to recognize that being a pursuer of projects is not equivalent to being a fully autonomous agent in the sense of 'autonomy' sketched out above. One's projects may, but need not be, the product of explicit deliberation concerning what vision of the good will engage one's efforts. They may instead be ingested with one's mother's milk, become by imperceptible degrees more firmly fixed over time within one's volitional makeup, and never be trotted out to be cross-examined at the bar of reason. If the liberal temperament has been prone to fasten on the appeal of commitment posterior to the full exercise of deliberative reflection, conservatives have responded by stressing the value of rootedness in a given milieu or tradition that is distinctively one's own and for which one feels an attachment not grounded in a conscious act of rational choice. Michael Oakeshott writes:

> To be conservative . . . is to prefer the familiar to the unknown, to prefer the tried to the untried, fact to mystery, the actual to the possible, the limited to the unbounded, the near to the distant, the sufficient to the superabundant, the convenient to the perfect, present laughter to utopian bliss. Familiar relationships will be preferred to the allure of more profitable attachments; to acquire and to enlarge will be less important than to keep, to cultivate and to enjoy; the grief of loss will be more acute than the excitement of novelty or promise. It is to be equal to one's own fortune, to live at the level of one's own means, to be content with the want of greater perfection which belongs alike to oneself and one's circumstances. With some people this is itself a choice; in

others it is a disposition which appears, frequently or less frequently, in their preferences and aversion, and *it is not itself chosen or specifically cultivated.*[7]

One need not take sides in the liberal/conservative debate to note that it could not be a live struggle were it not for the fact that project pursuit can be *either* reflective or nonreflective (or some mix of the two). The critic who alleges that a philosophical anthropology within which the human propensity to pursue projects occupies center stage is unacceptably argumentative and ideological is himself captive of an ideological mind-set such that nothing will count as a commitment unless it is the fruit of reflective deliberation. I do not doubt that people other than intellectuals deliberate concerning values, but I wish to emphasize that commitment to projects does not necessarily rest on such deliberation.

Can it then reasonably be denied that the vast mass of men at any time or cultural circumstance display the character of project pursuer? It is neither chauvinism nor parochialism to claim that most persons do display abiding commitments through which their volitions are regularly channeled. In all societies persons regularly attach themselves through their actions to the welfare of parents or children or clan or nation, display fealty to their gods, view the contours of the land that is theirs with special affection, show allegiance to the virtues and responsibilities of a craft or tradition. Because these constitute patterns of motivated activity that form the structure of a scrutable life, they merit recognition as projects.

It would be an error to extend these observations beyond their legitimate boundaries, to transform them into purported metaphysical truths. There is not any natural necessity that human lives exhibit the strong degree of unity that project pursuit confers. They can exhibit fragmentation of two different sorts.

The first is that of the Indiscriminate Evaluator, the person whose motivational thrusts are so sudden and transient that they elude all our attempts to understand them as emanating from a common core. Extreme schizophrenia is the pure form of this phenomenon, but it admits of degree: the breakdown of robust personal identity can occur partially or in stages. Whether extreme or mild, though, it represents deviation from the standard of a life that is rendered thoroughly coherent through the persistence of projects.

The second kind of fragmentation displays an abrupt break along clean lines. A conversionary experience conceivably could bifurcate a life in this way. The postconversion individual is imbued with drives and allegiances that give his life a definite shape, but they bear no resemblance to those that motivated the preconversion self. It would be natural for a convert to look back at the preconversion life as foreign, as one lived by someone else whose goals now seem puzzling and confused. The convert may speak of the decisive experience as a confluence of death/birth (as does, most famously, Paul, the erstwhile Saul). Here we find not the absence of unity, but two temporal segments, each of which displays an intelligible pattern, yet which are unhinged from each other.

Somewhat similar to spontaneous and unexpected conversion is the institutionalized practice of deliberately abandoning one form of life for another. The adoption by a postulant in a religious order of a new name, different modes of dress, etc., represents the taking on of radically different commitments that will thenceforward mold the transformed self. Similarly, the Hindu householder who has lived within a world devoted to economic and familial pursuits will, in his late middle years, cast these off and retreat into forest solitude to pursue enlightenment.

One ought not to be too quick, even in the case of radical conversion, to classify the resultant person as a different self. It might be the case that behind the apparent divorce from preconversionary projects there lurk abiding commitments that are recognizably those of the selfsame active being. Some questions to be asked are: Was it the case that the preconversion individual undertook actions to bring on the shift? Had he developed devotion to an ideal that could not be expressed adequately within the confines of his former way of life? Was there at any time a perspective from which he viewed the two as developmental stages of a common enterprise? Does he, postconversion, recognize obligations previously incurred as his (and not in the sense that one may feel obligated to pay off the debts that a parent or friend incurred)? Is remorse felt for preconversionary transgressions? Is he relieved that a deficient mode of his own activity has been repaired? If affirmative answers are given, then it is preferable to explain the case as exemplifying a complex kind of unity between two distinguishable episodes, each of which itself displays a different manner of unity[8] (e.g., the *Oresteia* vis-à-vis its component tragedies).

Abrupt and total cleavage within the biological span of a human life may be extremely rare; still, there do not seem to be adequate grounds for asserting that it does not ever occur, that it *could not occur*. One can at least imagine a kind of human existence in which genuine metamorphosis, rather than basic continuity in motivational structure, were the rule. Therefore, it seems inadvisable to legislate such continuity as an essential feature of human existence. Nonetheless, an ethic centered on project pursuit is not shallowly rooted. That persons usually and regularly orient themselves by reference to a set of commitments that evolve over time but do not suddenly appear and disappear is a *deep* fact—whether or not it is ultimately contingent. It is one that must be reflected in any conception of morality adequate to beings such as ourselves. Conversely, we should not expect our moral notions to be apt for beings who lack projects. For example, the practice of promising is only understandable within a context in which the one who is to comply with the promise recognizes it as having been made for reasons that are *his reasons;* and assigning value to individualism presupposes a conception of the individual as a purposive being whose goals display a sturdy measure of fixity.[9]

The argument here being presented for the recognition of basic rights rests on the fact of project pursuit and so is narrower in its scope than one that sees its starting point as the possession of sentience, or rationality construed as the fitting of means to (possibly evanescent) ends, or bare purposiveness. It has been maintained that human beings are, in fact, aptly characterized as project pursuers and that therefore rights have application. But it is admitted that were project pursuit not a characteristic feature within a community of beings, they could not reasonably be understood as having rights. One can therefore conceive of sentient beings or even thoroughly rational and purposive beings for whom no derivation of rights is possible. Naturally, theoreticians who take one of these qualities as the foundation of rights will demur. That dispute will be taken up subsequently, especially in Chapter 7.

The Bounds of Conflict

Individuals' aims can come into conflict. This truism is the starting point for virtually all ethical inquiry in the modern epoch. Philosophical normative ethics is the search for rationally justifiable standards for the resolution of interpersonal conflict; that is a definitional statement.

It is therefore with a sensation akin to vertigo that one turns to the ancients to find them disinclined to pursue ethics as a search for conflict-resolution schemes. In the *Nicomachean Ethics* Aristotle devotes a book to friendship (''Is this a work of ethics?'') and several paragraphs to *megalopsychia,* ''great-souledness'' (''This surely *cannot* be a work of ethics!''). But one looks in vain for prescriptions concerning responsibility toward the poor, toleration of nonconforming religious expressions, the duty of forgiveness, civil disobedience, legitimate appropriation of property, freedom of speech, obligations to future generations, the bindingness of contracts—or a host of other contemporary concerns that would be featured in a twentieth-century counterpart. A weighing of the respective merits of the political and the theoretical life in a work titled *Ethics* may strike the reader as jarringly solipsistic.

It is a commonplace to note that the Greek *ethike*, though a cognate of our 'ethics,' sharply differs from it in meaning. But a translation gap is not the primary factor that distances our concerns from those of Aristotle. The Greeks, after all, had a well-developed conception of law, one that we largely inherit. They, like us, understood law as the imposition of an order (perhaps rooted in nature, perhaps conventional) on the muddled affairs of men. Their horror of the conflict that would inevitably ensue in the absence of law was at least as great as ours, not having been tempered by a Rousseauian argument that law is among those impositions that have corrupted natural man. Nor was it beyond them to consider how alternate structures would differentially affect the likelihood and nature of conflict among different classes of men; that is precisely the theme of Aristotle's *Politics* (and numerous works of his predecessors and successors). Why, then, does interpersonal conflict play so diminished a role in the *Ethics?*

The response must be that Aristotle sees a different foundation for practical philosophy than do moderns. It is one in which virtues, not duties, are primary. That is not to deny, as commentators friendlier to Kant than to Aristotle often have,[10] that the concept of *duty* is foreign to Aristotle. It is quite clear from a reading of the Book V discussion of justice that his ethic has a place for the importance of acting on the basis of sound principles. Indeed, it is the discussion of justice, especially remarks concerning the optimal distribution of rewards and disabilities among conflicting claimants, that is most recognizably akin to the efforts of contemporary ethicists. Yet here too there is a difference. For Aristotle justice is not primarily a desirable feature of adjudicative decisions or of particular laws or even of institutional structures; it is a virtue of individuals, specifically the avoidance of *pleonexia,* "grasping too much." The duty to act justly springs from the inherent desirability of being just. To the diminished extent that moderns speak of the virtues, logical priority is usually the other way around: virtues are those traits of character that reliably lead one to discharge one's duties in acceptable—or exceptional—fashion.[11]

The Aristotelian conception of a virtue is a settled disposition to feel and act in intrinsically good ways. "Why be virtuous?" is a question that admits only of the question-begging answer: "Because virtues are those good-in-themselves components of a life that is itself inherently good." Decidedly nontrivial, though, are investigations of what traits constitute virtue and the process by means of which the virtues are successfully inculcated. To these he bends great efforts. There is, however, no temptation to argue that the virtues are instrumentally good because they generate socially useful actions. It may be the case that a society composed of preeminently virtuous persons will be well ordered, but that is not the rationale for virtue.

For Aristotle, then, practical philosophy is, in the first instance, concerned with the ability of individuals to give to their lives a persistent structure that does not easily bend to opposed enticements; that regularly motivates action and emotion comprehensible by reference to that structure; that serves as a standard of value for the appraisal of competing realizable outcomes; that will provide a basis for judging whether a whole human life has been a success or a failure; whose value is presupposed by all other judgments of value rather than being consequent upon them; and which is therefore not subject to trade-off for the sake of any higher-ranking good.

The purpose of this brief excursion into ancient philosophy is, of course, to demonstrate a striking resemblance between an ethic of activity in accord with virtue during a whole human life and an ethic of project pursuit. Projects are like Aristotelian virtues in giving motivational structure to a life and in providing the individual a standard of value for practical judgment. This is at least presumptive reason to reject the charge that to focus on the significance to practical reason of projects is to inter ethical inquiry rather than to pursue it. Although most contemporary ethical theory takes as its embarkation point the need for an external standard by means of which competing claims can be resolved, that is not the only way in which one can legitimately undertake to do ethics. Aristotle, for one, began differently.

It must, for better or worse, be admitted that congruence with this distinguished forebear is not exact. The most crucial difference is that between a conception of value as *thoroughly impersonal* and one in which at least some value is *personal*. As I read Aristotle, there is no place for genuine value coming to be for an individual through an act of commitment to ends that are distinctively his own.[12] The virtues, unlike projects, are *discovered* rather than *created,* the same for all men *qua* man rather than variegated among persons. He recognizes, to be sure, that people may undertake allegiance to other standards (for example, to an ideal of fame or a life of pleasure), but if they do so, then they are mistaken. No value, or at least no value that *truly deserves to be valued,* is thereby created. Value is prior to commitments, and one does well or ill insofar as one's commitments accurately exemplify or fail to exemplify that value.

I have opposed to this conception one in which at least some value[13] is posterior to choice, that is, is personal. There exist bona fide reasons for an individual to direct his life along a particular path, and some of these reasons would not have existed had he undertaken different commitments. Because these reasons are reasons-for-that-individual, there is no one (impersonal) standard to which all practical reason must alike bend. This is, then, in one acceptable meaning of the term, a *liberal* conception. It recognizes in each individual project pursuer value that springs from his ability to generate value through his own personal commitments. He is not merely a placeholder at which external value can express itself.

Aristotle is not a liberal, although neither is he exactly illiberal and although many of his insights can be incorporated into liberal theory. It is clear that no conception of *rights* (as something that persons have and that impose side constraints on the actions of others) is central to his thought[14] and, somewhat more arguably, it is only with a great deal of awkwardness that a recognition of basic rights could be added to an Aristotelian core.[15] It does not seem accidental that rights become a prominent unit of philosophical currency only in the seventeenth and eighteenth centuries as adjuncts of liberalism. Only when great stress is placed on the value of individualism will it appear credible to insist that individualism be safeguarded through placing systematic constraints on the activities of civil and ecclesiastical authorities. On the other hand, if all value is impersonal, then it seems quite reasonable to insist that society be ordered according to a design that will most fully and completely instantiate that impersonal value. The designers may be Philosopher Kings, bishops, Benthamite calculators of social utility, or whomever the regnant experts on value are taken to be.

Despite the important differences between an Aristotelian ethic grounded in "nature" *(physis)* and a liberal one centered on the significance of project pursuit, both reject a conception of ethics as primarily a search for interpersonal decision procedures. Instead, each takes as primary the individual's exercise of practical reason to realize value. How to live the good life rather than how to mesh the warring impulses of different lives is the focal problem, focal for the *theorist* because focal for the acting *individual*. Obviously, both problems must ultimately be addressed, but different answers are given to the question of priority. On one account, an individual is to direct his efforts to achieve a socially harmonious arrangement, and the tendency of his actions to bring about that harmony is what renders them meritorious. The alternative account begins from individual's reasons to pursue the ends that each separately values, and seeks to discover within or superimpose from without an orderliness running through these discrete conative endeavors.

For Aristotle, social harmony is partly the result of human artifice. It is the stateman's task to bring the seeds of cooperative activity to fruition, and where the statesman fails, chaos reigns. But those seeds of cooperation themselves have a natural basis in human nature. That man is a political animal means that human beings will choose to live among others of their kind, but also, even more important, that they *are a kind* and thus share an overriding common end. It is because of this end that there is such a thing as the virtue of man *qua* man, and not merely the different virtues of male and female, shoemaker and soldier, Greek and barbarian. (Admittedly, this incipient basis for a kind of egalitarianism is belied by other motifs in the Aristotelian corpus.) Each person seeks to attain the fully flourishing human state, and, since this is the same for all, a polity is not inherently an arena of clashing wills. It is instead an *enterprise association*[16] in which all are united in the pursuit of a common goal. That, of course, is an ideal; the reality is typically much messier. But because that ideal is rooted in the nature of things—and, most especially, in the nature of man—it can at least be approximated. Good laws and proper education are means toward that approximation.

A single standard of impersonal value is, therefore, Aristotle's key to interpersonal comity. Even were that standard accepted, though, the conclusion of a tendency toward harmony would not easily follow. For even if human virtue is the same for all persons, there nonetheless exist the claims of the separate virtues appropriate to different subgroups within humanity. The specific excellences of soldiers or philosophers are not identical to those of the good man *simpliciter* and may even conflict with the latter. Might one not have reason to accept somewhat less success as a human being in order to do splendidly well in one's calling? Aristotle does not seem able to provide any assurance that such could not be the case. (Were the stupendous triumphs of his perhaps not altogether diligent student Alexander an embarrassment to him on just these grounds, and could that be why Alexander and his exploits receive so little mention?)

Moreover, even the virtues common to mankind seem susceptible to conflict amongst themselves. If, at the cost of some measure of justice, one can develop a great deal of courage, is the bargain well made? If the pursuit of theoretical wisdom interferes with the demands of friendship or of political life, should *theoria* be assigned lexical priority such that its slightest increment will justify any degree of distancing from the other virtues? Or is there some ascertainable optimal trade-off ratio? If each virtue is inherently good in itself rather than made good by reference to some further standard, then how can any answer whatsoever be given to these questions? No principle of commensurability seems to be available. In the face of this dilemma, the usually forthright Aristotle hedges. On the one hand, he recognizes that the Socratic claimed unity of the virtues is implausible. On the other hand, if the virtues are separate, then they can impose conflicting claims not resolvable within the theory of the virtues itself, and which Aristotle does not otherwise resolve. I regard this as an unsolved probem within Aristotlelian philosophy.

If this is so, that is, if positing impersonally valuable ends does not guarantee the existence of a rationally justifiable conflict-resolution device, then personally derived value does not automatically make problems of modulating conflict more intractable than when all value is assumed to be impersonal. In either case, if more than one item of value is acknowledged, and if there is no miraculous, divinely imposed harmony of all values, then conflict can ensue. It is the task of theory to derive some principle by means of which conflict is to be limited. For a liberal theory it is to be done while acknowledging each person's rational motivation to value the objects of his own personal projects.

Therefore, it is much too abrupt to dismiss a project-based ethic as the covert abandonment of the (alleged) "moral point of view." Although it does not *begin* with the question "How are we to live together?" it, like any other theory in ethics, must eventually confront that question. It does not do so by constructing some one artificial standard by means of which all values are rendered commensurable; no such standard can carry conviction for a project pursuer. Instead, it proceeds with the understanding that value is plural and that practical reason is therefore essentially differentiated among persons. It is hoped that, nonetheless, there exists some acceptable basis for comity, but that result is not assumed at the outset. It must instead be developed out of a credible philosophical anthropology.

Project Pursuit and Liberal Theory

In fact, liberalism has traditionally recognized an irreducible plurality of incommensurable values. That is why, despite repeated efforts, it fails to fit smoothly at the joints with a monolithic utilitarianism. Liberalism accords to each individual a unique and irreplaceable value, and because individuals are many, so too are values. Rights are consonant with individualism because rights provide the most morally stringent protection of the worth that each individual exemplifies. Rights erect side constraints that preclude the sacrifice of one individual for the sake of another individual in order to maximize impersonal value. Indeed, many liberal theoreticians have been chary of admitting that there can be any such thing as impersonal value. I believe that to be mistaken for reasons that will be adduced at some length in Chapter 9, but the impetus toward extreme subjectivism is understandable. It is the intent to safeguard personal value, to reject the claims of a monistic impersonal juggernaut.

"Rational agents are to be treated as ends in themselves and not merely as means"; "Humanity constitutes a Kingdom of Ends"; "Individuals are inviolable"; "Persons are not interchangeable one with another"; these familiar Kantian and quasi-Kantian formulations are characteristically liberal.

It would be absurd to maintain that one who swears allegiance to them thereby abandons the practice of philosophical ethics. These strands congregate at a point that lies at the heart of ethical theory. Each is admittedly slippery, and one may acknowledge their persuasiveness while simultaneously wondering how they are to become components of a perspicuously clear account.

I maintain that attention to the status of projects carries explicatory weight at just this point. It lends enhanced sharpness to the vague notion of individuals not being interchangeable one for another. According to moral theories that acknowledge a supreme impersonal standard of value, we are all summarily enrolled in a common cause. It is the ceaseless and perpetual endeavor to maximize utility or whatever other good is sovereign. Each being is a soldier on the line, and though each stands in a different position and wields different armaments, everyone's cause is the same. While individuals may fall by the wayside, the enterprise goes on. However, it then becomes utterly mysterious why there should be anything suspect about sacrificing one of the troops for another just so long as more impersonal value is thereby attained. Interchangeability is inextricably built into that picture: all else equal, one producer of value can be replaced by another producer of value without any effect on overall value. That which leaves overall value unchanged is, tautologously, morally neutral.

Pace utilitarians, Charles Fried,[17] and other upholders of the Foil, recognition of project pursuit entails the denial of the existence of a Universal Human Enterprise in which we are interchangeable, replaceable participants. There can be as many enterprises as there are agents, and each agent acts rationally to apply a personal standard of value to those states of affairs that are within his power to promote or impede. Therefore, there is no single standard of value in terms of which all ends are commensurable. From what perspective could one justify the claim that A and all of A's ends ought to be sacrificed for the considerably greater charm of B and B's ends? Certainly not from the perspective of A; and even if this result would conveniently follow from B's appraisal of value, that result is in no way rationally binding on A. To generalize, no project pursuer can be shown to be rationally obligated to sacrifice for the sake of someone else's interests that which is essential to his own ability to construct a worthwhile life (here understood roughly as a life in which the persistent attachment to one's own projects can be expressed through fitting activity). Such sacrifice is *supererogation,* not *duty,* a distinction that emerges with some clarity in the context of a project-regarding ethic. Utilitarianism and other ethical systems that endorse an impersonal standard of value have a notoriously difficult time finding room for any distinction between duty and supererogation; the two seem exactly alike in the relevant respect of being instances of value maximization.

Just as project pursuit lends clarity to the rejection of interchangeability, so too does it help sharpen the distinction between regarding persons as ends in themselves versus regarding them merely as means. If an impersonal standard of value reigns, then lives possess instrumental value insofar as they are productive of whatever this standard takes to be of intrinsic worth. However, it is hard to see how lives can be of *more* than instrumental value, how they can be other than servants to the standard. For a utilitarian, persons turn out to be convenient loci at which and through which value can be realized. Because rightness of action is entirely a function of utility production, it is necessarily utility that counts primarily, persons only derivatively.[18] By way of contrast, an ethic in which project pursuit assumes a central place is one in which each project pursuer is constructing a life that has unique value because he *gives* it that value through his commitment to some ends as directive for him. Value emerges from commitment, not because the world is empty of value until an Existentialist Hero essays a venture of Radical Choice, but for the more prosaic reason that commitment engenders a personal standard of value in terms of which possible outcomes are appraised. The value that emerges is conceptually posterior to commitment, not prior to and thus conditioning choice.

Therefore: to require A to renounce his own cherished end E_1, and to enroll him as B's partner in the pursuit of B's end E_2 is to make A an adjunct to B's projects, an instrument for B to use toward B's ends. That is how I construe the locution of treating someone merely as a means and not as an end in himself. For A to regard himself as an end, A must conceive of his own life as being individuated by the commitments he has undertaken. A regards himself as a member of a Kingdom of Ends when he both respects the unique individuality that is his own and recognizes that all other project pursuers are themselves unique individuals, each with his own life to live, and each possessing reason to reject overreaching impositions from others. In a Kingdom of Ends, each project pursuer is accorded moral space within which he can independently attempt to realize a connected and coherent conception of the good life for him.

Rights are just this entitlement to moral space. By establishing boundaries that others must not transgress, they accord to each rights holder a measure of sovereignty over his own life. That is the sense in which individuals are said to be *inviolable;* even if one *can* act so as to deny another the status of project pursuer, one *must* not.

That is why I maintain that project pursuit is compatible with morality, specifically with a rights-based morality. Yet this parsing of Kant has not resolved the problem of conflict among persons; instead it has made it more acute. For if each individual has abiding reason to further his own projects, and if projects can run afoul of each other—and of that there is no doubt— then it would seem that a recipe has been provided for interminable and irreconcilable hostilities. If nothing stands athwart the jarring of contending projects, then either superior strength or mutual exhaustion can be the only respite from Hobbesian warfare. A Kingdom of Ends ceaselessly bashing one another about is not a pleasant prospect. It must then be asked: can we devise a constitution for this kingdom?

4

The Derivation of Basic Rights

The ends to which project pursuers can commit themselves are extraordinarily diverse. Precisely because of that diversity, because there is no one common good to which all other goods are subsidiary, the prospect of an ethic binding on all has seemed to be in jeopardy. Morality claims to be generally binding on actors, but how can that claim possibly be substantiated unless all have reason to adhere to its dictates? It has been argued that what A has reason to advance is E_1, that what B has reason to advance is E_2 . . . , and therefore that what counts as a *good reason* for A can decisively lack that status for B. Bogged down in this plethora of divergent and frequently competing rational motivations for action, it may seem impossible that anything that can be characterized as a common morality could emerge. At most, it seems, one might be able to chart the trajectories of prudential considerations that bear on each project pursuer as they flit their way across each other's path.

This pessimistic appraisal is too abrupt. Although the indexicality of practical reason must be granted, there is hope yet of discerning a common thread that runs through the efforts of diverse agents, an end that every project pursuer has reason to acknowledge simply in virtue of being a project pursuer. At least one suggests itself: the value of being a project pursuer. As a first approximation, consider the following argument:

1. A is a project pursuer.
2. Therefore, there is some end, E_1, that A values as directive for A's life.
3. If E_1 is a directive end for A, then A values that which is necessary for the promotion of E_1.
4. If A were not able to pursue any projects whatsoever, then A could not pursue E_1.

5. Therefore, ability to pursue projects is necessary for the promotion of E_1.

6. From 3, it follows that A values A's own ability to be a project pursuer; hence

7. By generalization, all project pursuers are rationally obliged to value their own ability to be a project pursuer.

The argument demands a close look at two points. The first is at step 3. A critic could maintain that this premise unacceptably takes it for granted that whatever attribution of value is accorded to some end will necessarily carry over to all means necessary for the attainment of that end. But this need not be so. Consider some agent, Ed, who places very high value on the circumstance of his becoming king of Thebes. In order to become king, however, it is necessary that he kill his father and marry his mother. Is it true that Ed is therefore rationally obliged to place correspondingly high value on the acts of killing his father and marrying his mother? Not apparently. He may find those prospects repugnant and so refrain from undertaking them while still valuing the end of becoming king of Thebes. That end is then blocked by other value considerations. It may be true that, all else equal, one who values the end thereby values the means, but to insert a *ceteris paribus* clause into each relevant step of the argument would be to weaken it unacceptably. The conclusion would then become:

7'. All else equal, all project pursuers are rationally obliged to value their own ability to be a project pursuer.

Without any firm guidance as to when the *ceteris paribus* clause is satisfied, the conclusion cannot be assumed to apply to the rational motivation of any actual project pursuers.

This criticism misfires. It is based on a general ends-mean analysis that does not apply to *directive ends*. Recall that those ends which are the objects of projects are directive in that they determine how other attainable outcomes are to be evaluated. A directive end does not bend to the prior determination of the value placed on means; the evaluation of means bends to it. Therefore, those ends that are truly the objects of projects will transmit their value to the means necessary for their advancement.

Although the argument can be validated at 3, it breaks down at 5. Suppose that what A values above all else is that someone or other swim the English Channel. It is a matter of complete indifference to A who swims it, himself or B, so long as someone does. Also, if one person swims it, that is as good as if two people swim it. If neither B nor anyone else were to swim the channel, A would value A's swimming, but if B were to swim the channel, then A would place no value on A's ability to swim. Because step 5 speaks only of the promotion of E_1, it does not restrict the promotion of E_1 to A's own activity. Therefore, A's ability to be a project pursuer, and thus his ability to pursue E_1, is not a necessary condition for the promotion of E_1. It seems then that whether a project pursuer values his own ability to pursue projects is contingent. It will often, but not always, accompany having a project.

This gap can be repaired. Commitment to an end is not merely the purely theoretical reflection that it would be good if that end were realized. It is instead the *practical judgment* that one has reason to act in order to bring about that end. A recognizes that there is reason for the promotion of E_1 but additionally, and more to the point, that there is reason-for-the-promotion-of-E_1-by-A. The unique relation that binds an agent to his own ends involves one having reason to bring about those ends. Otherwise they would not be *ends* (for action), but at most what Aristotle calls object of *boulesis,* "wish."[1] If A's attachment to E_1 is not merely the *wish* that E_1 somehow be made to obtain but instead the *commitment* to act in order to produce E_1, then A values his own ability to act for the sake of his own ends. He does, after all, value being a project pursuer. We can then reformulate the original argument (starred steps indicating emendation):

1. A is a project pursuer.
2. Therefore, there is some end, E_1, that A values as directive for A's life.
3*. If E_1 is a directive end for A, then A values that which is necessary for the-promotion-of-E_1-by-A.
4. If A were not able to pursue any projects whatsoever, then A could not pursue E_1.
5*. Therefore, A's ability to pursue projects is necessary for the-promotion-of-E_1-by-A.
6. From 3*, it follows that A values A's own ability to be a project pursuer; hence
7. By generalization, all project pursuers are rationally obliged to value their own ability to be a project pursuer.

This result is considerably stronger than it may at first seem to be. It was noted above that valued items need not form a mutually consistent, jointly realizable whole: ends and necessary means may have opposite value-signs. It is also the case for most objects of desire that they can be opposed within a person's volitional makeup by desires at a different level. That is, one who desires some outcome O may not value the circumstance of his valuing O, may even desire to be rid of the desire for O. For example, a cigarette smoker may desire to smoke cigarettes, may in fact be motivated by that desire to smoke cigarettes yet, at a higher level, disvalue the circumstance of his desiring to smoke cigarettes.[2] Volition at one level need not be in harmony with volition at a higher level, and so one may be moved to do X and simultaneously value someone's preventing the doing of X.[3] Indeed, the direction of desires can continue to oscillate at successively higher levels. Consider the prude who is troubled by his lascivious desires and wishes to quell them. Suppose that he becomes a recipient of the largesse of the Sexual Revolution such that he now wishes to put his prudery behind him, all the better to wallow in his instinctive desires. In such a case, a third-order desire attempts to countermand a second-order desire which itself wars against a first-order desire. It seems possible that the prude might then develop a fourth-order desire that goes against the third, and so on. Just how complicated this structure might become is limited only by the empirical facts of moral psychology and not by the logic of desire and valuation.

A significant feature attaching to one's assignment of positive value to being a project pursuer, though, is that it is not susceptible to disharmony in this way. Suppose that A is strongly motivated to pursue E_1 yet comes fervently to desire that he be rid of the appalling desire for E_1. Then A has reason, in virtue of this second-order desire, to bring about the state of affairs: A's not being motivated to pursue E_1. If the desire to eradicate all craving for E_1 comes to have directive force for A's life such that it has implications for the value A assigns to a wide range of possible actions, if, in other words, it has the status of a project for A, then A must positively value *being able to act* so as to eliminate desires for E_1. Therefore, *A's ability to be a project pursuer* necessarily has value for A.

The reason why projects in this respect stand apart from other kinds of valuation is that projects are those persistent desires which order a life and by reference to which other items are valued or disvalued. A being who has projects is one for whom there is a highest level that confers positive or negative value on lower-level desires. Or, if there is no highest level but instead an infinite hierarchy, projects are those valuational commitments that, at every succeeding level, are positively valued. That is why commitments undertaken at the level of projects resound through all lower levels and entail that positive value is assigned to being a project pursuer.

This may look a bit like sleight of hand. But it is not being claimed that project pursuit is some sort of Metaphysical Valium that causes all intrapersonal disharmony to vanish. Tension among the values to which a person is attracted can be expected to persist within a life; there are, after all, acute dilemmas for practical reason. To be a project pursuer is not to transcend tension but to confront it. One constructs a life of greater rather than lesser coherence by employing one's personal standard of value, itself created and recreated through one's acts of choice, to impose an ordering relation upon felt sources of disharmony. Success if usually a matter of more or less rather than all or nothing. But without the basis for an imposed coherence that projects provide, a person would be simply the battleground on which disparate inclinations, including higher-level desires, perpetually war.

The Value of Projects and the Value of Rights

Project pursuers, whatever their projects may be, value the ability to be a pursuer of projects. That means that they value having moral space. Because rights demarcate moral space, every project pursuer has reason to desire to be accorded the status of a rights holder. At this point, it is tempting to try the following ploy: each project pursuer is rationally committed to valuing a world in which he is accorded rights. Since all are rationally committed to a regime of rights, every project pursuer values at least one thing in common with each other project pursuer. However much they may disagree amongst themselves concerning the objects of their *particular projects,* they must recognize that upholding respect for rights is a *common good* that each has reason to advance.

The argument is invalid. What A is rationally obliged to value is not a world in which rights are generally respected but a world in which *A is accorded the status of a rights holder.* Similarly, B values a world in which B has rights; C, a world in which C has rights; and so on.[4] Each values rights for *himself* but because of the presence of that indexical reference, each is not valuing the same imagined state of affairs. Of course, A *might* value a world in which everyone is accorded rights—and B, C, . . . might also value that world—but A is not *committed* to anything so charmingly democratic. He need merely value his own having rights.

The argument that was essayed above is formally equivalent to:

1. Each runner in the race desires that he come in first.
2. For every runner, it is desired that that runner come in first.
3. It is desired that every runner come in first.

Both involve a Fallacy of Composition. Just as there is no runner who desires that every runner come in first, there is no project pursuer who (necessarily) desires that every project pursuer be accorded rights.[5]

The High Road to Rights by way of a bogus common good desired by all must, regrettably, be abandoned. What we are entitled to assume is merely that each wants moral space *for himself.* This is a slender point of departure;

wanting something to be true doesn't make it so. That A wants B to accord A the status of a rights holder does not by itself in any way provide B reason so to regard A. At least this much more is required to get the progression toward rights under way: B must be able to recognize that A wants to be treated as a rights holder. That is why, to take an obvious example, rights claims cannot meaningfully be addressed to animals or to forces of nature whose intrusion may be as undesirable as the instrusion of other men. (Puzzle: could one meaningfully address a rights claim to a solipsist?) Need confers rights only when what is needed is recognizable as a need by the one who is to meet it.

Crucially, though, even this is insufficient to generate rights. There is a great deal of slack in the concept of a *need*. Typically, when we say that some person P needs x, we are elliptically expressing the proposition that unless P has x, P will not achieve some good y. But y may itself be either urgent or trivial, and the judgment that P needs x in order to achieve y does not carry with it the further implication that P needs y. For example, someone might need a 1922 Denver mint coin to complete her collection of pennies, but not need to complete the collection. If x is needed for y, and y is not itself something that P needs, there is little temptation to suggest that P's needing x confers a right against one who recognizes P's need for x. Only it if had previously been ascertained that y is itself an intrinsic good of great value to P (or if y is needed in order to secure the intrinsically good z) might an assertion of P's right to x be advanced. "Needs" are an inchoate class that ill support a theory of basic rights.[6]

There is further reason why the recognition of needs, even pressing needs, is insufficient to generate rights. A might need to be able to pursue his projects, A might need that B refrain from interfering with A, and B might recognize that A needs B's noninterference; still, a rights claim against B will not go through unless B has some rational motivation to accede to A's desire that A be accorded the status of a rights holder. One can imagine a race of beings each of whom values the ability to pursue projects and whose ability to do so requires at least noninterference by others. Yet each is so constituted as to be totally unmoved by the plight of any other. Their frantic strivings to give effect to their projects are viewed with the studied unconcern we might have for the doings of goldfish in a tank. "Whatever *it* is acting to bring about is no concern of *mine*," one of these beings might say. I suspect that this is precisely how we would respond to each other if each person's projects were so different in kind from the projects of every other person that it would be inconceivable how anyone could succumb to motivation from *that* direction. Needs, even when recognized by others, are not an adequate springboard for a jump to rights.

The Tripartite Derivation of Rights

It is at this point that the generation of a theory of basic rights runs up against its toughest task: how can one go beyond the bare recognition *of* others as project pursuers to a rational motivation to respect them *as* project pursuers? The problem is especially acute, because what is being bumped up against feels disturbingly like the Is-Ought divide. How can it be crossed? I am unsure of the best path to take. Therefore, I suggest three. Perhaps some one of them can be validated, perhaps, luckily, the passage is over-determined, or, what I suspect to be the case, perhaps the most credible account of the grounds of rational motivation involves elements of each.

The first line to be taken is to note that we are not in fact the sort of beings described above: beings whose empathy is totally disengaged from the plights of their fellows. Rather, human beings are social animals whose survival is predicated upon their being the beneficiaries of altruistic concern of limited yet crucial scope. One of the most far-reaching facts about human beings, a fact that moral theory ignores at its peril, is that human beings are more inclined to feed their young than to eat them. Undoubtedly this propensity is rooted far more in biology than in delicate moral reflection. The organism is such that it is totally dependent on others of its species throughout much of its life cycle and significantly dependent throughout the remainder. Thus there is a sociobiological explanation of why the tendency to be moved by the needs of others, especially the needs of kin, has become a characteristic of the species. The value of empathetic response is, at least in part, survival value. On this quasi-Aristotelian account, one's propensity to be motivated to accord to others what they are known to need is a component of what it is for one to be human. Human rights emerge because there is not merely project pursuit but because there is specifically *human* project pursuit.

The argument from biology does not, taken by itself, carry much conviction. It seems palpable trickery to build into an essentialist construal of man what one wants to churn out when it comes time to do ethical theory. If one seeks a motivation for affording moral space to others, then package the conception of *Homo sapiens* as an animal by nature clever *and* by nature motivated through its recognition of the plight of its fellows. Presto! The gap in one's moral theory has healed itself. This is such an *efficient* investment of philosophical capital that it cries out for further deployment. We posit that man is not only empathetic by nature but also trustworthy, loyal, helpful, friendly . . . ; and forthwith deduce the necessity of Boy Scout morality.

The limitations of the argument from biology should be acknowledged. It has not provided an account of the motivation to respect rights that can count as a *justification*. Instead it has proffered a *causal explanation* with an alleged genetic base. Even it if turns out to be true that human beings are genetically programmed to display a certain measure of altruistic concern, it does not follow that one who refuses to give in to his altruistic leaning, or one in whom it is strikingly absent, is for that reason rationally deficient. It may be the case that there is a biological basis for the typical human propensity to value near-term satisfactions far greater proportionally than long-term satisfactions. A prudent man is one who has acquired control over the impulse to favor the near. Surely, though, we do not judge prudence to be a syndrome featuring defective reason; just the reverse. Finally, it should be observed that even if diminished empathy is judged to be a severe defect, it does not seem to be the kind of defect that the argument sought to exhibit. Someone who fails to be motivated by recognition of the needs of others turns out not to be guilty of moral viciousness so much as he is a sufferer from biological abnormality.

In spite of the above cautions, there remains to this approach an element that has merit. If it is the case that people *ought* to acknowledge and respect the rights of others, then it must be true that people generally *can* respect the rights of others. They can do so only if the recognition that others crave moral space within which to carry out their projects will somehow provide a *motivation* to cede that space. If a certain version of psychological egoism were true, that version maintaining that nothing can possibly move a person to action except desires for his own personal well-being, then no recognition of the needs of others could, by itself, have motivational force. The argument form biology is put forth as a corrective to that kind of egoism. If empathetic response comes naturally to human beings, then they are creatures who at least can be motivated by the recognition that others are project pursuers. A necessary though not sufficient basis for grounding rights has been uncovered.

I turn now to the second line of approach, one suggested by Thomas Nagel.[7] It is complementary to the first. Nagel argues that the ability to recognize oneself as *one person* in a world containing *other persons* is logically sufficient to provide the basis for transmission of rational motivation. A's having end E_1 provides A motivational force to pursue E_1, but also A's recognition that B has end E_2 provides A *at least some reason* to act so as to advance E_2. I deliberately say "some reason," because if value is not completely impersonal, then A's reason for promoting B's attainment of E_2 is not the same reason that B has to promote B's attainment of E_2, nor is it liable to be nearly as strong as B's reason. Nonetheless, A recognizes that there does exist reason for bringing about E_2. It happens that, in the first instance, the reason is B's; but it seems reasonable to suggest that that very recognition has motivational force for A.

The argument can be put in this way: one who recognizes R as a reason for E_2 is thereby logically bound to admit that it is not totally and in every respect indifferent whether E_2 obtain. R *is* why E_2 should obtain; otherwise R could not be conceived to be a reason. It should not be supposed that a dubious "moral point of view" is covertly—and question-beggingly—being inserted from which perspective one neutrally and dispassionately views the other person's ends with the same concern one has for one's own. The appeal is not moral but semantic. To understand what it is for someone else to have a reason is to recognize the existence of evaluative grounds that have not been created by oneself for oneself.[8] These evaluative grounds provide reason for judging that the world ought to be one way rather than some other. But to put forth that judgment as cogent, even if it is only a *prima facie* judgment, and even if it is overridden by other considerations, is to admit the transmissibility of practical reason from person to person. The scenario that has been suggested is: A acknowledges that B has reason (understood personally) to act in order to bring about E_2; thus there is (impersonal) reason to bring about E_2; thus A has some reason to advance B's attainment of E_2; however, if A's commitment to his own projects entails pursuing E_1, which is incompatible with E_2, then A does not have reason on balance to promote E_2.

This construal of the transmission of practical reason has much appeal. It provides a bridge between someone's *having a reason* and *there being reason,* that is, a bridge between personal value and impersonal value. It does not, however, collapse the distinction between the two. A theory in which personal and impersonal value are completely disjoint (or where one is absent altogether) is untidy. Because we can make sense of personal and impersonal value as both being *value,* there ought to be some link between them. The transmissibility of practical reason is such a link. Recognition that someone values end E is sufficient warrant for one to judge that there is value that attaches to E; one need not first note that the one who values E is indeed none other than oneself.

Consider the following analogy: knowledge that someone or other is in pain is knowledge that something, somewhere, hurts. Of course, if it is one's own pain, then the pain is personal, and one has reasons to bring about its alleviation that go beyond the reasons one has to bring about the alleviation of someone else's pain. But the word 'pain' is not understood equivocally as: pain is something that hurts when what is meant is one's own pain but something quite different when the reference is to another person's pain. Both hurt in exactly the same sense, although there is no danger of being unable to distinguish between one's own pains and other persons' pains. Similarly, it is being maintained that there are not two radically different ways of understanding reason for action: understanding a reason as mine, which is suffussed with motivational force, and understanding it as thine, which is entirely bereft of motivational force.[9]

It is not clear though that this approach is powerful enough to buttress a robust theory of rights. The reason transmitted from B to A can be vanishingly small. Even if A has some reason to accord B the status of a rights holder, it could be the case that this reason is routinely engulfed and outweighed by the far stronger reasons A has to pursue his own projects at the expense of B. The possibility envisaged is that every project pursuer has *some* reason to accord rights to others but that none has *sufficient reason* to do so. In such a world, two emotions that would be fitting accompaniments to virtually all action would be disappointment and regret: disappointment because one would know oneself always to be a potential recipient of other persons' care but would never come to experience that care; regret because one would constantly be called upon to sublimate one's own inclination to display respect for others. As possible worlds go, this one is not very pleasant.

There are other possibilities, though. Imagine a world of project pursuers in which each is able to recognize the existence of other project pursuers, in which each is vulnerable to interference by others, and in which each recognizes his own vulnerability. Finally, imagine the world being such that each has reason to undertake activity to eliminate interference by others. The imaginative powers required are not great; this is a passable portrait of the actual world. Because each project pursuer values his own ability to be a project pursuer, each has reason to act to bring about circumstances in which he will be able to lead a coherent life responsive to his own conception of the good.

What strategy then merits adoption? One candidate is an aim of enslaving or otherwise neutralizing all potential interferers. There are good empirical grounds for thinking that this is unlikely to work very well. There are a great number of them, and each is more or less as potent as oneself. That is why it was initially rational to seek out a strategy for promoting their noninterference. Worst of all is that adoption of the enslavement strategy tends to be self-defeating: if others become aware of the enslavement design, then they have reason to undertake preemptive measures.

A more promising strategy is one that is truly strategic, one responsive to transactors having reasons for action that mutually modify each other. The factors that underlie the strategic possibilities that confront each project pursuer are represented, in simplified form, in Figure 4.1. A and B are repre-

B's Policy

A's Policy	Active Aggression	General Neglect	Active Deference
Active Aggression	3, 3	8, 2	13, 0
General Neglect	2, 8	6, 6	11, 5
Active Deference	0, 13	5, 11	9, 9

FIGURE 4.1

sentative individuals whose efforts may, from time to time, conflict. If each were to proceed about his way, taking no notice of the other except when their activities led to clashes, in which case they would compete for success, they pursue the policy labeled "General Neglect." If each adopts General Neglect, they land in the middle box, in which both A and B receive a payoff of 6. (The numbers are meant simply to indicate differences in ordinal ranking. Nothing is to be inferred from the particular arbitrary cardinal assignments.) Either may instead adopt the policy of Active Aggression or Active Deference. By "Active Aggression" is meant the deliberate attempt to remove the other's ability to interfere with and thus impede one's own designs. By "Active Deference" is meant the deliberate attempt to avoid interfering with and thus impeding the other's designs. Although the diagram does not so indicate, both Active Aggression and Active Deference admit of degree. In particular, one may defer to a transactor over a particular range of the transactor's activities but respond aggressively beyond that range.

Mutual General Neglect is not a stable solution to the problems facing A and B. If each is acting independently of the other, then A will note that whatever B does, A will be better off by adopting the policy of Active Aggression. If B continues to observe General Neglect, then A can bring about a move due north in which his payoff becomes 8. Or, if B were to adopt one of the other two policies, A will still gain by commencing Active Aggression. Conversely, for A to adopt the policy of Active Deference will leave him worse off no matter what B does than if he had remained with General Neglect. Exactly the same considerations bear on B's choice of policy. In the parlance of the game theorist, Active Aggression *dominates* General Neglect, which in turn dominates Active Deference. If A and B each act in accord with rational self-interest, the solution they arrive at is the northwest box, with payoffs 3, 3. This result is an instance of the extended Prisoner's Dilemma.[10] Although there exist two boxes in which each would be better off (middle and southeast), they arrive at the Hobbesian "war of all against all." Each has reason to desire a different outcome, and each has reason to believe that the transactor desires a different outcome. Because both can be made better off simultaneously, there exists the possibility of gains from trade. That can be achieved if A and B switch from a system of independent policy determination to cooperative policy determination.

Since the dilemma is vintage Hobbes, the solution that immediately suggests itself is also that of Hobbes: a social compact in which A forswears interference with B contingent upon B's forswearing interference with A. Each incurs a cost—the forgoing of his own aggressive activities—but in turn receives a benefit—the other's forgone aggression. Because the benefit outweighs the cost, both profit. However, as Hobbes was well aware, the cooperative solution is rife with uncertainty. That social compact is an unambiguous improvement over the state of war does not, alas, render it a stable outcome. Once it is attained, A can jump from a payoff of 9 to one of 13 by unilaterally adopting the policy of Active Aggression. The same prospect presents itself to B, and each is aware that the other can reap a gain at his own expense. There is then a great temptation to abandon Active Deference, both in order to achieve an immediate gain and to avoid the loss that would be suffered if the other leapt first. Each would be aware that the eventual consequence would be a return to 3, 3; but this knowledge might not be enough to dissuade them from making the move. Deterrence would fail if either had very high time preference such that the gain that would be achieved in the time period before the opposite number could react is valued above the larger but more distant loss that would be incurred after the other did react. Also, deterrence could fail because, though each dreads the prospect of moving from southeast to northwest, each fears another prospect more. For A it is moving due west; for B, moving due north. Under conditions of stress and uncertainty, each may judge that the rationally indicated strategy is maximin. Each guarantee through the adoption of Active Aggression a return of no less than (and possibly much more than) 3, while no other strategy will guarantee as high a return.[11] So, the dismal result is that both players may, through perfectly rational action, land back in 3, 3.[12]

Because of just such reasons, Hobbes built into his system an enforcement mechanism to eliminate the instability that bedevils the cooperative solution. This is, of course, the Sovereign, who is granted a monopoly on the means of coercion that is intended to strike terror into the heart of anyone rash enough to contemplate violating the compact.[13] Because the Sovereign can inflict penalties far more ferocious than those available to any ordinary aggrieved party, deterrence is maximized and stability enhanced.

This solution, as critics have been quick to point out, is not without difficulty. Because the Sovereign's reprisal is not instantaneous, the problem of high time preference reemerges. Also, the Sovereign's services come at a cost. These can be understood as "taxes," and include the ordinary costs of paying for information and enforcement devices to secure the compliance of A and B. But the tax can also involve those disabilities that are inflicted on A and B by the Sovereign so that the latter can more expeditiously pursue his own ends. God may be a Sovereign who is purely disinterested, but men are not. Because some degree of taxation is inevitable, the full gains from trade represented by the southeast box are unattainable. If taxation is not too great, the result may yet be a situation in which each is better off: for example, the middle box. This is evidently the outcome that Hobbes envisions. However, if the Sovereign exacted 6 units from each, A and B would be back to a situation not better than was the state of nature: all gains from trade would have been expropriated. Nor is this the worst possible outcome from the perspectives of A and B; taxes of 7 or more units would leave them positively worse off than they would have been had they never deviated from mutual Active Aggression. They might subsequently try to return to that position but find that the process is irreversible due to the newly created monopoly of coercive means. In effect, a revised diagram would have come into being with uniformly lower payoffs for every policy decision. The prospect of this outcome may, if it is foreseen, lead A and B to abandon all thought of progression from the state of nature. This scenario is gloomy, much more so than Hobbes believed to be realistic, but it is not self-evidently faulty.[14]

Were all these difficulties solved, there would remain reason to think that Hobbe's own political theory is inadequate and that some variation is needed instead. It is rash to suppose that men mired in contending policies of Active Aggression could come to believe that cooperation promises more benefits, communicate that belief to their antagonists, and, by an act of will, effectively agree to cease hostility. A problem familiar since Hume is that the conventional undertakings involved in contract are unintelligible unless the parties to it already acknowledge (logically prior) reason to regard certain doings as performing the action of undertaking a morally binding commitment.[15] This is clearly so in the case of explicit contract, where A and B take their pledges as binding themselves to subsequent specified observances, and also for implicit understandings in which the parties successfully convey their intentions to be bound by reciprocal acknowledgements of the entitlements of others. The problem, though, is to understand how these contractual relations could ever be initiated. Suppose that A were to emerge from his bunker waving a white flag, or saying, "Why don't we make peace?" or assuming the most beatific countenance he can muster— or all three at once. Could these reasonably be taken by B as an indication of A's intentions to be bound to a policy of Active Deference contingent upon B's adoption of the same policy? Unfortunately, no. B has historically encountered A in contexts where each was attempting to enslave or otherwise neutralize the other. If B is a competent inductive logician, B will conclude that the best explanation of A's new antics is that they are yet another ploy to bring about B's subjugation. Therefore, B will perceive no reason to alter in any way his own optimal policy of Active Aggression. A will therefore encounter B's continued hostility and lapse back into his own accustomed poses of offense and defense.

Even this prospectus is too optimistic. It assumes that A has some initial motivation to undertake actions that are intended by him to convey to B the offer of reciprocal cooperation. But that assumption is itself groundless. The best explanation that A can fit to B's behavior is that B (correctly) construes every action by A as an assault upon B. A therefore believes that B will construe A's waving of the white flag as yet another aggressive act, and so A will not take his own action as the attempt to convey to B A's intention to effect an armistice with B. And if, *per impossibilis*, they found themselves waving white flags at each other, each would understand that episode as a venture in creative escalation. *Pace* Hobbes, civil society could not emerge from a state of war, because what Hobbes takes to be politics would, in that situation, be interpreted as war by other means. (American-Soviet negotiating sessions are a reasonably close approximation.)

What has been argued is that from a starting point of nakedly egoistic agents for whom all value whatsoever is personal, there is no egress. However, it is not necessary to adopt that starting point. Indeed, the earlier discussion of this chapter has provided reason to reject it. There is a biological basis, it was argued, to the denial that human beings are best modeled as fundamentally egoistic. Although each project pursuer does possess reason to favor differentially the ends to which he is committed, an inbuilt tendency to empathize with other persons must also be recognized. The two are not necessarily opposed sources of motivation; rather, it can be expected that empathetic response will be reflected in the choices of projects that agents make. Essentially social commitments, such as those involved in loyalty to friends and family, polis and nation, will predominate over those displayed in the hermit's life. If empathy is an inbuilt source of motivation, then sociality is incorporated within the pursuit of self-interest.

Further support for this anti-Hobbesian line of reasoning is drawn from the argument concerning the interpersonal transmissibility of practical reason. That argument was intended to make credible the claim that agents are not only able to understand what it is for there to be value-for-oneself, but also are able to recognize that there exists (impersonal) value. If the recognition of value as such carries with it motivational force, then each agent who recognizes the existence of value that stems from the volitions of others thereby has reason to act so as to realize that value. Hobbesian man is not only lonely; he is, in a fundamental sense, irrational.

Therefore, it is a mistake to commence political analysis with a state-of-nature scenario in which each individual is entirely consumed by his own conceptions of value-for-himself and regards others only as obstacles to his own designs. It is a mistake both because from that point of entry there is no egress whatsoever and because it is blind to an important source of value. Hobbesian egoism is the mirror image of the Foil: just as the latter acknowledges no value other than impersonal value, the former is wedded to a construal of all value as personal; the Foil can give no account of a person's special attachment to his own projects, and Hobbesian man is logically precluded from initiating relations of sociality. Each is radically incomplete. What is proposed by way of correction is a conception of project pursuers who are logically and biologically impelled to make a place within their projects for the concerns of others.

The offense/defense strategy outlined above should be replaced, then, by one which takes account of *all* the motivational pressures that impinge on project pursuers. A, in the course of trying to further his designs, encounters B, who is an obstacle to those designs. A therefore finds reason to try to neutralize the presence of B. However, A finds in B a source of value with which A has some tendency to empathize. This provides A with reason to attempt to promote B's ends. On some occasions the former motivation will be dominant, on other occasions the latter. And, of course, there may be episodes in which no conflict at all between them is perceived: where A's pursuit of A's designs does not entail the quashing of B's or where A can act to promote B's ends without any curtailment of A's efforts to advance A's own projects. Because A will evince *both* kinds of response to B, aggressive *and* altruistic, it will not be the case that the best explanation B can fit to A's activity is that of incessant hostility. A more complex theory will suggest itself, namely, that A is a sometimes aggressive, sometimes altruistic being. Nor will B conclude that it is an entirely random matter whether A happens to assume the aggressive mode or adopts instead the altruistic mode. B will probably observe that A most often adopts an aggressive posture when some action of B interferes with an ongoing pattern of activity in which A is engaged. That is, B will come to realize that A's inducement to display resistance is very great when B poses a serious threat to the success of one of A's projects. Conversely, B will observe that A tends toward altruism when B is engaged in conduct that is neutral with respect to A's designs, and A's inducement toward altruism is at its strongest when B is himself displaying altruism toward A. These factors are reciprocal.

It need not be supposed that the disposition to behave altruistically is initially very high; only that it is present to some observable extent. B notes that the usually aggressive A from time to time defers to B. B values A's deference and disvalues A's aggression. Thus, B has reason, all else equal, to adopt patterns of activity that will maximize the ratio of A's deferential actions to A's aggressive actions. If, by displaying less aggression and more deference, B can bring it about that A will in turn respond with more deference, then B has reason to shift from his initial choice of policy, one, perhaps, in which aggression overwhelmingly predominated, to a policy incorporating extended deference.

It may be responded that all else is *not* equal, that B retains his personal commitments to his own projects and that this will sharply limit the extent to which he will, on balance, be motivated to defer to A. That is true, but there also exists an impetus in the other direction. B's initial policy toward A will, if it is predominantly inclined toward aggression, provide B little opportunity to give effect to B's own empathetic tendencies. Because these are real, B has added reason to appreciate an advance toward cooperation. It will result in an increase of deference from A but also lessen the costs to B of acknowledging and responding to the value that emanates from A. That is, B regards his own deference as not simply instrumentally good but intrinsically good. This is an additional reason for B to moderate his policy toward A.

Once B does move away from his initial, predominantly aggressive policy, even if only slightly, that will alter the constraints under which A is operating. A will now find his own aggressive acts more costly than before because they risk the loss of the newly acquired increment of deference from B. A will correspondingly find his own acts of deference to be less costly because they are marginally more likely to be met with B's deference (a "good" for A) and less likely to be met with B's aggression (a "bad" for A). Therefore, the relative prices of deference and aggression have changed in favor of the former. Given these new constraints, A will choose to "buy" more deference toward B and less aggression.

This, in turn, alters the constraints on B, who will similarly respond with yet more deference and less aggression, thus once a gain altering A's constraints. Eventually this process will arrive at an equilibrium position at which each finds that the marginal cost of one more unit of deference is slightly greater than the benefits that would be attained. "Costs" here are to be understood as lessened ability to pursue one's own projects successfully, and "benefits," as both freedom from encroachment by others and opportunity to act in accord with one's own empathetic inclinations. Exactly where this equilibrium position would be situated is impossible to determine without more information. That additional information includes: the strength of A's empathetic motivation and B's, the extent to which A's projects conflict with B's, the extent to which A and B each requires cooperation from the other for successful pursuit of his own personal projects, the comparative skills of A and B in waging aggression. It is not the case that the equilibrium position will feature the same mix of aggression and deference in the policies of each. If, for example, A has a stronger tendency toward empathy than does B, A's project commitments inherently value altruistic doings more than do B's, or if A is less skilled at aggression than B, then the equilibrium position will be one at which A will adopt a policy more deferential than B's.[16] These complications aside, it is reasonable to conclude that the attained equilibrium will be neither perfect cooperation nor the war of all against all. It will be somewhere intermediate between the two.

The process of reciprocal recognition is illustrated in Figure 4.2. The reaction curves indicate how much deference each will supply at every level of deference provided by the other. Given an initial starting point of A_1B_1, A will adjust his response to land back on his reaction curve at A_2B_1. This will in turn induce B to move to A_2B_2, A to A_3B_2, B to A_3B_3, and so on until equilibrium is achieved at Q. Indeed, Figure 4.2 might understate the levels of deference ultimately achieved. It holds constant the preferences of A and B for deference. However, it is reasonable to suspect that as each experiences more deference from the other and provides more, their tastes for deference will increase. If greater familiarity with mutually accommodating behavior occasions an endogenous preference shift toward greater willingness to supply deference, Q' instead of Q could emerge as the observed equilibrium.

It should be observed that this process does not involve any explicit bargaining between A and B. The white flag has not been waved nor has a compact been signed, sealed, and notarized. Instead, each has found reason to respond to some initial display of the other's deference with like deference from himself. Convergence is eventually achieved at a point substantially distant from the point of outset. Neither A nor B intended at the outset to achieve this point, but it emerges from a pattern of response in which each is responding rationally to the cost-benefit schedule that faces him. This explanation of developing cooperative policies is of the sort Robert

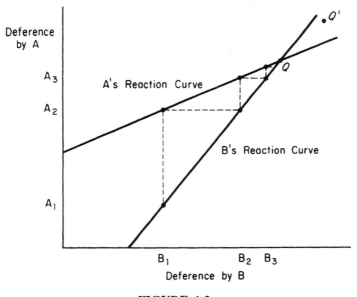

FIGURE 4.2

Nozick calls *invisible-hand explanations,* accounts that "show how some overall pattern or design, which one would have thought had to be produced by an individual's or group's successful attempt to realize the pattern, instead was produced and maintained by a process that in no way had the overall pattern or design 'in mind.' "[17] There may be some question as to whether what has been offered is, in the strict sense, an invisible-hand explanation: because both A and B desire deference from the other and have some initial willingness to defer, the solution was not entirely unintended. Still, neither A nor B viewed his own activity as directed toward the realization of the equilibrium state that emerges. (Whether or not one chooses to call this an *impure* invisible-hand explanation is a matter of little moment.)

It has been granted that Hume is correct when he maintains that contract as a basis for establishing a regime of mutual deference is unintelligible. In response, it has been demonstrated that policies incorporating a substantial amount of Active Deference can naturally evolve from a situation in which aggression predominates. Once that evolution has occurred, A and B are each the recipients of valued moral space that each has reason to accord to the other. Although no bargaining and no explicit trades have occurred, the equilibrium position, if viewed from the outside, will appear to be one contractually determined. (This appearance in part explains the attraction of social contract theory.) From that external perspective, rights will be viewed as a social artifact.

Opposed to that external appraisal is the argument that rudimentary mutual acknowledgement of moral space is not artifactual but rather the result of a natural process in which project pursuers confront each other and achieve a *modus vivendi*. That is why the argument of this book can be characterized as developing a theory of *basic rights*. No mutual acknowledgement on the part of all transactors of binding moral principles has been appealed to in order to show how each project pursuer can find reason to grant moral space to others. Nor were rights presented as the ingenious invention of some proto-Archimedes who took for himself the task of designing an instrument for conflict modulation. Rather, it has been claimed that moral space will be fenced off through individuals' exercise of a practical reason that recognizes both personal and impersonal value. This will naturally tend to develop over a wide, though not unlimitedly wide, range of situations in which persons can encounter each other. For example, under conditions of extreme scarcity such that A has no realistic expectation of success in his own projects unless B's designs are thoroughly neutralized, and vice versa, neither will have reason on balance to move one jot away from a policy of unremitting Active Aggression. But where conditions are somewhat more favorable, basic rights can emerge.

Although rights are not established *ex nihilo* via contract, parties who antecedently recognize reason to respect each other's moral space conditional upon like respect from the others can *ratify* that understanding through contract. That should not be understood as the move to a full-blown constitutional convention replete with the flourish of trumpets, but rather, at least in its inception, as a far more modest affair. The move to contract is for each to communicate to the other his own understanding that there exists an equilibrium position removed from aggression that he wishes to preserve from decay and, if feasible, build upon. Once a cooperative equilibrium has been reached, the parties to it have established the conditions for entering into explicit agreements that each will regard himself as bound by. That will once again alter the constraints under which the transactors are operating. Previously A had recognized that he could affect the level of B's aggression/deference through his own unilateral choice of policy; now he recognizes that bilateral agreement can generate further improvements for both.

The kinds of provisions that will emerge are familiar from classical social contract theory. The equilibrium will be less prone to disruption if each has full information concerning the policy choices that others have made. That will minimize the chance of inadvertently triggering an aggressive response through a misunderstanding of what the other will regard as acceptable behavior. Those vaguely understood policy choices can be sharpened by the formulation of explicit *principles* and *rules* for action that each pledges to observe.

Ease of achieving further cooperative exchanges will be enhanced by the creation of *institutions* within which transactions can efficiently proceed. Since it is known that changing circumstances will render some accustomed patterns of cooperation obsolete while opening up new paths for fruitful cooperative activity, the institutional design will incorporate flexibility of response.

Finally, the transactors will attempt to establish a mechanism for *enforcement*. If A enters into a cooperative undertaking with B, then A will desire assurance that B will comply with the terms governing that undertaking. To the extent that the existence of an enforcement mechanism increases B's likelihood of compliance, A receives that assurance. It should also be noted that it is advantageous to A that A's own compliance be enforced. That is because the conditions of exchange between A and B will, in part, be determined by the degree of confidence each has in the performance of the other. B will relinquish some good, G_B, in exchange for A's agreeing to relinquish G_A only if B values G_A more than G_B and additionally only if

$$p \cdot G_A > G_B$$

where p represents the subjective probability that B assigns to A's compliance with the terms of the agreement. The closer to 1 that p becomes, the more A benefits, because A need give up a smaller value G_A to satisfy the inequality. So, even if both A and B are absolutely committed to compliance, each has reason to desire the existence of an enforcement mechanism ensuring to the other his own compliance. Transaction costs are thereby lowered, with both parties benefiting.

Beyond the Two-Person World

Further development of possible structures that contract can assume is the task of general political philosophy rather than that of an inquiry into the foundations of basic rights. The preceding discussion should serve to indicate some of the avenues that a political philosophy grounded on the recognition of basic rights can take. However, one further complication must now be faced. Heretofore it has been assumed for the sake of simplicity that two parties are engaged in bilateral transactions. It is now time to extend those results to the multiperson community.

Consider A, B, C, D, . . . , all living in close proximity to each other, and each able to advance or impede the project pursuit of anyone else. For reasons already adduced, repeated interaction will tend to generate bilateral cooperative equilibria between A and B, A and C, B and C, etc. These equilibria may be different for different pairs. As the number of interacting parties grows larger, the number of bilateral equilibria increases geometrically: with two parties it is one, with three it is three, with four it is six and, generally with n it is $n!/((2!)\,(n-2)!)$. Each of the n persons has reason to attain and observe an equilibrium arrangement with each of the others; but as the numbers increase, it becomes progressively harder to acquire and retain information concerning what level of aggression/deference is optimal with respect to each of the others. One way to economize on information costs is to move from a network of distinct bilateral equilibria to a single *multilateral equilibrium.* The larger the numbers become, the greater the incentive to make this move.

It was noted above that in the two-person world the attained equilibrium need not be one in which both parties adopt the same aggression/deference policy toward the other. The multiperson world is interestingly and importantly different in that regard. While persons will still differ in terms of their motivations to aggress or defer, counteracting such differences is the informational constraint that leads each party to prefer a regime featuring a multilateral equilibrium to a regime of numerous bilateral equilibria. It becomes too costly to insist on achieving a distinct equilibrium with each other person, and therefore there is an impetus to move toward a single optimal multilateral equilibrium. In a very significant sense, then, the multiperson world exhibits a bias toward *egalitarianism:* each party has reason to accede to a generally established policy of cooperation.

This general policy need not be the deliberate product of design. Again, an invisible-hand explanation can be provided to account for its emergence. Consider some representative agent A who regularly encounters numerous other persons. If A finds it too demanding to frame distinct policies for transactions with each other agent, A will tend to adopt some one policy that he employs in dealings with all those of whose response patterns he is unaware. If his initial choice of policy leads to a perceptibly suboptimal pattern of responses, he will increase/decrease the deference he habitually displays until he hits upon the policy that maximizes his expected returns. Similarly, B is engaging in a like process, and so on for C, D, and all the others. As more and more of them tend to converge on a particular policy mix, there is an increased incentive for those who have not yet adopted that policy to do so. Eventually it becomes very costly to adopt a mode of behavior that deviates more than slightly from the generally accepted norm: one is "ostracized," unable to establish a desired measure of comity with those whose forbearance one needs. So, even if the norm that emerges happens not to be the one that person D would most prefer to be generally observed, D finds himself with strong reason to bend his will to that norm. By an invisible-hand process, disparate inclinations are brought to convergence upon a generally acceptable standard.

This has more the *look* of a theory of basic rights than does what had previously been developed. One thing that might be demanded of a theory of rights is an explanation of how one individual comes to have reason to recognize another's entitlement to *some expanse* of moral space; that explanation was previously offered. But another thing that might be demanded of a theory of rights is a rationale for according to each rights holder an *equal expanse* of moral space. That has now been broached. The constraints of multipersonal interaction provide reason for each person to insist on being accorded the same level of forbearance from others that he is willing to accord to each of them.

This pressure toward equality of basic rights may, of course, fail of consummation in practice. Instead of one multilateral equilibrium being attained within a community, it can be the case that the community is segmented into distinct classes. Within each class a particular policy of reciprocity emerges as the internal norm, but relations between members of two different classes will exhibit unequal status arrangements. Male and female, black and white, capitalist and proletariat, young and old: each pair may exhibit *intergroup* policies concerning the granting of moral space that diverge from either *intragroup* policy. It is foolish to maintain that the impetus toward equality of basic rights will regularly be decisive; empirical evidence to the contrary is all too available. Where classes enjoy differential allotments of moral space, the information constraint has generated several multilateral equilibria among groups. This is a result intermediate between one multilateral equilibrium embracing every member of the community and multiple bilateral equilibria. This result, unfortunately, can prove to be stable.

There is then no invisible-hand explanation of the emergence of thoroughgoing respect for equal basic rights within an entire community, much less for relations among separate communities. That unsurprising conclusion indicates that if equality of basic rights is to emerge in practice, it will do so as the intended product of human decisions. There is a *moral case* to be made for equality in basic rights, and every disadvantaged individual has reason to advance that case vis-à-vis the advantaged. He can argue:

> I am every bit as much a project pursuer as you are. Just as you demand moral space within which you are able to advance your projects free of encroachment from me, I too need moral space within which I can create a life

according to my lights. Yet you are unwilling to grant to me the same measure of freedom from interference you claim for yourself. You may be able to *force* me to accede to this inequality through your superior strength, but you are unable to *justify* it to me. There neither is nor could be some interpersonal standard of value which I have reason to accept that ranks your ability to pursue your projects above my ability to pursue my projects. To the contrary: what is maximally important to me is my ability to construct a meaningful life for myself through my own ability to commit myself to directive ends. Therefore, you can never provide me with adequate reason to accept your claim that you are entitled to a fuller measure of rights than am I.

This response may fail to persuade the superior, but not because of any lack of cogency. Each project pursuer, whatever his projects may be, is fully on a par with every other project pursuer in having reason to value the advancement of his own projects above the advancement of all others. And each is aware that every other project pursuer has exactly the same reason personally to value his own project pursuit in virtue of its being his. None is rationally obliged to accept inferiority in protected moral space, and none can make good a claim to superiority. Even if equality of rights does not emerge as the equilibrium result within an actual community, it is nonetheless a *moral equilibrium* derived from reflection on the logical structure of practical reason.

It may be felt that this is insufficient, that what is required is an argument that will *obliterate* the arrogance and prejudice of those who refuse to acknowledge the claim of equal rights for all project pursuers. This, though, is to misconstrue the efficacy of philosophical activity. Robert Nozick writes:

> The terminology of philosophical art is coercive: arguments are *powerful* and best when they are *knockdown*, arguments *force* you to a conclusion, if you believe the premises you *have to* or *must* believe the conclusion, some arguments do not carry much *punch*, and so forth. A philosophical argument is an attempt to get someone to believe something, whether he wants to believe it or not. A successful philosophical argument, a strong argument, *forces* someone to a belief.
>
> Though philosophy is carried on as a coercive activity, the penalty philosophers wield is, after all, rather weak. If the other person is willing to bear the label of "irrational" or "having the worse arguments," he can skip away happily maintaining his previous belief.[18]

The philosopher *qua* philosopher has no alternative other than to allow him to skip away. But the philosopher *qua* moral agent can, along with other moral agents, strive to instantiate his conception of the good and just society. This can in part, but only in part, be achieved through doing philosophy. Contra Marx, the point is *both* to understand *and* to change the world; and the former can—marginally—advance the cause of the latter.

Moral Space and Fanaticism

An invisible-hand explanation has been proffered to account for emergence of the recognition of entitlements to moral space, and to this has been attached a moral argument indicating that each project pursuer has reason to insist that his allotment of moral space be equal to that of every other project pursuer. But the argument for the existence of equal basic rights for all project pursuers still leaves one fundamental question unanswered: How extensive ought these equal basic rights be?

I do not believe that this question admits of any a priori answer. Communities may differ with respect to how much deference is optimal as the norm demanded from all its members. It follows, then, that two communities may differ in the scope of the rights each acknowledges to be possessed by all its members, yet it being the case that each has attained the optimum result for that community. That is the nugget of truth contained within the otherwise dubious theory of moral relativism. However, neither the question of *how much deference* ought to be included in the community norm nor the question of *what form deference should take* is entirely indeterminate. In Chapter 5, I discuss in some detail the form that basic rights take. Here I shall make some remarks concerning their breadth.

Each project pursuer will value more deference shown to him over less. Ideal would be a world in which he could pursue his own projects while everyone else defers to him. Also, each project pursuer values being required to show less deference to others over being required to show more deference. The ideal is a world in which he need never defer to anyone else, although he may, supererogatorialy, elect to defer even though not required to do so. If there exists, however, a constraint of equal basic rights, then whatever degree of deference is demanded from everyone else must also be accorded to everyone else. Your not having to defer to anyone else may be far from ideal if, correspondingly, no one need defer to you. That is why the state of nature is suboptimal.

For each individual there will be some optimal amount of deference he is willing to extend in order to receive a like quantity of deference from others. This amount, though, need not be the same for all persons.

P_1, P_2, P_3 represent the preferences of different individuals for the amount of deference incorporated within the community norm. Points along the or-

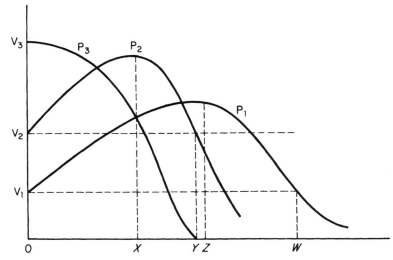

More Deference

FIGURE 4.3

dinate stand for the amount of deference customarily required, with 0 being the Hobbesian state of nature, and points along the abscissa stand for the value assigned to some given level of customary deference.

If communities were entirely homogeneous, then there would be a unique position along the ordinate that would be optimal for everyone. For example, a community peopled exclusively by P_1's would find it optimal to demand Z units of deference from everyone. Similarly, a community of P_2's would find a requirement of only X units ideal. However, a heterogeneous community including both P_1's and P_2's will not be able to arrive at a position along the ordinate that maximally satisfies everyone. There is no unique solution for a heterogeneous community to the problem of formulating a multilateral policy.

There is, though, a specifiable range within which any acceptable policy determination must fall. Although Z is ideal for P_1, any quantity of deference demanded that is less than W will be regarded by P_1 as preferable to the state of nature at 0. P_2, the "rugged individualist," demands a smaller quantity of deference. He will regard a requirement of more than Y units of deference as intolerable, preferring to it the state of nature. P_2, though, will be willing to "do business" with P_1, because there exists a range over which both will be benefited by comparison with the benchmark of 0. That range is represented on Figure 4.3 by the length between X and Y. Whatever policy is arrived at by the equilibrating process will be somewhere along that length. Its precise determination can be expected to be a function of the number of P_1's and P_2's within the community and their respective bargaining strength.

P_3 is a different case. This is the individual for whom 0 is the optimum position and who will find any measure of deference shown to him as an unsatisfactory return for having to reciprocate with a like amount of deference to others. Following R. M. Hare,[19] I shall call P_3 a *fanatic*. A fanatic is anyone who prefers the existence of Hobbesian war of all against all to every possible condition of equal basic rights for all. It is apparent that no sufficient reason can be provided to the fanatic for entering into civil association with others; at most the fanatic, so long as he remains a fanatic, can be bludgeoned into displaying minimally acceptable conduct toward others.

Were everyone a fanatic, interpersonal comity would be impossible. And if there existed many fanatics, civility would be tenuous at best. Moral theory may decry this result but is powerless to evade it: against the fanatic there simply is no argument good enough rationally to convince him of the error of his ways and lead him back into the pacific community. Argument must give way to prisons and guns. However, what *can* rationally be arrived at is a choice of policy that will not lead others into joining the fanatic in the abandonment of civility.

Suppose that the P_1's had their way in demanding Z units of deference from everyone. The fanatic, P_3, would, as always, have no rational stake in such an arrangement and would resist its imposition as best he could. But it is also the case that P_2 would thereby find himself worse off than in a situation in which no rights at all were acknowledged. P_2 would then have good reason to join P_3 in the rebellion against a regime of rights. Because this redounds to the disadvantage of the P_1's, they had good reason *ex ante* to decline to impose position X even if they possessed sufficient force to bring it about against the will of the P_2's.

Let us suppose, as seems reasonable, that each member of a community who places value on rights being respected within that community has compelling reason to bring to fruition and preserve a situation in which the vast majority of his transactors also have a rational stake in that community. That is, he wishes to minimize the number of persons who will find it in their interest to join the fanatic in abandoning sociality. There are two ways in which this quest for social stability can be pursued.

The first is to give up the constraint that basic rights be equal. If inequality is sufficiently pronounced, even the fanatic can be brought within community boundaries. For example, if P_3's were required to show only X units of deference to everyone else but received in return W units, then they might regard themselves as adequately compensated.[20] This is a solution of sorts; but even if it is not rejected for being morally odious, it carries with it grave drawbacks. P_1 and P_2 will now find that they receive less deference per unit of deference extended (because they have to extend W units to P_3 while receiving only X in return), and so their policy preferences will shift to the left. They will find it less agreeable to defer if not all others defer equally. Also, P_1 and P_2 will be provided an incentive to dissemble concerning their true preferences. If either can pass himself off as a fanatic, then he will be able to decrease the amount of deference required from him while increasing the amount he receives. A policy of appeasing fanatics leads to greater quantities of fanaticism being supplied. For a whole host of reasons, then, the attempt to neutralize fanaticism by countenancing inequality in basic rights appears to be grossly ill-advised.

The alternative approach to social stability is ruefully to accept the fact that a certain residue of fanaticism will accompany any recognition of equal basic rights. Since the fanatic is impervious to friendly suasion, he must be dealt with by other means. A major priority, though, will be to encourage as few others as feasible to accompany the fanatic in his rebellion against civil society. That is accomplished by adopting a policy that minimizes the number of persons who find the deference they receive from others insufficient compensation for the deference they must supply. Adverting again to Figure 4.3, this consideration recommends a leftward move from Z to somewhere in the range between X and Y. To state the result more generally: *a stable regime of equal rights for all requires that the amount of required deference be close to the level of deference ideal for the least deferential members of the community.* Rights impose forbearance, but if too much forbearance is demanded, the foundations of rights-respecting sociality are imperiled.

In Chapter 1 unease was expressed at the vast proliferation of novel "rights" currently being advocated by spokespersons for one cause or another. These alleged new rights intuitively were seen as debasing the very language of rights. Now some theoretical backing to that intuition has been supplied. To lend support to maximalist claims of basic rights is to undermine the conditions within which a rights-respecting society can flourish. Basic rights are the heavy artillery in the moral arsenal; because they are powerful, they must be brandished sparingly and with care. If A has a right to certain treatment, then B *must* comply. It is exceedingly unfortunate if the compliance costs imposed on B are so great that B does better to abandon all stake in a morality of rights rather than comply.

This is an argument not to limit the *stringency* of rights but rather to limit their *scope*. Nothing should be acknowledged as a basic right unless it is the case that the vast majority of community members is rendered better off if they and all others respect that right than if no one were obliged to respect it. For a project pursuer, being well off is to be understood as being able to pursue one's own projects in a setting where encroachments by others are sharply restricted. This, at long last, provides us with a tolerably clear basis for explicating what is comprehended within a defensible conception of 'basic rights': basic rights are those moral constraints that impose minimal demands on the forbearance of others such that individuals can pursue projects amidst a world of similar beings, each with his own life to lead, and each owing the same measure of respect to others that they owe to him.

5

Two Concepts of Liberalism

What, then, are the basic rights that project pursuers possess? It has been argued that they amount to minimal demands on the forbearance of others, but is it *exclusively* forbearance that individuals can demand from one another as a matter of basic right or should claims to recipience of goods be acknowledged as well? A familiar way to phrase this distinction is as a contrast between "liberty" rights and "welfare" rights. Alternatively, rights are spoken of as "negative" (entailing noninterference with an activity) or "positive" (entailing the provision by some individual or institution of a valued item).

Liberalism has bifurcated into two distinctive variants in its response to the question of whether persons possess positive or welfare rights along with negative or liberty rights. *Classical liberalism*, a modern form of which is libertarianism, maintains that all rights individuals possess (or: a vastly preponderant share of the rights that individuals possess[1]) are negative in character. Welfare liberalism maintains that individuals possess extensive positive claims on others, and that these positive claims are on a par with negative claims not only with respect to their prominence on the moral landscape but also with respect to their justification. That is, whatever reasons we have to acknowledge that individuals may not be interfered with are also reasons for holding that individuals are entitled to aid from others. If it is *need* that validates claims to noninterference, then it is also need that confers a right to be provided the requisites for a satisfactory life. Or if it is alleged that individuals would *contract* amongst themselves in a suitably described setting, perhaps the Rawlsian original position, to respect each other's liberties, then they would similarly contract to guarantee to each other some specified level of welfare goods.

The argument to rights by way of project pursuit resides thoroughly within a liberal tradition. It is based on the proposition that individuals can and do commit themselves to long-terms ends which they have primary reason to advance. These ends are directive in that they determine what will count as a potential item of value for that individual. Individuals therefore are to be understood as project pursuers. That status is not to be assigned to units more encompassing than individual persons such as tribes, nations, economic classes, or all of humanity; neither is it assigned at the subindividual level to particular genes,[2] the left and right lobes of the brain,[3] or time-slices of persons.[4] Those who pursue projects thereby have reason to value their own ability to be project pursuers and so have reason to try to establish conditions of reciprocal recognition and respect for the interest each has in being able to pursue his personal ends. These conditions are provided by rights—liberal rights.

Persons require noninterference from others, metaphorically described as "moral space," to be able to pursue their own designs. Therefore, it is initially plausible to insist that basic rights be understood as negative or liberty rights that forbid coercive encroachment. However, it is also the case that individuals need more than liberty in order to carve out for themselves satisfactory lives. Conditions of minimal well-being are also needed, and these typically depend on having means of access to economic goods. Because project pursuers have reason to value both the liberty to promote their own ends and the material means to secure those ends, it may seem that the argument to this point tips decisively to the side of welfare liberalism.

The Argument from Need

Although it may be the case that basic rights afford protection to those interests of individuals which are especially important, which individuals *need*, it does not follow that everything which individuals find important will justifiably be theirs as a matter of right. Importance is at most a necessary condition for being the object of a right, not both necessary and sufficient. Therefore, it is invalid to argue, as does D. D. Raphael:

> One cannot exercise the initiative of a human being (which is what the rights of liberty are intended to protect), or indeed remain a human being at all, unless the basic needs of life are satisfied, and if a man is not in a position to do this for himself, it seems to me reasonable to say that he has a right, as a human being, to the assistance of others in meeting these needs.[5]

It is important to see why this argument, representative of a prominent strand in the case for welfare liberalism, fails. There are at least three respects in which it is defective.

First, even if some item is a vital component of a worthwhile human life, there will be no presumption whatsoever that one has a right to it if it is not the case that others are able to provide it. The impossibility of provision can be either causal or conceptual. An example of the former is a needed transplantable organ when no spare organs are at hand. The latter sort of impossibility is more difficult to specify but of considerable moral significance in that it stakes out the boundaries between self and others in the sphere of practical activity. It is reasonable to maintain that no satisfactory life, viewed either externally or internally, can be lived by someone who lacks altogether a conception of a good that is directive for his activities. The complete cynic, for whom no end is worthy of pursuit, not even the development and defense of his own cynicism, is a pitiable figure. But the propriety of pity does not carry over into a justifiable claim on others to provide that which the cynic sorely lacks; a conception of the good is something that individuals must provide by themselves and for themselves if they are to have it at all.

Similarly, persons require motivational energy to propel themselves actively to realize that which they hold valuable. They require sufficient fixity of purpose to hold to plans of activity over extended periods of time such that they are not subject to diversion by every passing whim or caprice if their lives are to exhibit coherence and fixed identity. Persons also require flexibility of response so that previously held conceptions of value worthy of pursuit can be modified in the light of new information and evolving structures of attachment. All of these can justifiably be regarded as basic needs of human beings, yet they are not moral commodities that those who are well supplied can be asked to donate to those whose stock is low.

John Rawls writes, "Perhaps the most important primary good is that of self-respect."[6] Note that self-respect is yet another good that, though of inordinate value, cannot be conferred on one by some other person or by some set of institutions. At most, these external agencies can provide conditions within which individuals are rendered able to develop and act on a conception of a good that, in turn, promotes a sturdy sense of self-worth. But the primary good of self-respect is not one that is amenable to external provision. The Rawlsian theory of justice involves principles for the allocation of liberties, opportunities, and economic goods to persons; yet Rawls is careful to say that "justice as fairness *gives more support* to self-esteem than other principles."[7] It does not and cannot mandate the provision of self-respect.

The point concerning impossibility of provision of some highly valued good needs little more than to be stated in order to gain acceptability. However, though evident, it is not innocuous, for what it reveals is the limits of a welfare liberalism. There are components of the good for man that cannot be provided. Society can arrange itself so that individuals are *not impeded* in producing and sustaining these goods, can provide channels through which *support and encouragement* by others is directed toward persons whose capacity for achieving these goods will thereby be enhanced, but it cannot offer these goods to all who are in need of them as a matter of right. Classical liberalism can be understood as recognizing, at least implicitly, this limit. For by promoting an ideal of thorough-going liberty within which persons can develop coherent life schemes, and thus a firm sense of self-worth, classical liberalism stands opposed to the placing of obstacles in the way of individuals' cultivation of moral commodities that, in the last analysis, must be internally generated.

A second defect of Raphael's argument is that it takes into account only the magnitude of the need a potential recipient has for a good without giving corresponding attention to the magnitude of sacrifice that must be exacted from others in order to provide that good. In other words, it is entirely oriented toward *demand* and ignores factors concerning *supply*. It may appear intuitively plausible to suggest that persons have a right to some good that they very much need when it is the case that others can easily supply it at little cost to themselves. But when the demand side of the equation is held constant and the supply side allowed steadily to increase, there comes a point at which it is no longer obvious, or even credible, that there is any right of recipience to the good and thus a correlative duty to provide it.

A strict utilitarian will concur with this judgment but will claim that this point is reached only when the equation is exactly balanced: when the marginal cost to the provider of supplying one more unit of the good is equal to the marginal value of that unit to the recipient. That utilitarian cost-benefit equilibrium rests on the presupposition that there exists an impersonal standard of value (in this case, the standard of overall utility) to which all agents have reason to adhere, and in terms of which the ends of all persons are commensurable. In Chapter 2 it was argued that this presupposition merits rejection, that individuals rather have reason to subscribe to a personal (at least partly) standard of value. The individual called on to be a donor is not rationally obliged to weigh impartially his own ends and those of the would-be recipient. He acts rationally if he assigns special value—personal value, value-for-himself—to his own ends simply in virtue of their being his. Therefore, there can be no general obligation to give up that which is of considerable instrumental value to the pursuit of one's own projects on the grounds that someone else has pressing need for those items.

Our moral intuitions seems to support this theoretical position. Suppose that the population of the Indian subcontinent could be brought up to a level of tolerable material subsistence, however that be measured, if the United

States were to divert some 70% of its gross national product toward that end. Few persons (or is it "few persons in the United States"?) would take that fact to confer a right upon hundreds of millions of Asians to receive that sum.[8] The need is certainly genuine, and the ability to alleviate it present at least in large measure, but the inference to a welfare right is highly dubious.

Cases yielding the same conclusion can also be adduced at the micro level. The autocratic father may urgently require that his adult daughter remain at home with him as companion, captive audience, domestic servant, and token of his capacity to command respectful deference. She would prefer a life of her own with far more independence and self-direction than the paternal roost affords, but the father would be devastated should the daughter "abandon" him. Is there then a case to be made for a right on his part to her perpetual servility?

You have two good corneas and I have none. No other source of bodily parts is at hand. Do I then have a right to one cornea? (I'll generously leave to you the choice of which one to give up.) The operation will be a bit painful to you, although not otherwise demanding, and afterwards you will have trouble hitting a major league curveball, should baseball be a preferred activity of yours. However, it is undeniably the case that my being totally blind is a much graver hardship than would be your loss of sight in one eye. It is unlikely, though, that any such consideration will persuade you that I have a right to one of your corneas.

It is not being denied that the recognition by A that B lacks some crucial good which it is in the power of A to provide (though at some substantial cost to A) is a reason for A to provide that good to B. We might very well want to say that Americans *should* donate some appreciable share of their income to impoverished Asians, that it would be *morally praiseworthy* for them to do so, or that you would be acting wonderfully well if you choose to give up one of your eyes so that I could see.[9] These judgments of moral approbation, though, do not imply a right on the part of the beneficiary. That it would be *outstandingly good* for A to provide some good to B, or even that A *ought to* provide the good to B, is not equivalent to the judgment that A *must* provide B with the good. All arguments that needs as such confer rights are flawed in this respect.

A third defect of Raphael's argument, related to the preceding one, is that it fails to distinguish between that which is held to be needed and the manner in which there is an obligation to respond to the need. Suppose that B needs, with the relevant degree of urgency, good G. The extent to which B's need entails on the part of A some obligation toward B ranges from *not at all* to its being *mandatory* for A that he bring about conditions sufficient for B's attainment of G.

The argument from need to rights characteristically rests on the claim that the former of these extremes is implausible. To hold that need is entirely irrelevant to the moral relationships in which persons stand toward each other is to plump for a desiccated view of the moral realm. Of what account would morality be if it were unresponsive to undeniably pressing constraints on individuals' abilities to make a start at constructing for themselves minimally satisfactory lives? If morality is to be *practical* in its traditional sense, to hazard judgments concerning how men ought to conduct themselves in a world in which they are vulnerable to circumstance, then it must address the ways in which vulnerabilities can be rectified through the concerted action of persons within a moral order. Accordingly, it is asserted that need *does* confer rights, and that others must (subject to a few complicating qualifications such as knowledge of the need, ability to meet it, no greater unmet need resulting as a consequence, and so on) provide that which would otherwise be lacking.

But this is too quick. Even if it be admitted that B's need does figure within the moral calculus such that it is not in every respect a matter of moral indifference for A whether B secures G or not, it does not follow that A must do whatever will suffice to bring it about that B have G. There are ways of construing A's obligation toward B with respect to G that lie between the two extremes. At least two deserve mention.

First, it may be held that A need not go as far as providing G to B but must *assist* in the provision of G. This is a natural way to construe the obligations on individuals engendered by most of the positive rights put forth by welfare liberalism. Suppose that what B needs is income, or a job that will generate income. If there are many other persons besides A who have the capacity to provide B with income or employment, then it is arbitrary to maintain that A alone is required to make provision to B. And it would seem a case of conspicuous overkill to maintain that each of the *n* persons who is able to aid B has the obligation to do so in full; B does not need *n* jobs or *n* streams of income. Rather, the phrasing that suggests itself is that B's right to G creates a *shared* or *social* obligation. Each of the other parties can be called upon to contribute a fair share to the maintenance of B's well-being, such that their acting together will be sufficient to bring about B's having G.[10] It will be the case then for welfare liberalism that the obligation actually to provide G falls on the state; individuals will be obligated to contribute their suitably defined share to governmental institutions.

But there is a second way in which individuals can be required to be responsive to a need without it being the case that any one of them must supply that which is needed—or without the collectivity as a whole being obligated to do so. A takes account of B's need for G if A intentionally brings about a condition *necessary* for B's attainment of G, even though that condition is not simultaneously sufficient. If B needs clean water to drink, A may walk down to the stream, fill up a quart jug, and carefully carry it back to B. Alternatively, A may respond to B's need by refraining from dumping raw sewage into the stream (which, for purposes of simplicity, can be supposed to be the only source of potable water available to B). In the former case, A *provides* B with drinking water; in the latter, A *refrains from preventing* B from having the water. The argument from need will not be morally impotent if it generates rights to treatment of the latter sort, rights, however, that fall short of mandating provision of the good G.

It is clear from preceding stages of the discussion that there are some needs to which no right of provision can correspond. Self-respect is one such good. No one can provide another with the day's ration of self-respect as one can a quantity of water. Self-respect, if it is to be attained at all, must in the last resort be internally generated. "The last resort": the phrase is to signify that how others act is not altogether inconsequential for one's ability to develop self-respect. To be treated contemptuously by others as a pariah whose conception of the good merits scorn and denigration will predictably cause all but the hardiest egos to waver or capitulate. Although no one can confer this good on anyone else, it is certainly the case that others can act to impede its realization.

Accordingly, were we to acknowledge a right to self-respect, it logically could not take the form of a right to provision. There is, however, no logical bar to arguing for a right to certain conditions necessary for the development of self-respect. Persons would thereby be placed under an obligation not to degrade others or render them servile in a manner that would obliterate chances for respect of one's own ends and one's status as a moral agent. Admittedly, there would be complications, perhaps insuperable, in applying a right to self-respect so generally stated. Suppose that Jones sets for himself the life task of squaring the circle; he would be absolutely bereft and hold his life to be devoid of meaning were he to be led to believe that he is unable to attain this goal. Would Smith be violating Jones' right if she sent him clippings from a geometry text? Or if she refrained from encouraging Jones to continue his quest in spite of the fact that the first hundred dozen attempts had failed? We might say that only those conditions *typically* necessary for self-respect, those that a vast majority of human beings find essential, must be afforded as a matter of right. But that would seem to be too weak a protection: members of a small racial or religious minority M could then permissibly be degraded in virtue of their inclusion within M because most persons do not require respect for M-members. These, though, are digressions; the intent of the example was not to argue for the existence of a right to (the conditions necessary for the attainment and maintenance of) self-respect. Rather, the argument was conditional: *if* there is a right to self-respect, it can *only* be a right to certain necessary conditions and not to sufficient conditions.

The distinction between classical liberalism and welfare liberalism is often misleadingly characterized as revolving around which needs or, more generally, which interests are to be accorded primary moral status and, therefore, to be safeguarded by ascriptions of rights. Classical liberalism, it is said, recognizes that persons require security in person and possessions, and so it posits the familiar Lockean triumvirate of rights to life, liberty, and estate. No one may properly intrude on the enjoyment of these, where intrusion is understood as coercive interference.

Welfare liberals agree with classical liberals that individuals have a strong interest in not being interfered with, but emphasize that noninterference hardly exhausts persons' vital interests. The liberty to untrammeled use of one's estate will be of little value to the beggar who has no estate; his primary concern is the acquisition of material goods in the first place. The proclaimed right to life will ring hollow to the man who lacks the means to procure medical care necessary for his survival. Welfare liberalism claims to be consistently carrying out the unfinished program of classical liberalism. Rather than restricting attention to a *select* class of human needs, it maintains that *all* needs possess moral weight in virtue of their being needs, and therefore they create rights. It is not only liberty that is generally valuable but also health care, housing, employment, education, recreation, and so on. If there are liberty rights, then there are also rights to these welfare goods.

This way of putting the contrast between classical and welfare liberalism trades on a fundamental confusion. It is mistaken to say that one version is responsive to a narrow array of interests while the other ascribes moral weight to a much wider range of interests. The difference is almost not at all with regard to *which interests merit moral protection* but rather with the *manner in which moral protection is afforded.* Classical liberalism recognizes rights to conditions *necessary* for the attainment of valued items, while welfare liberalism is concerned to bring about *sufficient* conditions for their attainment. If the older version of liberalism is myopic, it is not because it is blind to the value of things like employment and medical care. If it is to be faulted, it will be because the degree of moral response to these interests is held to be inadequate, and not because the interest itself is dismissed.

Consider the status of an alleged right to employment (or, more grandly, a right to "meaningful and productive employment"). It is tempting to classify this as one of the "new rights," one unknown to the liberalism of an earlier century. That classification would be importantly mistaken. Whether or not classical liberals used the term 'right to employment', they clearly believed that there was such a right, and that it was violated whenever private parties, or more commonly, state institutions acted to restrict the liberty of persons to engage in chosen occupations. The feudalism that tied a serf to the manor and the patriarchy that sought to restrict women to a domestic existence as the appendage of husband or father were both, at different historical stages of the career of liberalism, condemned. So, too, were grants of patent and monopoly that restricted access to various lines of work. If people need employment, then they need the liberty to contract for whatever employment is available. The liberty right vouchsafed by classical liberalism is a moral response to this need and therefore fully deserves to be accorded recognition as a right to employment.

That is not, of course, to maintain that classical liberalism anticipated the welfare right to employment. In its recent incarnation the right to employment does not merely uphold a condition necessary for the securing of employment, but one that is sufficient. The government is called upon to provide jobs to all those not employed by the private sector. In theory this is to strengthen the classical liberal's right to employment by recognizing additional obligations toward the unemployed; alongside the liberty right of free contract are positive rights to the provision of a job. Nothing is taken away, but something is added.

Practice, however, significantly diverges from theory. Welfare liberalism in fact has largely acceded to major erosions in the liberty right to employment. Minimum wage laws tend to receive strong support from contemporary versions of liberalism,[11] but these laws restrict persons' freedom to secure employment without in any way providing additional sources of jobs. Moreover, the persons who are inconvenienced will almost always be those for whom the securing of any employment at all is difficult. Brain surgeons and master carpenters will rarely be touched by the existence of minimum wage laws, but seventeen-year-old black high school dropouts will often be guaranteed an absence of work opportunities. Occupational licensure laws also restrict access to employment, and these too are typically sanctioned by welfare liberalism. Therefore, it is not at all obvious that the right to employment espoused by welfare liberalism is stronger or more encompassing than the version set forth by classical liberals.

The two varieties of liberalism do not differ essentially in the interests they hold worthy of protection but rather in the nature of the protection that is to be accorded. The decision between them will have to be made on grounds of which response is the more adequate in doing justice to the gravity of the interests at stake. And these are grounds on which the case for welfare liberalism seems especially strong. It can be put in the following terms:

> To judge an interest *important* is to judge that it should be *met*. Simply to eliminate a group of obstacles to its attainment will be of value only when those are the only obstacles. It is small comfort to a person who lacks some vitally important good G to be informed that he has complete liberty to pursue G if possession of that liberty is insufficient to ensure his attainment of G. Liberties that are unaccompanied by the ability to make effective use of the liberty are of negligible value. What should be of preeminent moral concern is not how many or how few conditions necessary for the securing of G are satisfied, but whether in fact the need for G will be met. To take seriously an interest is to bring it about that the interest will, if possible, be satisfied. Only the recognition of positive rights entails an obligation of *provision*.

This argument is presumptively strong because it links the theory of rights to a theory of personal value. If rights are to be the hard currency of moral exchange rather than counterfeit coin, rights must be something that persons have reason to value. They will value a right to the extent that it enhances their ability to act successfully on their conception of the good. (A right to an equal share of aluminum mined on the moon will be assigned little value by its holders.) If possession of a right is fully sufficient to guarantee the attainment of some valued component of a person's good, then the person has reason to value that right. But if a right to G will predictably fail to lead to the securing of G because it protects only some of the conditions necessary for G, others of which will remain unsatisfied, it becomes mysterious on what grounds such a right could be held to be of value. Insofar, then, as the rights espoused by classical liberalism fall short of ensuring the enjoyment of goods, their lofty position in the moral pantheon is in jeopardy.

That is not to claim that liberty rights are altogether insignificant. Rather, it is to specify with some precision for whom they will be of value: individuals who need nothing more than liberty of the relevant sort in order to pursue G with a high probability of success. They will be persons for whom the other necessary conditions have antecedently been satisfied. Typically, this classification will include members of the upper and middle economic and social classes and will exclude those whose economic and social position is marginal. Marxist theoreticians have found it entirely unsurprising that the staunchest upholders of liberty rights come from the classes that will be most advanced by their recognition; ''bourgeois rights'' are advocated by the bourgeoisie because they are, in a very direct sense, *for* the bourgeoisie. Welfare liberals decline to embrace the full Marxist critique of a liberal order, but they go along with the Marxists in asserting the moral indefensibility of a class-biased scheme of rights, where 'class bias' is defined in terms of de facto differential advantage. Their preferred way of surmounting this bias is to buttress a structure of negative rights with a collection of positive rights such that they are jointly sufficient to guarantee to all persons the various goods which are held to be objects of rights.

If a cogent case is to be made for classical liberalism, it will have to meet the charge that assigning favored status to liberty rights is morally arbitrary. It will require arguing either (1) that liberty of action is a more valuable moral possession than are other necessary conditions for achievement of one's ends or (2) that the provision of welfare goods carries liabilities that do not similarly attach to the provision of liberty. The two prongs are complementary; each aims at showing that liberty is, in some sense, unique and that liberty rights inherit this uniqueness. To the extent that such a case can be developed, the presumptively powerful argument supportive of welfare liberalism will be defused.

The Liberal Ideal: Noninterference or Aid?

Because rights generate correlative obligations of compliance, the justification of an alleged right necessarily displays two aspects. It must ground the object of the right in some compelling interest of the potential right holder, and it must also demonstrate that those who transact with the potential right holder have reason to acknowledge and respect the interest in question. If either is absent, the justification fails. That is why an argument that proceeds directly from needs to rights is, at best, incomplete. The fact that B needs G may afford A no reason whatsoever to act in a way that enhances B's likelihood of securing G. Or, less arguably, it may have some bearing on A's choice of activity without mandating that A provide G to B. The more onerous the demands placed on A, the less reason that A has, *ceteris paribus,* to accede to those demands.

A requirement of noninterference with the liberty of persons to pursue some good will typically be less costly than a requirement of provision.[12] For that reason, an argument for a liberty right can go through in circumstances where the argument for a corresponding welfare right does not. Specifically, that will be so when a bona fide interest has been established but where

$$C_L^G < I^G < C_W^G$$

C_L being the cost to a representative individual of acknowledging a liberty right to G, C_W the cost of acknowledging a welfare right to G, and I^G the moral weight of the interest in G.

It is intuitively plausible to suppose that, for many I^G, the inequality holds. Consider two cases cited above. It is undeniable that impoverished Asians have a strong interest in securing means of subsistence, yet few will argue that this fact imposes an obligation on Americans to ship abroad 70% of their GNP. However, it is very persuasive to maintain that Americans (and others) are obliged *not to interfere* with the efforts of Asians to secure economic sufficiency. It would therefore be impermissible to send a flotilla to commandeer a share of the none-too-bulging Bangladesh granary, or to forbid by governmental edict relief agencies from sending cash or commodities to that country. It is also morally impermissible to enact protectionist legislation that in any way interferes with the liberty of foreign nationals to trade with whomsoever they choose in order to secure income. (If this implication of a right to noninterference seems more questionable than the other two, it may be because our familiarity with protectionist practices lends them a veneer of respectability. A century ago imperialistic exactions enjoyed similar familiarity, as did the practice of slavery a century before that. Surely there is more than a little inconsistency exemplified by those who argue for protectionism coupled with foreign aid.) If Asians possess any rights against Americans for subsistence, then they at least possess a liberty right.

Similarly, my interest in acquiring a serviceable cornea imposes on others at least the duty not to prevent my getting the part from a willing donor. If someone chooses to give me an eye, bequeath it in his will, or sell it for an agreed sum, then it would be a violation of my liberty right should a private individual or the state act to impede such a transaction. The acknowledgment of a liberty right to secure the cornea does not, of course, entail that, should no donor be forthcoming, you are morally required to turn over to me one of your two good corneas.

The criticism of classical liberalism was that the rights it sets forth are too modest to correspond adequately to the gravity of interests at stake. But what the preceding discussion shows is that modesty is a virtue. Because C_L^G is typically much less than C_W^G, individuals will often have reason to acknowledge liberty rights, though not welfare rights. Welfare liberalism claims to take seriously the interests on which rights are founded; perhaps it does. But it fails to attend with equal attention to the rational motivation of persons to accede to a rights claim. By insisting that a right to G worthy of the name must entail the provision of G, welfare liberalism jeopardizes the underpinnings of a structure of basic rights. Rights are moral claims with which others *must* comply. Because the demand for compliance is (maximally) strong, an interpersonally acceptable structure of rights has to restrict the area over which compliance is mandatory. Otherwise individuals will find that they have no rational stake in the maintenance of a regime of rights.[13] This was the conclusion of Chapter 4. It can now be seen that classical liberalism is concerned *both* to recognize rights that correspond to grave interests *and* to ensure that all members of the moral community have a stake in securing for themselves and others the rights so defined.

It may be objected that this line of argument is question-begging. It has been argued that moral demands which are stringent must therefore not be excessive. But what is to count as "excessive"? Unless this preliminary question is answered, it will be impossible to determine whether welfare liberalism requires too much of persons—or classical liberalism too little. After all, the surest way to avoid excess imposition is to demand nothing at all of anyone. Such a retreat into Hobbesian anarchy is not what any liberal defends. Let it be granted that obligations corresponding to rights lie on an Aristotelian continuum between deficiency and excess. Until the mean is specified, it is impossible to determine the extent to which negative rights should properly be augmented by positive rights.

A second line of objection is to demur at the equation of positive rights with severe impositions. The critic can admit that some positive rights will fall heavily on others: e.g., those very carefully selected as examples for this chapter. However, the critic will be prepared to respond with his own examples in which the balance of benefits and burdens is quite different.

1. A small child has slipped into a swimming pool and is in danger of drowning. One person is sitting by the side of the pool doing the Sunday *New York Times* crossword puzzle. By getting out of his chair, walking a few steps, and reaching into the pool, he could save the child. That, though, would mean abandoning the crossword puzzle for a minute or two. Does the child have a right against this man to be saved? Is there a positive obligation to save the child or no more than an obligation not to prevent anyone else who wishes to do so from saving the child?

2. Persons who lack the means to purchase antibiotics will suffer from diseases that are easily curable. Thousands of impoverished individuals will live longer and happier lives if the rest of us are taxed a few pennies each, the proceeds to go toward supplying needed drugs. Do the indigent have a right to

medical relief that is inexpensive and easily tendered, yet which has great therapeutic benefits?

These are cases in which it seems entirely persuasive to maintain that I^G exceeds C^G_W, and that therefore a welfare right to G should be admitted. It is barely, if at all, more inconvenient directly to provide the good than to pledge noninterference with respect to attainment of the good. (Won't it disturb one's concentration if rescuers are scurrying around the sides of the pool?) If important needs support a structure of minimally imposing *liberty* rights, then they should equally well support minimally imposing *welfare* rights. There is no presumption that all and only welfare rights are very burdensome on others or that all and only liberty rights embody suitable moderation in demands placed on others. Therefore, it cannot be concluded that a rationally defensible version of liberalism will be one in which liberty rights are dominant.

Both strands of objection implicitly concede that the direct argument from needs to rights is defective. Because that argument is so prominently deployed as a chief prop for welfare liberalism, the concession is significant. It implies that if there are welfare rights, then they must be like liberty rights with respect to the degree of burdensomeness imposed. The welfare liberalism that could emerge from such a basis would be a modest extension of classical liberalism rather than a sharply revisionary view of what rights people have.

Classical liberalism does not, however, rest merely on the claim that liberty is more easily provided than many other things individuals require. Rather, it insists that liberty is unique among goods necessary for project pursuit in that it *must be provided by others* if it is to be enjoyed at all. The conditions necessary for an agent to lead a successful life may be divided into three mutually exclusive categories. In the first are those items which only the agent himself can generate. These include motivational energy and self-respect. If they are lacking, then no one else can provide them.

In Category 2 are goods of which the agent may avail himself through his own efforts or which may be provided to him by others. Food, clothing, shelter, and most other economic goods fall within this classification. It is, of course, the case that individuals who "provide themselves" with these goods typically do so within a framework of institutions involving the voluntary cooperation of others. To purchase one's food at a grocery store requires the cooperation of others in a way that solitary berry-picking does not; do-it-yourself neurosurgery is not likely to be as successful as the services involving the efforts of thousands of persons provided at a major medical center. The division of labor in complex modern societies leads to more efficient provision of some goods and to the very availability of others. Without in any way wishing to downplay the significance of specialization within the social order, there is still a point to saying that individuals who command resources that can predictably be transformed into or exchanged for desired goods and services provide those goods and services for themselves. As it were, the social levers are already there waiting to be pulled. By way of contrast, a person who commands no appreciable stock of resources may yet receive valued items, but the levers then must be pulled by others. The distinction is between the ability to purchase or secure an item through one's labor and securing that item as a gift or through coercive extraction.

Category 3 includes those conditions which the agent cannot bring about for himself but which others can provide. These include fame, adulation, friendship, and other services that make essential reference to others. Paramount, though, among these is *noninterference.* Whatever it is that one desires to do, one requires the absence of interference by others. Noninterference is thus a good that is both *universal* and *general:* it is universal in the sense that it is of value to every project pursuer and is general in that it is valued irrespective of the nature of the ends that one endeavors to advance. Moreover, it is needed *from everyone.* Of course, not everyone is in fact able to intrude on one's pursuit of ends, and so there will be no point to insisting on the noninterference of someone who totally lacks the power to affect one's designs. But that is to say that a Benign Nature is arrayed so as to limit possibilities of interference, and is not to deny that such noninterference is needed. Should *anyone* interfere with A's pursuit of end E_1, then A is thereby harmed.

Among the members of Category 3, noninterference is unique. Unlike, say, fame, it is of basic value to everyone irrespective of the particular nature of the ends to which one commits oneself. And even if it be argued that friendship is also a good that must be present for a life to be minimally satisfactory, it is not a good that must be supplied by everyone. One or several friends will satisfy the condition quite nicely. Perhaps—though this is arguable—more friends, all else equal, are always better than fewer; and perhaps a community exemplifying universal mutual affection is the best of all possible moral orders—if it be possible at all. However, it cannot be *demanded* of persons that they contribute a full share to the maintenance of a superlatively good social design, both because such a contribution is supererogatory rather than a matter of duty, and also because goods such as friendship cannot be procured via edict. Friendship (or affection, or solidarity, or fraternity) presupposes an antecedent regard for persons and their ends. To be a friend is voluntarily to enroll oneself in the projects of another, to regard his good as one's own simply because it is his good and not because there happens to be a coincidence of aims. Noninterference entails no such presupposition. It involves the recognition of other persons as distinct individuals committed to their distinct projects, but assumes no sympathy with person or project. No aid for a design that is not one's own (and to which one may be indifferent or antipathetic) is required, only the avoidance of instrusion.

What these considerations seem to indicate is that classical liberalism is *not* myopic in its strong emphasis on liberty rights. The moral theory that it puts for forth is continuous with the account of practical reason as responsive to personal value that was sketched out in Chapter 2. If E_1 is A's end, then there is reason-for-the-promotion-of-E_1-by-A that is not similarly reason-for-B. If C is a condition necessary for A's attainment of E_1, then A has reason to bring it about that C obtain. B, though, does not possess equivalent reason to bring it about that C obtain. If C falls into Category 2 (i.e., C is a condition which either A or B could satisfy), then it is A on whom the practical necessity of satisfying C primarily falls. However, should A have a right against B that B provide for the satisfaction of C, then it would be B and not A for whom reasons to provide C would be maximally weighty (or they would face reasons of equal weightiness). To posit the existence of such a right, then, is at odds with the essentially individuated character of practical reason. Classical liberalism is quite properly hesitant in acknowledging the existence of such rights.

Because liberty falls within Category 3, its provision is a very different matter. B's noninterference with A's pursuit of E_1 is something that A cannot provide for himself; it must be tendered by B. Unlike the previous case, the responsibility for providing the good is necessarily external to the recipient of the good. To demand liberty as a right is not in conflict with the recognition of the separateness of persons and their projects. Rather, it is responsive to such separateness: because persons are separate beings individuated in part by virtue of the particular projects to which they commit themselves, they are rationally entitled to insist that they be let alone to pursue their own designs and not be enlisted as adjuncts to the projects of others. Classical liberalism is the moral endorsement of persons' individuality.

Reference was made in the previous chapter to Kantian formulations of liberal individualism. It is now possible to spell out in somewhat more detail how thoroughly consonant with the structure of a Kantian ethic is the preeminence of liberty rights. Kant insists that universality and generality are formal properties of all binding ethical principles. We have now seen that a moral requirement of respect for persons' liberty satisfies the generality criterion in that the value of liberty is not dependent on individuals' particular choice of projects. It doubly satisfies the universality criterion: every project pursuer needs liberty, and liberty is needed from everyone. The formulation of Kant's Categorical Imperative that enjoins one to treat all persons as ends in themselves and not merely as means can be read as requiring the recognition that each project pursuer is a being who accords to his own projects a special personal value, and that respect for persons entails that they not be precluded from acting as project pursuers.

It is open to the welfare liberal to identify other goods that are like liberty in being capable of provision only by others, and that are general and universal in the relevant senses. These goods, once identified, may serve to ground rights in as deep a theoretical base of individuated practical reason as are liberty rights. This course is open to the welfare liberal—if there are any such goods to be discovered. Prospects, though, seem dim. It is clear that the usual listing of interests that are to be satisfied by individual or, more commonly, political provision does not come close to qualifying. Most of these interests are in Category 2, not Category 3. Those in the third category lack either generality or universality or both. One can, then, with some confidence, predict that future development of the theory of welfare liberalism is unlikely to shake the primacy of liberty and liberty rights.

It would be too abrupt, however, to proceed from the *primacy* of liberty rights to an extreme libertarian stance that countenances *only* liberty rights, whatever the circumstances in which human beings find themselves. It has been argued that noninterference is requisite for successful civility. Therefore, individuals have reason to supply noninterference to others conditional upon the like receipt of noninterference from them. It has not been argued nor, I believe, can it be that no acts of positive performance are such that persons can claim them as their rightful due. (See Chapter 6.) Even were that so for advanced capitalistic liberal democracies, itself a highly debatable point, it would be parochial to extend by fiat that recipe to all settings for social existence. Respect for the individuality of persons as project pursuers with their own lives to lead is compatible with the acknowledgment of dependency relations that validate positive claims on others.[14] Moral theory, including the theory of rights, must be chary of prescribing for all times and all places in an apodictic voice. Principles derived from philosophical anthropology and the a priori form of practical reason admit of widely varying applications. Morality is not a Procrustean bed into which, willy-nilly, social existence can be trimmed to fit.

Basic Rights, Moral Rights, and Legal Rights

Philosophy is at home in the realm of the abstract; this book is no exception. Because that is the case, it is especially important for philosophers to indicate with some care the level of abstraction at which their analysis is deemed to apply. Otherwise it can all too easily seem that the investigation is being carried out in terms wildly inappropriate to its object. The danger is especially acute for a work that purports to address the theory of rights. We routinely speak of "rights" of various different degrees of concreteness and specificity. *Legal rights* derive from a community's body of law and its institutional arrangements for promulgation, interpretation, and enforcement of law. Legal rights are highly specific to a particular legal order. Against them are *moral rights,* existing in some sort of complexly symbiotic—or adversary—relation with legal structures but not simply the product of positive law. Finally there are the "grand rights," referred to variously as "natural rights," "human rights," or, as I prefer, "basic rights." They are rights whose scope of application is maximally broad, that are not the product of explicit conventional design but antecedent to it, and that are morally regulative in the highest degree. If the word 'right' can be employed in these widely differing ways, it will be crucial to keep them straight and not, for example, speak as if legal rights are nothing other than moral rights transcribed into a law code.

It has been the goal of this book to develop a theory of basic rights, and the strategy has been to allow a conception of basic rights to *emerge* from the discussion rather than to *stipulate* a definition at the outset. To the extent that this strategy is effective, one will come to see what basic rights *are* as one comes to understand what moral order persons have reason to *acknowledge* and to *value.* Now that much of that exploration has been carried out, it will be more useful than it would have been previously to say something directly about what basic rights are—and what they are not.

Basic rights have been presented as the guarantors of moral space to individuals who, in virtue of being project pursuers, have reason to value their ability to be project pursuers. I have not claimed that project pursuit is an essential property of human beings. Nor was it claimed that the world must invariably be such that individuals can establish conditions of reciprocal recognition and respect for the interest each project pursuer has in his ability to be a project pursuer. Therefore, I am unable to maintain, as do some "human rights" or "natural rights" theorists, that in every conceivable setting in which the interaction of human beings occurs there is a rational basis for claiming rights and extending them to others. Given that proviso, it can still be said that the scope envisioned for basic rights is considerable. Human beings *do* by and large endeavor to carve out coherent lives for themselves via commitment to regulative personal ends; this is not a shallow fact likely to obtain only within a narrow cultural and historical spectrum. Conditions within which reciprocity is feasible *do* regularly obtain, else the survival of the species would be nothing short of miraculous. Therefore, even if basic rights do not obtain always and everywhere, they very nearly do.

It has been argued that recognition and respect for persons as project pursuers translate primarily into rights of noninterference. That, though, is not to be glossed as an assertion that successful civility among individuated persons is incompatible with all demands that go beyond a call for noninterference. There is no one rigid mold of liberal society into which every community of human beings will nicely fit. Still, that is not to say that the value of liberty is, in a strong sense, culturally relative. Men need liberty not because they subscribe to some particular good esteemed by some particular culture but because they are beings who *have a good* and who thereby generate personal value. The moral adequacy of a society of project pursuers can be appraised by reference to the protection it affords to individualism: this is an almost universal truth. It is difficult to imagine a civil order in which individualism thrives but in which liberty rights are not a prominent component of that society's moral grid. Therefore, it will not oversimplify much to cast the fundamental moral imperative of a well-ordered society as:

Each person is to have an equal right to the most extensive basic liberty compatible with a similar liberty for others.[15]

What will count in any given social order as satisfying the basic rights of persons is not determinable once and for all. Rather, contingencies peculiar to the time and place will bear heavily on the acceptability of assignments of rights and obligations. What ends persons are able to comprehend and embrace as their own will vary, and so too will what is reasonably to be regarded as interference. Respect for basic rights, then, will assume different forms, and these culturally relative modes will define persons' *moral rights*.

It will help to make clear the distinction between basic rights and moral rights (as moral concepts operating at different levels of abstraction) by citing several examples. The basic right to noninterference will assume different forms in response to beliefs concerning the nature of the causal order. If it is believed that acts of blasphemy will incite the gods to rain fire and brimstone (or plague, or famine as other accounts have it) down upon the entire community, then blasphemy will not be classified as a purely self-regarding act but rather as an instance of blatant interference with the lives of others. Its proscription will not be illiberal or irrational, simply empirically mistaken. Similarly, if no causal connection is observed between dumping one's raw sewage into the common water supply and the occurence of disease, then no one could justifiably claim a moral right against the other that the sewage not be dumped. It is not self-evident what the correct scientific theory is, and therefore one will not be able simply to read off the moral landscape what moral rights persons have.

Variance in moral rights need not rest on factual mistakes. Even if all relevant causal connections are known with a high degree of accuracy, there yet remains considerable scope for different understandings concerning which causal effects constitute *interference*. It will not do to define 'interference' as an act of causally contributing to an adverse effect on someone or other. That is both too weak and too strong. It is too weak because it excludes *threatening* or *risky* behavior; should I choose to play Russian roulette with your head and the chamber that comes up happens to be empty, then I would not have interferred with you.[16] It is too strong because it is impossible for persons to avoid all adverse causal effects on others. Driving a car releases hydrocarbons that are causally contributory to cancer and other diseases. So, too, does burning wood to heat one's hovel. Any close contact with others creates the possibility that some microorganism will travel from one's own body to that of another person who will thereby be made ill, and so on. In order for life to be possible, social determinations will have to be made concerning which causal effects will be deemed cases of (impermissible) interference.

These determinations are not derivable via a precise algorithm, but neither are they arbitrary. A society's determinations will hinge on its history, conventions in force within the society, its material conditions, and also on its background moral attitudes. The introduction of an automobile's fumes and noise into a pastoral setting whose most advanced transportation device is the donkey could plausibly be viewed as an interfering act that violates moral rights. The introduction of the same vehicle into Los Angeles would not be. (Alternatively, leaving donkey droppings in one's wake will be impermissible in Los Angeles but not in the village.) To have carcasses of beef in plain view in one's butcher shop window may be entirely innocent in Boston but not in Bombay. Cases can easily be multiplied. What they point to is the open-endedness and cultural relativity of the concept of a *moral right*.

Legal rights are consequent upon the existence of a determinate legal structure. Just as moral rights are more determinate than basic rights, legal rights are characteristically more determinate than moral rights. It will often be possible to say when a legal right came into existence, by whose authority, and what penalties attach to its violation. Even where the right in question does not proceed from a datable statute but is an outgrowth of common law "from time immemorial," one will be able to specify which institutions are charged with the responsibility of defining and protecting the rights that issue from the law. Moral rights grow spontaneously from the warp and woof of a society; legal rights are manufactured to design. In one crucial respect, though, they are alike: both the moral and the legal rights recognized within a social order are to be evaluated with reference to how adequately they instantiate the basic rights that individuals possess. It is basic rights that are morally and epistemologically prior.

The characterization presented above of the three levels of rights is, admittedly, rough. Things are lumped together that in a fuller account would have to be distinguished. For example, it is not the case that all legal rights are equally general. Fundamental constitutional protections are regulative with respect to statutes which in turn are regulative with respect to particular judicial decisions. The preceding remarks were not intended to advance discussions in the philosophy of law but rather to provide a perspective for construing the concept of a basic right. Those remarks may also help explain the skepticism commonly expressed toward the espousal of any rights other than legal rights.

Legal rights are conveniently concrete, with carefully delimited principles of application. Their practical significance is also manifest; in a well-ordered society legal rights are regularly enforced in a predictable manner by effective state institutions. It is, therefore, clear why persons have reason to value their legal rights. Because the content and value of legal rights are so readily apparent, it is tempting to take legal rights as the paradigm in terms of which the genuineness of all other alleged rights is to be judged. If "basic rights" and "moral rights" are found to lack the specificity and enforceability of legal rights, then they are not bona fide rights at all. It is then a short step to consign them to the dustbin of ill-defined concepts.

Rights theorists have themselves often provided the ammunition for their own undoing. Corresponding to *positive law,* it is said, there exists a *natural law;* as the former generates positive (legal) rights, the latter generates natural rights. Natural lawyers are persons trained to search out applications of natural law to particular situations through utilization of much the same legal tools that positive lawyers employ. Enforcement of natural law and the consequent protection of natural rights is not guaranteed, but neither is the enforcement of positive law. In both cases the proper functioning of institutions is necessary. Yet, if natural law is the product of a natural lawgiver, then there is hope for an enforcement that transcends all earthly imperfections: "But if the Prince, or whoever they be in the Administration, decline that way of Determination, the Appeal then lies no where but to Heaven.''[17]

Whether or not the concept of a natural law is a useful adjunct to moral theory is disputable. However, to conceive of natural law as analogous to positive law, only written instead in Plato's (or Locke's) Heaven, is to court confusion. The abstraction of a defensible natural law precludes its direct application to concrete situations that are immersed in a sea of particularity. Casuistic attempts to the contrary will, inevitably, appear as arbitrary and capricious, thus undermining the appeal of a doctrine of natural law—and of natural rights.[18]

Basic rights and moral rights are rationally defensible—but not if they are taken as a detailed blueprint for systems of positive law. Basic rights cannot be expected to function as legal rights do, entailing imperatives that are directly applicable to human affairs. It must not be supposed that there is one unique instantiation of basic rights that is everywhere optimal. Rather, basic rights are conceptually valuable because they derive from the nature of human beings as project pursuers having a community existence among other project pursuers. Because basic rights abstract from particular forms of social life and from particular project attachments, basic rights do service as a moral standard by means of which various social arrangements can be evaluated. Moral appraisal is blinkered by culturally relative practices and values unless there exists a rationally accessible vantage point that is antecedent to specific cultural forms (and yet not dismissive of them). Because philosophers have an interest in surmounting what is transient and provincial—if not to ascend to the summit of the Eternal and Essential, then at least to grasp the less transient and less provincial—they are significantly served by a concept of basic rights.

Anarchism and Liberalism

Liberal theorists are not alone in placing great stock in basic rights construed primarily or exclusively as liberty rights. Philosophical anarchism also insists that individuals be left unconstrained in their endeavors to carve out for themselves meaningful and satisfying lives. As with the liberal, the anarchist rejects the enthronement of a monolithic impersonal standard of value or the hypostatization of a common human enterprise that commands the allegiance of everyone. Precisely because of the way in which he construes these liberal postulates, the anarchist is led to reject the liberal theory of the state. An institution that claims a monopoly to define and impose demands on persons who have not explicitly consented to be governed—and to that the anarchist *will not* consent—necessarily violates men's rights. Coercive imposition of a legal order is inherently intrusive on moral space, claims the anarchist, and therefore no state can enjoy legitimacy.

Those disinclined to give serious weight to the claims of individualism can easily shrug off the anarchistic critique. Utilitarians, for example, will note that maximization of overall utility requires the provision of public goods, and that these will be very much underproduced in the absence of coercive mechanisms to extract from individuals full cost shares for the goods. Because anarchism decisively fails the maximization test, it can be dismissed as a utopian (but strangely unlovely) fantasy. However, one who takes rights to engender side constraints upon action has already abandoned the conception of morality as an exercise in unconstrained value maximization. If there are public goods that can only be attained through coercive impositions, these goods must be forfeited should it be the case that such impositions are found to violate rights.

The importance of anarchism for political practice may be negligible, but its importance for political theory is great. Anarchism tests the limits of political liberalism through its questioning of whether the marriage between individualism and political order is compatible. Nothing could be clearer than that governments, even the most benign and limited ones, engage in massive acts of coercion. If the state by its very nature is a violator of basic rights, then liberalism does not represent a moral equilibrium; either political order or individualism must go.

Liberal theorists often respond to the anarchist challenge by ignoring it. One who does not, who is the conspicuous defender for our time of a liberal politics against the anarchist challenge, is Robert Nozick. The first third of his *Anarchy, State, and Utopia* is a complex justificatory exercise in demonstrating the existence of a path by means of which a minimal (i.e., liberal) state could emerge from anarchy without anyone's rights being violated in the process. The argument pivots on an intricate point concerning legitimate compensation for the prohibition of risky activity, the compensation taking the form of—citizenship! The argument is as ingenious as it is tortuous, and critics have hacked at it at one point or another.[19] But even if Nozick's devolution of the minimal state can be sustained in the face of criticism, the liberal theorist must be made uneasy by reliance on so involuted a chain of reasoning to uphold the legitimacy of a rights-respecting polity. Should the chain break down at any point, would the realm of the political thereby be thrown into disrepute?

The Nozickean demonstration takes anarchism as the benchmark from which progress toward the state commences. The onus is upon the defender of the political to show that at no step of the progression are any of the side constraints imposed by persons' rights violated. It is taken for granted that anarchistic society itself is compatible with the recognition of and respect for basic rights.

Just this assumption deserves to be called into question. Is anarchism an appropriate moral benchmark, or is it instead the case that the moral legitimacy of anarchism itself is in jeopardy? The distinctions raised above concerning the levels of abstraction at which various conceptions of rights function indicate, I believe, that the onus of proof should descend onto the shoulders of the anarchist. It is by no means evident that persons in a hypothesized or actual state of nature can coherently be characterized as in full possession of their basic rights.

Basic rights cannot be directly applied to the interactions of human beings. Rather, they are enjoyed only insofar as they are instantiated in the concrete forms of moral and legal rights. Recall the preceding discussion of *interference:* it was argued that there is no criterion of what constitutes interference that can be "read off" the face of the world. Rather, it must be *determined* what is to count as interference within a social order, and that determination is not the product of *inspection* but of *decision*. There is no "fact of the matter" as to what constitutes interference independent of persons' decisions—which is not to deny that factual considerations delimit the range within which reasonable choice can fall. Unless there is some determination or other (although there may be no one "best" determination) of where the boundaries of interference lie, then liberty rights will be empty of content.[20] It is intolerable to admit that one's maximally weighty moral claims are suffused through and through with vagueness and indeterminacy.

It can be responded that what constitutes interference is a matter for decision, but it is a decision that each agent is called upon autonomously to make for himself in the light of all available evidence and with full rationality. But even if persons had complete evidence and perfect rationality, there can be no presumption that they would arrive at congruent standards. Indeed, given different histories, technologies, and commitments, the presumption is rather that individuals acting *qua* individual would arrive at widely differing construals of the liberties that men enjoy by right. If it is important that conceptions of allowable liberty be compacted within a narrow band that fixes the reference similarly for all members of a moral community, then it must be the community *qua* community that constructs standards.

It *is* important. Rights have an essentially interpersonal character. Persons have reason to claim rights for themselves and acknowledge them in others because each has a fundamental interest in the ability to be a project pursuer amidst a world of others with the same interest. Each is rationally motivated to bestow some measure of deference conditional upon receipt of that measure of deference. However, any such moral order would be altogether unrealizable if there were not some basis for a common understanding of what that measure is. Moral community breaks down if no criterion exist for distinguishing secured liberties from acts of encroachment. Because nature does not supply that criterion ready made, it must be created by the undertakings of men in society.

Atomistic beings who lack a socially generated and shared understanding of the bounds of liberty can neither meaningfully claim rights for themselves nor respect them in others. Solitary individuals who independently discern for themselves the rights that nature endows, and who then come together in voluntary compacts should they choose to do so, all the while respecting the rights of each other: this anarchistic fantasy is incoherent. Basic rights are conceptually independent of any *particular* social structure, but basic rights as instantiated in the actual transactions of human beings presuppose sociality of *some sort* or other. In this respect moral rights are like language. Just as the existence of a language presupposes a linguistic community, the existence of moral rights presupposes a moral community.

If anarchism were nothing other than the ascription of rights to atomistic, disconnected individuals, then the case against anarchism would now be complete. But anarchism need not present itself in so naive a fashion. A more sophisticated version will insist on a morally crucial distinction between a *social order* and a *political order*. Sociality as such is in no way condemned; indeed, it will be conceded that social existence is a prerequisite of moral consciousness. Persons who live in communities will come to adjust their activities in response to the behavior of others, thereby creating legitimate expectations of patterns of interaction that carve out allotments of moral space for each. The intricate nexus of social interdependency that evolves in this manner is simultaneously a moral order.

But society is not politics. Nowhere in the process of social formulation and reformulation of moral concepts is it requisite that there be a state that coercively imposes a mandatory demarcation of rights. Here, too, the analogy to language is apposite: just as a language can develop and flourish within a linguistic community in the absence of a Royal Academy empowered authoritatively to rule on what is or is not grammatical, so, too, can a community-wide conception of rights develop and flourish in the absence of a government that designs and hands down law to its obedient subjects.

The sophisticated version of anarchism makes appeal to the efficacy of a *spontaneous order*. The analysis and defense of spontaneous order in the work of F. A. Hayek has given us reason to rethink the assumption that a benign social order must primarily be the intended product of design.[21] Hayek argues that spontaneous acts of adjustment by independent agents will regularly generate desirable social outcomes that could not have been foreseen or intended at the outset and that were thus not capable of production according to plan. The moral rights operative within a community, the anarchist contends, are the priceless by-products of such a spontaneous order. This Hayekian argument[22] merits respect. If it is absurd to posit atomistic individuals who independently generate moral rights, it is equally absurd to suppose that governmental machinery can crank out rights *ex nihilo*. Moral rights, like language, like economic structures, evolve from the shared lives of persons within communities. It is *not* incoherent to envision a community minus formal institutions of governance in which moral principles are nonetheless widely disseminated and respected.

Anarchistic society of a certain sort is, then, conceivable. But whether it is a *morally justifiable* form of social order, let alone the *unique* justifiable form, is another matter. There is strong reason to believe that anarchy is unstable, that the rights it advances are less able to act as gurantors of moral space than are the rights that characterize a polity, and that the process of spontaneous social evolution is itself incompatible with respect for rights in anarchy.

The last criticism, if it can be made out, is especially embarrassing for the anarchist. The theory of anarchism has relied heavily for its coherence on the concept of a spontaneous order. Should it turn out that rights and spontaneity are necessarily at odds with each other, then the foundations of anarchism are shaky indeed. Yet it seems that there is a genuine tension between the two that is irresolvable from within the confines of anarchy.

Consider a process of evolution such that at time t_1 action A is socially understood to be noninterfering but at t_n A is socially understood to be an impermissible act of interference. Suppose that t_1 and t_n are the temporal extremes of the process (i.e., one moral equilibrium is upset at t_1 and a new one established at t_n). What is the status of a performance of A during the range $t_2, \ldots, t_{n-1}$? If A constitutes the violation of a right, then it *must not* be done; but if it is an innocent act, it *must not* be proscribed.

There seems to be no good answer that can be given. By hypothesis, the spontaneous order does not yield a judgment because it is between determinations; yet the morally serious question of whether one may do A cannot merely be sloughed off. "Wait until a new equilibrium has been established." But that might be a *very* long time (spontaneous adjustment, whatever its virtues, is not necessarily quick), and what rationale can be given for proscribing an action that is not (yet) socially understood to be in violation of rights? "You are free to perform A until a spontaneous determination of its impermissibility has been achieved." But such determinations are not instantaneous, and therefore A's moral acceptability would remain unaffected by an ever-increasing consensus that A entails the violation of rights.[23]

The anarchist seems to be in limbo during the stages of a spontaneous moral shift. Because the process of adjustment is perpetually going on in one area or another, he is *always* in limbo. Only if evolution were to cease once and for all when an initial moral equilibrium is achieved could he escape from this Heraclitean flux. That, though, is a will-o'-the-wisp. The anarchist is forced to concede that rights will suffer from continuous indeterminacy. This is a debilitating defect for a theory that maintains that rights are morally portentous. Because persons have reason to endorse an order in which rights are respected, they have reason to endorse a social decision procedure for specifying as precisely as possible what respect for rights does and does not entail. They therefore have reason to establish institutions that are empowered to promulgate and maintain *law*.

For law to be something other than advice or hopeful solicitations of compliance, it must be *enforceable*. Enforcement requires institutional structures authorized to act coercively with respect to miscreants. This is not a backdoor move to introduce gendarmes through the front door. Persons who have a stake in an order in which rights are acknowledged have a stake in the enforcement of those rights. It is not logically necessary that the agency through which rights are defined also claim a monopoly on powers of enforcement, but the *authority* that determines what is to count as a right-inforce thereby determines which coercive acts can be classified as the enforcement of a right and which are the initiation of aggression. Whether the power to enforce is kept at home or farmed out, the legitimacy of enforcement originates from the legitimacy of law.

It appears, then, that a morally adequate order will be one in which conceptions of liberty will germinate from and be nourished by the shared social life of persons in a constant process of adjustment with respect to each other. But precise demarcations of allowable liberties will require the existence of an agency that deliberately and decisively determines what is law. There is, perhaps, room for quibbles concerning whether every such agency will possess *all* the defining characteristics of a "state" or only *most* of them. But at this stage of the debate the challenge to liberalism posed by anarchism begins to vanish.

One final remark: the existence of the political realm is not inherently incompatible with a regime of rights. It does not follow that polities usually or often are characterized by scrupulous concern for the rights of the citizenry. That proposition will meet no opposition from any true liberal.

6

Property Rights Within
a Liberal Order

A liberal order adequate to the interest individuals have in being able to live as project pursuers places a moral premium on noninterference. Traditional civil liberties descend as a corollary of this postulate. Freedom of speech and assembly, in conjunction with an unconstrained press, is conducive to individuals' articulation of their conceptions of the good, for attempts to enlist the cooperation of others in ends which are rendered attainable or enhanced through joint efforts, to secure access to information that bears instrumentally on one's pursuit of designs, and to secure entry into a forum through which one's conception of a good can be modified in the open air of unconstrained conversation. Freedom of religion directly attaches to one major area within which individuals seek to construct meaningful lives through commitment to regulative ends. Freedom from arbitrary search and seizure physically represents and gives force to the individualistic notion of "moral space."

From within a liberal perspective it is virtually uncontroversial that these liberties and others of similar provenance must be afforded wide play by any rights-respecting polity. However, controversy seems endemic to the corresponding determination of what *claims over property* a society based on rights should acknowledge. Casual inspection of contemporary literature in political philosophy reveals that debate among liberal theorists centers overwhelmingly on the principles by means of which rights to property are to be allocated. John Rawls' influential *A Theory of Justice* undertakes to derive from a contractarian basis those principles that constitute the justice of social institutions. He identifies two: the principle of maximum equal basic liberties and the difference principle (for the allocation of economic goods and social offices). They are held by Rawls to stand in a lexical order; in every case of conflict the former principle takes precedence over the latter. One might expect, then, that critics and commentators would be most keen to address themselves to the more favored principle of maximum equal liberty, with perhaps a word or two for the subsidiary difference principle. Precisely the opposite is the case: a rough guess would be that the Rawls industry has churned out twenty searching examinations of the difference principle (i.e., the principle that directly bears on the justification of inequality in the distribution of property) for each attempt to appraise the significance of the maximum equal liberty principle.[1]

Robert Nozick's *Anarchy, State, and Utopia* also squarely resides within philosophical liberalism, though in a neighborhood distant from that of *A Theory of Justice*. Respondents to Nozick have also kept themselves uncommonly busy, and their primary focus has been Nozick's *entitlement theory* (of justice in property holdings). The development of that theory, though, is accorded many fewer pages by Nozick than are his defense of the minimal state against the anarchist's challenge and his sketch of a theory of utopia in the final section of the book.

Lest it be supposed that these remarks are intended as an indictment of readers too slipshod to keep an eye on the main chance, I hasten to add that the commentaries are duly responsive to cues issued by the authors in question. Rawls himself spends far more time on explicating, deriving, and defending the difference principle than he devotes to its lexically prior mate. And Nozick clearly takes the entitlement theory to be the linchpin of his libertarian (i.e., classically liberal) theory of politics. Should his account of property rights founder, not much could be salvaged from the wreckage. It is then not appropriate to condemn the surrounding literature as distorted.

The allocation of property within a liberal order undoubtedly is a salient theoretical issue. It bears quite directly on the "uncontroversial" rights referred to above. The "speech" of which individuals are free to avail themselves will reach listeners to the extent that one has access to property through which one's words are disseminated; a still, small voice is notably amplified by a megaphone, a printing press, or a network of several hundred television stations. What will count as search and seizure will be determined, beyond the boundaries of one's epidermis, by what one *has*. Moreover, one's command of economic goods directly affects the projects one can pursue and the likelihood of success one enjoys. So property arrangements are clearly significant for political theory. Significance, though, cannot itself explain why property is the bone of contention par excellence; there must be some other reasons why theorists otherwise in substantial agreement concerning the core principles of a liberal order find themselves so very much at odds in their attempts to work out a satisfactory account of property rights.

Property and Its Puzzles: Some Sources

It is not as if one were called upon to develop a morally satisfactory theory of property rights that stands radically apart from and is unaided by all other constituents of the theory of basic rights. Whatever it is that molds our conviction that *rights* occupy a strategic position on the moral landscape will simultaneously establish the framework within which a defensible account of *property rights* is to be constructed. Rights are the moral recognition of persons' fundamental interest in the ability to be project pursuers. It is through the mutual and reciprocal extension of equal degrees of required deference, primarily understood as noninterference, that individuals in society rationally respond to this interest. It follows that a system of property rights will be acceptable only if it generally enhances the ability of persons to achieve and maintain the status of project pursuer. If the distribution of property within a society will, under some particular formula for the allocation of property rights, be such that a significant percentage of individuals will find themselves unable to formulate and pursue meaningful projects for themselves without regularly interfering with the socially determined liberties of others, then that system of property rights stands condemned. At least this much seems tolerably clear.

Unfortunately, it is far from clear (or, at least, far from a matter of consensus) how to limn the details that will lend a recognizable shape to this vague outline, how to determine *which* property arrangements fully accord with the demands of the theory of basic rights. Property, more than other items on the moralist's agenda, seems elusive. Why though should that be so? The following six observations may help to indicate the difficulties that confront attempts to develop a satisfactory theory of rights to property.

1. It seems impossible to frame acceptable principles for the allocation of property rights by reference to the standard of noninterference. That is because what will count as interference is itself a function of rights to property and so cannot noncircularly be employed to establish those rights. Consider an extreme case: suppose that title to all property was conferred on one person, the king, and no one else owned anything. It would follow that should anyone make use of any item except with the sufferance of the king that person would be guilty of interference. By way of contrast, the king would enjoy rightful use of whatsoever he pleased, no matter how inimical that use should prove to be to the interests of anyone else. It would not be interference because the king would only be using that which is *his*. True, this one-sided distribution of property has little to recommend it and need not be given serious consideration as a potentially *just* arrangement.[2] But it

does serve to indicate that whether an act of "interference" is impermissible depends on the moral legitimacy of the claim with respect to which the alleged interference takes place.

2. It is tempting to say something like this: "There is a *natural* boundary that largely, if not entirely, determines what can be judged to be interference with a person: it is the boundary of the person's own body. One's body is, nontautologously, one's *own;* for others to attempt to control it or exercise force on it is to interfere, in the most primordial sense of the term. Assault *on* one's person is assault *of* the person. This is a benchmark from which every account of men's liberties must commence."

Although there are problems[3] with drawing out of this statement a coherent view of natural liberties, some of which will be addressed in this chapter, the position expressed is intuitively compelling. There seems to be nothing arbitrary or otherwise suspect about declaring whose right arm this is: it is the arm of the person to whom it is attached. We need no subtle theory of distributional justice to parcel out claims to (undetached) bodily parts, nor do we need a highly developed theory of rights before we are able to hazard a judgment that persons have a basic right to bodily integrity.

But the solid basis, "in nature" as it were, to sovereignty over one's own body underscores the absence of similar solidity to persons' claims over property. Consider some patch of land. It is straightforwardly *external* to each person; no one can *have* that land in as basic and incontrovertible a sense as one has one's right arm. It is not *me* or a *part of me;* at most it is *mine.* "At most"—but how is title even in the restricted sense established? Suppose that I came across the land first and cultivated it. But is it not morally arbitrary who should chance upon it first? It seems merely the luck of the draw. If that is so, why should you, the second (or ten-thousandth) person to spot the land, be obliged to accede to my claim of ownership? How does seeing something first make it one's own? When Galileo became the first person to see the rings of Saturn, did he thereby gain ownership of them? True, he didn't set foot on them or utilize them for production, but what makes *these* factors criteria of ownership? Perhaps it is the "mixing of one's labor with the land" (Locke) that confers ownership. Does that mean that nomadic people who have utilized the land as a right of way for untold centuries lose all claim to its use once the first clever farmer shows up and scatters some seeds? And why suppose that labor confers property rights in perpetuity? Plausibly, it confers title only so long as productive use is actually being made of the property. (Does a night's sleep thereby constitute an interruption of title?) Or perhaps labor confers rights that are nonexclusionary; as soon as someone else shows up who is willing to mix *his* labor with the land, then he gains shared rights to the land and its product.

Once such a path is broached, it seems that all hopes of termination recede beyond the moral horizon. Or, rather, what recedes are all hopes of *nonarbitrary* termination. It is clear that if persons are to survive, then they will have to be afforded use of the natural resources around them. Some parceling out is necessary—but none seems mandated by persons' natural claims. Recognition of claims to property is unlike the recognition of privileged entitlement to use of one's own body. Whatever allocation of property will best allow people to get about their business will, it seems, satisfy the demands of justice.

3. A corollary of the above is to say that no one can *deserve* any item of property in virtue of one's own performances vis-à-vis that property. Things, to be sure, are out there, and one can, through one's efforts, consume or transform them. But because the initial act of appropriation is arbitrary and not itself something that a person can deserve, it seems to follow that any resultant set of de facto property holdings will not be such that persons can be said to deserve that which they happen to hold. Social institutions would therefore not seem to be under any constraint to respect the property status quo. If ideals of justice or economic efficiency prompt principles for the redistribution of goods, no one who ends up with a lesser quota will be entitled to claim that he deserves the greater share he formerly held.[4]

4. Even if it were the case that the act of appropriating and/or productively employing a previously unowned resource conferred a property right to that thing, it would not follow that the property arrangements historically consequent upon initial appropriation are morally justified. It is all too evident that most valuable resources have a geneaology starkly featuring episodes of plunder and dispossession. Whether or not some Neanderthal man established just title to an expanse of land millenia ago bears not at all on the propriety of present ownership relations. We can be as sure as one can be about such matters that there exists no unbroken chain of just transfers leading up to the present and thus no legitimate holding based on just initial acquisition. This would seem to imply the practical, if not theoretical, irrelevance of an entitlement theory of just holdings such as that presented by Robert Nozick.[5] It is not merely that injustices pervade current property relations but also that there is no possibility of applying principles of rectification that will restore title to the rightful owner. The causal chain leading up to current holdings must be irretrievably lost from view except for events that have transpired recently. Even if that chain could somehow be miraculously reconstructed in toto, it would be impossible to redistribute claims to those who, counterfactually, would have held them had justice in transfer been sedulously observed. The occurrence of previous unjust acts bears causally on which sperms and ova would have joined together and thus on

which persons would have come into existence to enjoy their rightfully held property. It is impossible to redistribute an item to someone who never was and never will be.[6] As a means toward Paradise Regained, rectification is a nonstarter.

These considerations further reinforce the view that property relations are morally up in the air and that allocation *de novo* according to a morally grounded program cannot be in violation of anyone's rights. Of course, what that program should be is a matter of extraordinarily heated ideological controversy. No doubt there are better and worse answers, but the ubiquity of controversy is itself an indication that property rights *remain* to be settled and do not attach neatly to persons and their actual holdings.

5. For many of the familiar civil liberties it is the case that one person's enjoying the liberty does not exclude another person from enjoying the same liberty. For example, freedom of religion is a right that everyone can have, and have in the same degree. It is not the case that there is only so much freedom of religion to go around, and my having more necessarily means that you have less.[7] One who acknowledges another's liberty thereby pledges not to interfere with that liberty, but he does not relinquish his own claim to that liberty.

It appears to be quite otherwise with property rights. If one person has a property right to the full enjoyment of item *I*, then no one else can have a similar right to *I*. If I may use, transform, sell, destroy, or bequeath *I*, then you may not. Liberties to treat *I* as one's property are fundamentally exclusionary in a way that other familiar liberties are not.[8]

It may be said by way of retort that the alleged disparity between the two sorts of rights is simply a result of the ambiguity of 'property rights'. If 'property right' is construed as a right possessed by some one individual over some one item, then property rights will be exclusionary. But exactly the same will be true of other rights; for example, A's right to determine the manner in which A formulates and expresses A's religious convictions excludes from B the liberty to determine A's religious activities. However, 'property rights' can refer to the basic right of individuals to acquire and use some property or other. In this general sense of the term, it is possible for everyone to enjoy property rights that are suitably nonexclusive. The objection, then, is that there is no disanalogy in this respect between liberties involving property and other liberties.

That response, though, is incorrect. It is true that all rights are in some degree exclusionary, else they would not entail correlative duties that demarcate individuals' moral space. However, property rights, whether taken as rights to particular items in the world or as general rights to acquire and use, exclude in a distinctive way the activities of others. Consider the following two particular "things": (1) item *I*, (2) A's religious practices. Reference to *I* can be made independently of reference to any particular person who stands in any particular relationship to *I*. *I's* ontological status is that of a freestanding entity whose relations to other such entities are external. By way of contrast, the religious practices in question (understood as tokens rather than as types) make essential reference to A and thus stand in a relation of ontological dependence to the person whose religious practices they are. To identify the practices necessarily presupposes the identification of the person. Freedom of religious expression is not to be understood as one's freedom to control something that has an independent status in the world, but rather the freedom to direct *one's own activities* insofar as they partake of a religious aspect. This is a nonexclusionary freedom in the sense that everyone who chooses to undertake patterns of religious activity thereby brings into being religious performances which are consequent upon the choice. No independently existing object is taken out of the public realm of unowned things and added to one's private stock. But to acquire a property right to *I* *is to remove I* from the public realm or from someone else's domain of holdings and to add it to one's own. Where formerly *I* existed as a potential object of appropriation by others, once the private property right to *I* is acquired, others are, in an important sense, excluded from the use of it.

If we instead conceive of property rights not as rights to particular items but as general rights to acquire and use (something or other), there is once again a sense in which property rights appear to be uniquely exclusionary. Whether or not you choose to exercise your freedom to engage in religious activities does not affect the range over which I am free to engage in religious activites. But the number of persons in your vicinity who are at liberty to acquire property, and the extent to which they put that liberty into practice, will definitely bear on the range over which you are able to engage in the acquisition of property. Your liberty to appropriate unowned land will not be exercisable if other people have gotten there first and have snatched up all the land that there is.

To put it slightly differently, the game of acquiring property is, in the near term, *zero sum*. Whatever one player gets is lost (as a potential item of appropriation) to the others. Speech, religious activity, and other such objects of civil liberties are *positive sum*. No matter how devoutly and frequently you worship, there is no resultant drain on my prospects for religiosity. Because the sum of property is fixed in the near term, it seems a requirement of justice that this sum be deliberately allocated in accordance with principles of fairness. A benefit allocated to one person is a burden (or at least the absence of a benefit) to another. But where the range over which liberties are assigned is not fixed in quantity, no such division is required.

Everyone may engage in as much speech or religious activity as he pleases; no cost is thereby imposed on anyone else.

Of course, the quantity of property is not fixed in the long term. Persons' productive activities result in the creation of new goods that add to the total stock. Destructive activities correspondingly reduce the stock of goods.[9] Because project pursuers have ends that stretch indefinitely into the future, they have reason to take account of long-term prospects for the availability of goods. Accordingly, the allocation of rights to productive property will be more like distributing seed corn than like carving up a pie. Principles of dynamic efficiency will supplement principles of fairness. But these will be principles that are *chosen* by the social unit in the light of its preferred moral and economic theory. Because valid claims to property are constituted by that social determination, prior holdings do not seem in any way to constrain the social choice process.

6. In recent years, persons who specialize in the analysis of property relations (lawyers, economists, philosophers) have developed a conception of property markedly different from that characteristically employed by laypersons. To the ordinary person, 'property' refers to material things that people own. But to the specialist, property dissolves into "bundles of rights" that can be apportioned in a myriad of ways among persons or institutions, and such bundles need not correspond in any close way with the pretheoretical conception of ownership. Dozens of persons might hold rights with respect to a thing, and which of these persons, if any, is to be considered its "owner" seems to be a quite trivial matter of convention. Moreover, rights can attach to nonmaterial forms of "property": shares in the stock of company, tenure as a university professor, one's reputation, a patent. These rights to intangible property can also include less than full ownership: one has the right to hold one's university chair during good behavior, but not to sell it to the highest bidder or to destroy it.[10]

The conceptions may seem to differ primarily along the dimension of precision, with the specialist having a predictable tendency to wield more finely honed conceptual tools than does the layperson. It is not immediately obvious, though, why this difference in precision should be expected to bear importantly on the moral theory of property rights.

Upon reflection, however, it appears that the moral foundations of a theory of property become considerably more tenuous with the specialist's "bundle of rights" than with the ordinary person's notion of owned things. It is tolerably clear how possession of *things* might be established; Lockean man in the state of nature picks up an acorn and carries it off with him, thus making the acorn *his*. Or he comes across a patch of virgin land, clears and cultivates it, and sets up boundary markers that inform all other passersby that he *owns* it. Lockean man thereby acquires full rights to the acorn or land, subject only to general requirements of noninterference with others. Should he choose to transfer title, he is free to do so, in which case all rights to the property pass to the designated person.

One can pick up an acorn—but how does one pick up a bundle of rights? One can fence in land, but in which respect is that to fence in *rights* to the land? It would seem a gross conceptual confusion to equate material things with bundles of rights. A theory that might adequately justify claims to property *qua* thing cannot be assumed similarly to justify claims to property *qua* bundle of rights. The only bundle of rights that can intuitively be identified with ownership of a thing is the bundle that constitutes complete control over that thing. Less inclusive bundles are an embarrassment for the property-in-things account. If picking up the acorn confers full rights concerning its disposition, what must one do to acquire the full bundle of rights *minus* the right to bequeath the acorn? (Pick it up somewhat diffidently?) Is there some process by means of which one can acquire only a right to eat the acorn but not to sell it or use it as a paperweight? A Lockean theory in which property is things that are owned seems incapable of addressing such questions.

The specialist, however, will be immediately ready with answers. Moral and legal rights, he will say, are the product of social determination. They are not simply exuded by things nor by people's use of things. Property rights are social creations, and they can be packaged in whatever bundles the social unit elects to recognize. There is no one mode of packaging that is in any way "natural" or dictated by the hypothesized appropriative acts of persons in a state of nature. Although *material objects* may have been used by human beings and other species from time immemorial, *property* only begins to exist when social collectivities come to generate shared conceptions of rights.

Modest Steps Away from a Thoroughly Socialized Conception of Property

The six considerations brought forth above are a bit of a jumble, neither amounting to a unified theory of property rights nor even clearly consistent with each other. Nonetheless, to present them together has some point. Each of the observations has a measure of plausibility, and each has been deployed or implicitly relied upon by some analysts of property.[11] Of greatest significance, though, is that each, in its own way, pushes in the same direction. A classically liberal theory of property rights holds that natural relations obtain between persons and objects in the world. These relations precede civil society and thereby establish claims to property that are prior to social determination. It is this theory that each of the six observations tends to undercut. It is charged that relations to objects are morally arbitrary, are hazy, are irremediably tainted by a history of usurpation, are not such as to constitute reasons for deference by others, or are not convertible into suitable bundles of rights. The ineluctable conclusion seems to be that property, with its associated rights, is a social construction and thus amenable to allocation in accordance with a society's most highly warranted moral and economic theory.

I shall grant that moral and legal rights to property must arise as the product of social decision rather than be read off the moral landscape. As was argued in Chapter 5, this is true of *all* moral and legal rights, property rights being no exception. It need not be conceded, however, that property is *purely* a social construct, that basic rights to property do not in any respect constrain social determinations. That is, however many thorny problems stand in the way of piecing together a satisfactory theory of property rights, problems that may not be of equivalent magnitude in the development of an account of other civil liberties, it does not follow that there are no basic rights to property which are morally regulative. Social determinations of property rights are not, I shall argue, completely open-ended but are *sharply limited* by persons' interests in living as project pursuers protected from interference by others.

It is not at all mysterious why persons should come to take an interest in property—or rather, to avoid begging any crucial questions, come to take an interest in things in the world. Consumption of food, clothing, and shelter are necessary for survival. The characteristically human development of ends that transcend one's own survival (or the survival of one's genes) places yet further demands on objects in the environment. Taking delight in aesthetic expression will require chalky rock and a cave wall on which to etch one's inscription—or an electric guitar. The desire to extend one's diet will be advanced by the construction of a bow and arrow—or purchase of a Cuisinart. Purposeful action and command over things are virtually inseparable.

Persons, then, have a natural interest in having things. The relation of *having* is conceptually more basic than and not to be confused with a *property right*. It amounts to the actual ability to employ some object in the furtherance of one's designs and does not presuppose the existence of any structure of rights. Having I and enjoying property rights in I are conceptually and empirically distinguishable. The thief *has* his booty but does not *rightfully possess* it; the thief's victim possesses property rights to what he does not have. However, these are not two unrelated concepts. It is because of persons' interests in *having* objects that there is an interest in being accorded property rights.

Property rights demarcate moral space within which what one has is marked off as immune from predation. Access to and command over goods that can confidently be expected to be available throughout the course of one's efforts is required for successful project pursuit. Security in one's possessions—what one has—is of value to everyone, and, therefore, each individual has some reason to extend deference to others with respect to their holdings conditional upon the receipt of like deference. The creation of social institutions that recognize and define principles of noninterference with persons' holdings transform *having* into *rightful possession.*

What is perhaps most noteworthy about this brief story is its complete equivalence in form to the derivation of general rights to noninterference in Chapters 4 and 5. The only addition to the familiar account that renders this an examination of *property* rights is the insertion of the proposition that the ability to pursue projects entails the having of goods. Presumably, that addition is uncontroversial. Therefore, to posit basic rights to property is neither more nor less warranted than is the positing of basic rights *simpliciter*. *If* there are basic rights, then there are basic rights to property. Rights for whom, though—and to what?

Property rights can, theoretically, take the form either of liberty rights, rights to the untrammeled use of what one has, or of welfare rights, rights to the provision of items. It was argued in the preceding chapter that liberty rights merit preeminent status in a moral community that values individualism. Nothing distinctive to concepts of property has emerged which would call this into question. It is true that moral and legal rights to property are socially determined, but this is equally true of *all* moral and legal rights. Liberties of every sort are amorphous until the contours of interference are determined, and because persons must ultimately *decide* what is to be counted as interference, there is an inextricably social aspect to any system of personal liberties. However, the range within which social determinations can permissibly be made is itself limited by persons' existence as project pursuers for whom value is personal. Each project pursuer is justified in attaching special value to the ends that are his, not because, in the grand scheme of things, those ends score highest, but simply because they are his own. Every person has a stake in a regime of rights that responds to the incommensurability of personal value by maintenance of an order that is neutral among persons. One way of interpreting the requirement of neutrality is to call for equality in the property holdings (or their value as measured by a numeraire such as money or an index of primary goods) of all persons. The egalitarian contends that to allow one person to own more property than another is differentially to favor the projects of the former. Only if society ensures essential equivalence in holdings will it be treating individuals in neutral fashion.

Let us leave aside problems of how to measure "equality." [12] Is it the case that neutrality among persons and their projects requires the enforcement of equality, or at least requires institutional structures such as the progressive income tax and transfer programs that work to reduce inequality? Although some personal projects, for example, the leading of a life of rigorous asceticism, are not advanced by ownership of more than a minimal amount of property, it is undeniably the case that a person's ability to achieve his goals is generally an increasing function of his wealth. Inequality of assets is incompatible with equality in prospects for successful project pursuit. This is the sense in which egalitarianism can locate itself within an ethic based on project pursuit.

Such an interpretation of the neutrality requirement is, however, decidedly a *misinterpretation*. For what it advocates is an order characterized primarily by rights of provision rather than rights to liberty. It locates in the collectivity a duty to bring about the attainment by each project pursuer of material requisites for successful project pursuit. That alleged duty runs contrary to the claim that each project pursuer has a uniquely *personal* reason to bring about the success of his own projects. If command over a stock of material goods M is a necessary condition for A's pursuit of his end E_1, then A has reason to bring about A's possession of M that is not similarly reason-for-B to bring about A's possession of M. But if the members of the social unit were jointly obligated to bring about A's having M, then it would be equally incumbent upon each that A come to have M. The onus of procuring M would not rest primarily on A. Such a collectivization of project pursuit is flatly incompatible with individualism.

There are two ways in which persons can be treated equally within a collectivity. One is for each person's projects to be *equally embraced* by the collectivity, with the provision of aid in equal amount rendered to each. The other way is for the collectivity to *embrace no projects* but instead to acknowledge the (liberty) rights of all persons to pursue whatever projects they will. Of the two, only the latter is truly neutral among persons. It is to recognize that individuals have interests in their own ends, but it is not to insist that others undertake the service of those ends. Anyone may, if he should choose, enlist in the service of another person, or he may, if he should choose, entirely distance himself from another's particular designs. The collectivity as such has no say in either choice. All that it can demand is that the liberty, as defined by a common standard of noninterference, of each to live as a project pursuer is not invaded.

The former manner of equal treatment is not neutral. It is to make everyone a shareholder in the enterprises of everyone else. One can be called upon to make a positive contribution to the efforts of another even if one is indifferent or antipathetic to that person's projects. Nor is the call one that can politely be declined: it is not the call for supererogatory charitable performance but the assertion of a *right* to be aided. One will not be free to distance oneself from the ends of others; those interests *must* be advanced. Whether or not the requirement that one take a positive role in advancing the projects of all others is equally applied within the moral community, it is not the proclamation of neutrality among persons. It is instead the insistence that everyone's projects are to be valued, and they are to be valued by everybody.

In Chapter 2 it was argued that the demand for impartiality is seriously misplaced in much of contemporary ethics. To insist that persons are morally obligated to weigh impartially their own ends along with the ends of everyone else is to ignore the claims of personal value within practical reason. Impartiality can only be properly introduced into morality at a higher level as the impartial recognition of each individual as a project pursuer who has reason to be partial toward those ends that are his.

A similar analysis reveals that the demand for equality is often misplaced in very much the same way. To insist that persons are morally obligated to bring about equal allocations of material goods is to ignore that each person has primary reason to supply for himself those goods which are needed for the advancement of his own projects. And, just like impartiality, equality properly construed enters into ethical theory at a higher level of application. Each project pursuer has reason to secure those goods he values. Therefore, each has reason to value a liberty to acquire and use goods *equal to the liberty* to acquire and use that every other project pursuer enjoys. Not equality in holdings but equal liberty to acquire holdings is entailed by the normative theory of basic rights.[13]

Basic rights take concrete form as they are instantiated in moral and legal rights. The basic liberty right to acquire and use property is made concrete through the social recognition of conventions that define which actions constitute appropriation and transfer of property. It may be entirely arbitrary which among many conceivable legal forms is recognized as, say, a contract of exchange. That there be some form or other, though, is not arbitrary. Property rights demarcate boundaries that others must not transgress, and therefore persons need to know where those boundaries lie. A system of law

124 PERSONS, RIGHTS, AND THE MORAL COMMUNITY

is a means by which claims to items of property are acknowledged, recorded, and made known to the general public.

For law to exemplify basic rights, it must be neutral among persons in the sense developed above. That is, it must not be designed so as to favor the ability of one group of individuals to acquire and use property over the ability of another group. "Unowned items are appropriated by seeing them through blue eyes and touching them with white skin": this would not qualify as a neutral standard of appropriation. Unfortunately, it is extraordinarily difficult and perhaps impossible to specify necessary and sufficient conditions for neutrality within a system of property rights. Any set of arrangements, it seems, will be such as differentially to advantage some over others. A requirement that records of sale be entered into the county archives will favor those geographically close to the courthouse. If contracts are consummated by a handshake, the man without arms will be disadvantaged. Natural and acquired differences among persons are likely to be translated in any conceivable setting into a system of rights that will in fact favor some persons over others.

If de facto neutrality is neither perfectly achievable in practice nor precisely specifiable in theory, it does not follow that neutrality is to be jettisoned as a regulative moral ideal. The *intent* of a legal prescription is often knowable, and to the extent that a law is intentionally designed to favor one set of persons or ends over another, it is in violation of liberal basic rights. The enforced transfer of resources from blacks to whites from urbanites to farmers, from plutocrats to consumer advocates *so that* whites, farmers, or consumer advocates will be better able to pursue their designs is entirely illegitimate. On the other hand, should it turn out to be the case that whites or farmers or consumer advocates enjoy greater success under a system of law, although favor for their distinctive ends in no way motivated the shape of that legal system, then neutrality is not violated. Of course, it will often be difficult in practice to ferret out the intent of a piece of legislation, and interested parties will have reason to dissemble: "I do not support price supports for milk because I happen to be a dairy farmer but because I want there to be enough milk for every thirsty child in America!" Politics is not the mechanical application of an algorithm, but it will often be readily knowable whether a piece of legislation is compatible with the maintenance of a liberal order.

Redistribution and Rights

Liberties with respect to property do not dictate any particular pattern of property holdings but rather provide a framework within which the free actions of persons bring about and upset patterns.[14] Among these various patterns a liberal order must remain thoroughly neutral. There will be no such thing as "having more than one's fair share" if there is no socially imposed standard for allocating shares. People will allocate to themselves and to each other via their own uncoerced activity.

It follows, then, that ideals of "distributive justice" have no political standing. If the domain of "justice" is coextensive with the rights that persons have, then any sets of property holdings that emerge from rightful activity are, by definition, (distributively) just. If, however, justice extends beyond obligations that persons *must* fulfill to that which it would be good, praiseworthy, or best for them to do, then justice is, to that extent, a moral ideal that persons may, but need not, follow. In that sense, it may be laudable that persons act justly, as it is laudable that they pursue scientific truth, listen to Mozart recordings, jog five miles a day, develop deep friendships, read philosophy books. None of these, however, is mandatory. Persons may not be compelled to be wise—or to be just.

A state that engages in massive programs of redistribution in order to advance an ideal of distributive justice that extends beyond respect for rights thereby violates rights. If it is not the case that the wealthy Ms. A *must* give 10% of her income to the impoverished Mr. B, then the state is unjustified in coercively extracting 10% of her income in order to transfer it to B. It would be equally unjustified in interfering with the voluntary charitable activity of individuals who seek to aid persons such as Mr. B. All this follows as a simple corollary of the theory of basic rights.

What is not so simple to determine, however, is whether the redistribution of wealth from A to B can ever be justified in virtue of positive rights possessed by B. It was argued in Chapter 5 that liberty rights are preeminent, but care was taken to leave an escape clause such that *some* recognition of welfare rights may be compatible with the existence of a liberal order. A policy of studied noninterference was endorsed as the general rule, but a place was left for rights to provision as an exception to that rule.

When will that exception take effect? In a word, rarely. In all cases in which it is open to persons to act so as to secure for themselves holdings in property sufficient to enable them to live as project pursuers, the responsibility to provide is theirs. The responsibility that devolves on others is that of noninterference with such efforts. In a regime in which individuals have full liberty to act to meet their own needs, it will usually be the case that they are able to do so. No minimum wage or occupational licensure laws will restrict access to employment; zoning ordinances and building codes will not restrict access to housing; agricultural price supports will not restrict access to food; legal moralism will not restrict access to activities that are "victimless crimes." Nor would an ethos of welfarism spawn an army of bureaucrats whose livelihood rests on the perpetuation of generational cycles of dependency within a welfare class. It is not unreasonable to suggest, then, that persons within a liberal order would generally find themselves able to secure what they urgently need, even if not all that they would like to have.

Moreover, a liberal order is not to be conceived of as a collection of atomistic egoists who whiz by each other in a moral vacuum. Persons are not *required* to attach themselves to others in special relationships of caring and concern, but the good for most persons will surely include affective bonds. Those who stand in relations of love, communality, kinship, friendship, or fraternal solidarity with others can expect to aid and be voluntarily aided by them. Needs will typically be met because others care to meet those needs. Some may fall through the cracks of these social bonds, but concern for that fact will itself prompt the formation of eleemosynary agencies that will seek out and aid such persons. Because individuals are free to join themselves to others in caring relationships, it is not inevitable that those unable to meet their own needs will find those needs unmet.

To the extent that a civil order of maximal liberty is one in which persons can provide for themselves and are able to secure the willing aid of others, welfare rights remain in the background. There is, however, no assurance that liberty will universally guarantee to each person the requisites for satisfactory prospects of project pursuit. In the most genuinely liberal society, unless there are rights to provision, it is possible for some to starve while others dine on the tongues of hummingbirds. Is it the case that those in exigent straits may demand welfare goods *as a matter of right?*

The answer, I think, is yes. If a person is otherwise unable to secure that which is necessary for his ability to live as a project pursuer, then he has a rightful claim to provision by others who have a surplus beyond what they require to live as project pursuers. In that strictly limited but crucial respect, basic rights extend beyond liberty rights to welfare rights.

Some will, of course, charge that this grossly understates the role of welfare rights within an adequate moral theory. The burden of most of Chapter 5 was to meet that complaint by establishing the paramount status of liberty rights. Others will argue that I have erred in the other direction, that an acknowledgment, even at the margin, of rights to provision erodes the liberty of persons to lead their own lives using their own property as they see fit. Any welfare right possessed by A is simultaneously a restriction of the liberty of B. If A's exigency entails that B must provide goods to A, then B is no longer at liberty to control the use of those goods. The thoroughgoing libertarian who regards all restrictions of liberty as impermissible whatever the grounds on which restriction is based will reject the claim that there are any welfare rights.

Such a libertarianism is indefensible. It disconnects the theory of basic rights from its foundation in a theory of practical reason for project pursuers. Individuals have reason to value the maintenance of a regime of rights because they value their own ability to pursue projects. Should that ability be placed in jeopardy by a system of rights such that one can *either* continue to respect others' rights *or* be able to pursue projects *but not both,* then one would no longer have a rational stake in the moral community established by that system of rights. One would be in the situation of the "fanatic" discussed in Chapter 4. If acknowledgment of rights is rationally motivated by concern for one's future as a project pursuer, it will be plainly irrational to pledge support to a regime in which one's prospects for project pursuit are extinguished.

It might be responded that acquiescence to a standard of rights is made in the *ex ante* anticipation of being able to lead a satisfactory life within the framework established by those rights. If it should turn out to be the case *ex post* that this belief was in error, then one is nonetheless bound by one's act of prior explicit or implicit consent to adhere to what has, unfortunately, turned out to be a bad bargain. One has wagered and lost, but the gambling debt must still be paid.

This response rests on a model of a social contract ratified at some initial starting point t_1 which then remains in force indefinitely and from which one may not at a later time t_n withdraw one's consent. That model is highly dubious as a basis for moral and political theory. How are the privileged t_1 and the associated act of consent to be identified? Even more crucial, why should it be supposed that consent given at t_1 provides one with reason at t_n to agree to suicide as a project pursuer at t_n? Whatever reason one had at t_1 cannot be assumed to remain a reason for oneself at t_n in total isolation from all considerations of what one's interests are at t_n. Rational consent to adhere to an order of rights is better conceived to be *continuously offered consent* rather than a once and for all binding of the will.

Even if the model of undertaking enduring obligations at t_1 be accepted, it begs every important question to suppose that the obligations persons are rationally motivated to undertake are unconditional. Precisely because persons have reason to value future existence as project pursuers, they will assent to respect for others' integrity as project pursuers only insofar as their own is not thereby called into question. It will not be expected at t_1 that persons who at some later time find their careers as project pursuers jeopardized will have a continuing stake in an order of rights unless that order acknowledges welfare rights to minimally adequate provision. That which individuals require to live as project pursuers amidst a community of other project pursuers is primarily liberty, but that fact does not rule out the need for a safety net that captures extreme cases. To the extent that successful civility requires the provision of aid, welfare rights merit a place alongside liberty rights.[15]

State establishment of a welfare apparatus is not inconsistent with, and may be required by, the maintenance of a liberal order. Public institutions can rightfully direct the transfer of resources among citizens. It follows by similar reasoning that there can be a limited place within the law for "Good Samaritan" (or, perhaps better, "Minimally Decent Samaritan"[16]) legislation. Individuals acting in their private capacity can rightfully be required to make provision to others when one's own project pursuit is not thereby substantially impaired but where that which is provided is crucial to the welfare of the beneficiary. So, for example, laws requiring that one rescue someone in peril provided that the rescue attempt will pose no danger to oneself or laws requiring one who is aware of an assault in progress to notify the police are compatible with the spirit of liberalism. There may, of course, be other reasons to reject Good Samaritan laws, but impermissible infringement of liberty rights is not among them.

Whether the above endorsement of welfare rights should be considered a defense of redistributive functions vested in the state is arguable. If redistribution is the prescribed transfer of control over resources from one person to another, then a case has been made for redistribution. However, it has not been maintained that ultimate authority over the dispensation of all goods resides within collective institutions, or even that the state is authorized to transfer *any* rights to property among persons. The entire argument has rested on the proposition that each individual has a residual claim to the surplus property of others, this claim taking effect only in cases of extreme exigency. A correlative of this proposition is that basic rights to property are not unconditional but are limited by the otherwise unsatisfiable needs of others. Therefore, when the state effects a transfer, it is not destroying one set of property rights while creating another but is simply enforcing the residual claims that persons possessed all along. For that reason, it is misleading to speak of "redistribution" as if rights are vested in a collectivity that can do with them what it wishes. Nothing said above is intended to suggest that basic rights to property are collective rather than private. The transfers which have been endorsed are as morally innocuous as mandating the return of stolen goods from the thief to his victim.

Collectivist Critiques of Private Property

It has been argued that the primitive *having* relationship underlies basic property rights, just as project pursuit underlies the general structure of basic rights. Social conventions determine the concrete form that basic rights will take in a given society, but that is not to say that rights inhere in the collective. Because people come upon things, use them, transform them, and trade them in the furtherance of their projects, people have basic property rights which must be acknowledged by a rights-respecting society.

Contemporary economic, legal, and philosophical theory may hold that property is best conceived as a bundle of rights rather than as material objects in the world. It is not inconsistent with this theory to maintain that moral claims to such bundles of rights originate in the having of things. Insofar as moral and legal systems recognize persons' interests in controlling objects that they have and respond to this interest by specifying principles that publicly acknowledge persons' holdings, moral and legal bundles of rights are created. They do not arise *ex nihilo*, however, but are consequent upon what people have and use in the furtherance of their projects.

When a socially established order of rights comes into being, that occurrence does not obliterate the having relationship in which persons stand to objects. Rather, it makes possible the having of new sorts of objects, abstract objects called 'property rights'. Note that this is not a reductionistic program in which the having relationship disappears, to be replaced by a more basic one. Rather, it is augmented: one not only *has* land but *has* the right to let the land lie fallow, *has* the right to sell the land, and so on. New prospects for purposeful action with regard to one's property are thereby created. One can not only sell the land but *sell one's right* to sell the land, or. . . . In this way bundles of increasing complexity come into being, and bits of a bundle can pass into the control of different persons. Much thereby changes: relations to property that are inconceivable in a simple setting are part of the everyday order of an advanced commercial society. Much also remains constant, however: people rationally take an interest in what they *have*, whether it be an object, rights with respect to an object, rights with respect to rights, and so on. There is nothing, then, in the "scientific" conception of property that requires modification of the derivation of property rights by way of primitive *having*.

A more serious challenge to the liberal theory of private property is posed by attacks on *initial appropriation*. If private appropriation of objects is somehow incoherent, then subsequent use and transfer of objects inherits this deficiency. The entire system of private rights in property will seem to founder. Yet it is far from easy to explain how acts with respect to an item one discovers can constitute *ownership* of that item. Ownership of a thing entails the existence of moral boundaries with respect to that thing which others are not at liberty to transgress. Yet why should B regard any performances that A makes with respect to item *I* as properly restricting B's liberty? Suppose that A is the first person to come across *I*. Is it therefore incumbent upon B to acknowledge that A has full liberties in perpetuity to use *I* while B has no such liberties? It is not apparent why this should be so. Being the first to see or touch *I* seems arbitrary from a moral point of view. Mixing one's labor with *I* is similarly an uncertain basis for ascribing ownership. Why should we say that when A mixes his labor with *I* he acquires *I*? Why not instead declare that he simply loses his labor?[17]

In response, it can quickly be admitted that the fact that A rather than B comes to have *I is* morally arbitrary. But what is not arbitrary is that persons have things and that they value the having of things. No particular pattern of holdings is morally sacrosanct, but it is fundamental to the moral theory of property that persons will, in virtually every imaginable setting, assign value to acquiring and using objects. Similarly, that E_1 happens to be A's end and E_2 B's is morally arbitrary. But undergirding the whole theory of basic rights is the fact that project pursuers have ends and that they therefore have reason to act so as to advance those ends. And, of course, having ends entails having some *particular* ends, such as E_1 or E_2. It is, therefore, far too quick to dismiss all circumstances of having, whether of objects or ends, as "morally arbitrary" and thus rationally inconsequential on the grounds that those circumstances could have been otherwise. What is *in fact the case* carries moral weight.

If A comes to possess *I*, to use *I* in the service of his projects, and thereby values the having of *I*, then A has *appropriated I*. *I* is *his* in the sense that he rather than B or anyone else has *I*. A has reason to frame his projects so that they incorporate the use of *I* rather than the use of some other object that A does not have. And the result is purely general, applying equally to B's use of item *I** which B has come to possess. From it flows reasons for the intersubjective recognition of each person's interest in being unimpeded in the use of what he has. A has reason to acknowledge and respect B's having *I** conditional upon B recognizing and respecting A's special interest in *I*. Appropriative acts are necessary for project pursuit and are the basis by means of which the intersubjective recognition of individuals' interests in the objects that they have generates basic rights to property.

Note that ascribing a unique ownership relationship to the person who comes to have a particular thing is no more arbitrary than ascribing a unique valuational relationship to the person who comes to have a particular end. A has special reason to value end E_1 in virtue of that end being his; he also has special reason to value I in virtue of that object being his. In virtue of being a project pursuer, A has reason to act to bring about a moral order within which others will refrain from interfering with A's advancement of E_1; in virtue of being a project pursuer, A has reason to act to bring about a moral order within which others will refrain from interfering with A's having I. A has reason to reject the imposition by the collectivity of an impersonal standard of value that will determine whether A is entitled to advance E_1; A has reason to reject the imposition of a system of collective control over all goods that will determine whether A is entitled to have I.

The theory of basic rights cannot view communities as vast agglomerations of tabulae rasae waiting to be written on by an authorized seer or social unit. Persons come to civil society with ends that are theirs, however those ends were generated and shaped. The system of moral and legal rights that are socially determined in society must respect the ends that persons have rather than assert a baseless authority collectively to determine what ends persons have reason to pursue. Similarly, persons come to civil society with things that are theirs. A socially defined system of property rights must be responsive to what persons have. In no respect does a civil order entail the collectivization of property which is then available to be doled out to persons according to social plan.

One reason why acts of appropriation may seem arbitrary is that there is a good deal of slack in the notion of what a person has. The slack tends to be greater with real property, less with chattel property. Suppose that A views from a mountaintop a vast expanse of virgin territory, rides around half of it, places boundary markers to set off a quarter of it, grazes his cattle over an eighth of it, fences in a sixteenth, clears a thirty-second, and plants a sixty-fourth. How much of the land that A first saw does he "have"? When the morally minded B comes by, how much of the land should he feel obliged to acknowledge as belonging to A? If B eventually settles downstream from A, and A dams up the stream to create a pleasant lake for himself, have B's property rights been invaded?

There are no clear answers to these questions. Or, rather, there is no one best answer that can be deduced from the theory of basic rights. Persons will be unable to know and act on property rights that are ill-specified, and therefore it is requisite for the success of an order of rights that some determination be made. Social conventions are necessary to give concrete form to concepts such as appropriation, sale, bequest, and externality. The argument is familiar from Chapter 5 and will not be repeated here. It should not be misunderstood as an ascription to the collectivity of primordial rights over all property, rights which are subsequently doled out to individuals— no more so than the argument of Chapter 5 vested all liberty rights in communities which could then grant or withhold them from individuals. Both with liberty rights in general and with property rights in particular, what is socially determined is merely the concrete form that will be assumed by the basic rights that persons bring to civil society.

It is quite possible to draw out an alternative theory of property in which the scope of collective determination is much broader, in which the origin of all rights to property is founded on collective decision. All that is needed is the appropriate kind of starting point:

> Imagine that you and I (and the rest of us) embark upon a voyage of discovery, forsaking our previous wealth and position to enter upon the quest. Coming unexpectedly upon a new world, we scan it from afar and learn that it contains only a single resource, manna, which has some remarkable properties. Most important, manna is infinitely divisible and malleable, capable of transformation into any physical object a person may desire. Further scanning reveals, however, that manna retains one basic similarity to familiar earthly elements—it is impossible to squeeze an infinite quantity of a desired good from a single grain of the miracle substance. Indeed, there won't be enough manna to satisfy the total demands of all the members of our party. A struggle for power is inevitable. Nonetheless, things could be worse, and so we decide to make this new world our home.
>
> As we approach the planet, the spaceship is alive with talk. Since manna is in short supply and universally desired, the question of its initial distribution is on everybody's mind. We instruct the automatic pilot to circle the planet for the time it takes to resolve the question of initial distribution and proceed to the Assembly Hall to discuss the matter further.[18]

The story that Ackerman tells from this point on is quite entertaining, although it has a predictable conclusion. After a few false starts (space travel evidently affects the rational processes), it is eventually agreed that the best way to distribute the one million grains of manna on the new world among the one million citizens in the spaceship is—one grain per person! It is not implausible to maintain that the conclusion is morally indicated.

Has Ackerman rigged the story? Yes. Does that cast doubt on the account of justice in property holdings that it yields? Again, I believe, the answer is yes. Consider the following features of the tale:

1. All the citizens on board the spacecraft apparently have an equal share in the craft and its mission. At least nothing is said to indicate that one of them starts off *owning* the craft and that others are crew or invited guests or

that someone has put together the mission with the understanding that he will receive some previously agreed-on share of what is discovered. (Would Queen Isabella have bankrolled Columbus on such terms?) It is implied instead that they are acting in every respect as a collective.

2. The manna is just *there*. It has not been grown by anyone from manna seeds, dug by anyone from manna mines, caught in manna nets, or raised from manna pups. Manna is, after all, manna.

3. Project pursuit will not commence until colonization has taken place and manna has been doled out. The deliberations are stylized as those of persons preparing to begin pursuit of personal ends and not as deliberations among persons already engaged in purposeful activity.

4. There will be no property rights to manna until a collective determination has been made. Manna is now merely the subject of neutral dialogue and is not being contemporaneously consumed, transformed, or traded. There is no *having* of manna that temporally and logically precedes the establishment of rights to manna.

5. It is assumed that there is some "correct" pattern of holdings that can be discovered through conversation. "Incorrect" suggestions are put forth and easily (too easily?) disposed of. But once the "correct" solution is broached, even those who are at first reluctant soon come to see its inescapable rightness, and they object no more.

6. Just as each citizen aboard the ship has some claim to manna, the totality of their claims exhausts the stock of manna. The collectivity has full rights over—owns—all the manna, and no one else has any claim to it.

Not surprisingly, these features abstract away all those conditions serving to justify the private appropriation and exploitation of property. Individuals are not taken to be project pursuers for whom their personal ends are directive but are rather a million cogs in an enterprise association whose preordained purpose is collectively to arrive at an impersonal standard for manna distribution. Each stands as a bare ego, having no relationships to things which can be brought to the process of social determination and thereby condition its results. Persons are not to any degree individuated via unique relationships to that which they are using to advance their ends. The only form of distribution that plausibly can be recommended for nonindividuated egos is the allotment of equal shares.

It has been argued throughout this book that a theory of basic rights must take its bearings from the actuality of project pursuers whose ends are personal, who are engaged in purposeful activity to realize those ends, and who have goods that they employ in the pursuit of their ends. If that underlying conception is correct, then the spaceship model for the allocation of property rights must be rejected.[19]

Even on its own terms, the model exhibits internal tensions. It assumes that *individuals* do not rightfully appropriate goods; property rights are entirely a product of collective choice. But the choice of *which* collectivity? It will be convenient if no other group ever has anything to do with the planet and its stock of manna. That need not be the case. Suppose that there are a dozen other ships within a parsec or two of the planet; must a neutral dialogue be undertaken with them over interstellar radio before anyone is entitled to land and start using manna? If yes, must all potential manna consumers in the galaxy similarly be brought into the dialogue? If no, why must a citizen on one's own ship stay to listen to interminable speeches when he would prefer to be on the planet harvesting manna instead? Suppose that no other spaceship is in the vicinity. However, years later, after the planet has been thoroughly settled, one shows up. Must neutral dialogue be cranked up again, with shares subsequently awarded to the newcomers? If so,[20] then appropriation of property can *never* take place. Entitlements are up in the air again once someone new arrives. If, however, appropriation can take place, then one collectivity—the one that secures first occupancy, that mixes its labor with the manna, or whichever—enjoys a uniquely privileged status.

Arguments that property rights are a collective asset rather than private typically take the following form (though not usually with quite so thin a disguise):

No undertaking by a private individual can ever conceivably constitute an act of appropriation that other individuals are obligated to respect.

Therefore, appropriations are made by collectivities, and all individuals are obligated to adhere to collectively determined allocations of rights.

What goes entirely unexplained, of course, is what it is about collective units that transforms *their* performances into acts of appropriation, such performances being unavailable to private parties. It is *at least* as problematic to see how a social unit can come to acquire something as it is to see how an individual can. Indeed, it is much *more* so: individuals are project pursuers who incorporate the utilization of objects into their pursuits, thereby manifesting a recognizable interest in the *having* of things; social entities as such pursue no projects and have no interests.

If there were only one collective entity and if each person had volunteered antecedent consent to be enrolled in whatever enterprises the collectivity undertook and to adhere to whatever standard of value the collectivity should erect for itself, and if such consent were continually renewed, *then* there would be some basis for judging that rights inhere primarily in the group and not in individuals. In the absence of such a monistic foundation for moral theory, it is incumbent upon those who construe property as a thoroughly socialized construction to explain how it is that social units can justifiably claim for everyone what no individual can claim for himself.

The Rawlsian Difference Principle

A book on the theory of liberal rights written after 1971 must inevitably confront the imposing edifice constructed in John Rawls' *A Theory of Justice*,[21] either to embrace its method and results or to offer principled grounds for rejecting them. No other work in this century has articulated so complete a philosophical framework for liberal society and has influenced so wide an audience.

The Rawlsian two principles of justice are given the following first statement:

First: each person is to have an equal right to the most extensive basic liberty compatible with a similar liberty for others.
Second: social and economic inequalities are to be arranged so that they are both (a) reasonably expected to be to everyone's advantage, and (b) attached to positions and offices open to all. (p. 60)

The principle of maximum equal liberty and the difference principle are ordered lexically: that is, no trade-off between them is permitted. Maximum equal liberty must be secured before the difference principle takes effect. The second of the principles receives the name 'difference principle' because Rawls construes 'everyone's advantage' as ruling out all differences in wealth except insofar as they serve to raise the position of the least well off.

It is apparent that the principle of maximum equal liberty is entirely compatible with the argument of this book, both because it responds to the interest each project pursuer has in the ability to direct his own life free from the interference of others and because the lexical priority of the principle assigns preeminent status to liberty rights. The difference principle, however, fits uneasily with my argument and, as I have argued elsewhere,[22] with Rawls' own principle of maximum equal liberty. It seems to assume that after institutions are arranged to afford all persons maximal equal liberty, there will remain a vast stock of goods and opportunities to be distributed by the collectivity in accord with the favored principle of distributive justice.

As is well known, Rawls' formal derivation of the two principles of justice is carried out by means of a hypothetical "original position" in which persons select basic social structures. Their deliberations are stylized as occurring behind a veil of ignorance that shields from each deliberator all knowledge of his own particular circumstances, including his natural endowments, conception of the good, and the likely role he will occupy in the resultant society. It is claimed by Rawls that such selective ignorance will ensure that whatever result is achieved will be just: "Since all are similarly situated, and no one is able to design principles to favor his particular condition, the principles of justice are the result of a fair agreement or bargain" (p. 12).

A vast literature has been produced in which the Rawlsian decision procedure has been subjected to scrutiny from every possible angle. A commonly offered criticism is that the risk aversiveness Rawls postulates for his contractors is extremely unrealistic.[23] More fundamental, though, than the question of whether Rawls adequately demonstrates that it is his two principles that would be selected in the original position is the question of what bearing *any* hypothetical agreement has on moral theory. It is not enough to argue that results achieved behind the veil of ignorance are necessarily fair: a fairly agreed-upon distribution carries no moral weight unless the parties to the agreement are entitled to distribute shares. Should A and B gang up to confiscate C's wealth and then distribute that quantity amongst themselves, not even the most scrupulous subsequent attention to fairness would morally justify the resultant distribution. Nor would it if A and B generously offered to C an equal part in the deliberations. If specific goods come morally attached to specific persons, then they are not available for collective disposition.

The Rawlsian original position abstracts from prior relations to objects and so is essentially open to the objections lodged above against spaceship justice. The elaborate artifice of the original position comes to nought unless it can be shown that authority to distribute does reside within the collective. That presupposition cannot, upon pain of circularity, be derived through the formal apparatus of the original position. Therefore, Rawls appends to the formal argument an extensive informal argument intended to make plausible the claim that collective distribution of goods does not run counter to individual rights.

Rawls does not conceive of material goods as manna waiting to be effortlessly gathered but acknowledges instead that what persons come to get is largely a function of their talents and of their effort. How, then, can it be denied that persons are morally entitled to the product of their activity? Rawls' answer is that the holdings thereby created are *morally arbitrary* and thus do not constitute legitimate claims which must be acknowledged in any process of collective decision making. Differential abilities among persons are themselves arbitrary, the result of a morally neutral "natural lottery."

The extent to which natural capacities develop and reach fruition is affected by all kinds of social conditions and class attitudes. Even the willingness to make an effort, to try, and so to be deserving in the ordinary sense is itself dependent upon happy family and social circumstances. (p. 74)

Patterns of holdings that emerge from the spin of the genetic and social wheel are natural facts that confront social institutions, but they possess no cachet that renders them morally untouchable:

The natural distribution is neither just nor unjust; nor is it unjust that men are born into society at some particular position. These are simply natural facts. What is just and unjust is the way that institutions deal with these facts. (p. 102)

The Rawlsian argument for the moral permissibility of distributing economic goods according to a socially derived criterion, the difference principle, does not rest on a claim that there is some characteristic peculiar to property such that it and it alone falls under the public aegis; rather, the entire realm of the morally arbitrary is subject to collective determination. That, however, includes everything that individuates one person from another: physical attributes, character, intelligence, and relations to property. Indeed, even the ends that persons have will be regarded as arbitrary. That A comes to devote himself to E_1 and B to E_2 will be the product of a myriad of causal factors that have, on the Rawlsian account, no inherent moral significance. Only the bare deontological ego stripped of all its attachments and everything that sets it off as distinct from other egos remains as nonarbitrary.[24] If nothing that is tainted by the stain of moral arbitrariness can be allowed behind the Rawlsian veil, then persons can bring to the contractual process only their existence as persons. Since each is exactly the same as everyone else in the only sense that is relevant, the possession of moral personhood, no one will have any basis whatsoever to claim private control over anything. For any item *I*, A and B necessarily stand in an identical relationship to it. There could be no sufficient reason, then, for maintaining that A rather than B ought to control *I*. Only through a determination made by all agents acting collectively can there be rationally justifiable grounds for allocation with respect to *I*.

Some theories that profess to be liberal perceive no problem with an affirmation that all dispositions of property reside ultimately in the collectivity. Yet the implications of Rawls' informal argument extend far beyond property, as commonly conceived. Everything that in fact individuates one person from another becomes common property: "We see then that the difference principle represents, in effect, an agreement to regard the distribution of natural talents as a common asset" (p. 101).

Rawls does not explicitly list personal conceptions of the good as also being common assets, but that is the clear implication of his argument. If A's virtuosity as a pianist is a talent that does not, in a morally privileged sense, belong to A, if it can properly be harnessed for the good of everyone, then A's commitment to pursue a life in music is equally a social asset. That end is A's only in the restricted sense that it happens to characterize A's volitional makeup, but not in the sense that A has a claim to moral space within which he is free to act in the pursuit of that end. Whatever foundation there is in morality for A to direct how the end will find expression is equivalently foundation for B to direct how "A's" end will find expression. "In justice as fairness men agree to share one another's fate" (p. 102). This characterization is only partially accurate: in justice as fairness men do not have a fate prior to the collective determination of what that fate will be.

In pursuit of the elimination of that which is morally arbitrary, Rawls has, unfortunately, undercut the supporting structures on which a viable liberalism must rest. It *is* arbitrary that A has the abilities, character, and projects that he does, and thus it is arbitrary that A has reason to pursue those ends which are his rather than those ends which are B's. Rawls would preclude A from demanding a liberty to serve those ends which are distinctively his own because Rawls will not grant that contingent facts carry moral weight that is prior to and determinative of justice in social arrangements. Should it be judged that the common good would be better served by obliterating the conception of the good that A adventitiously has come to possess and by replacing it with another (e.g., the least well off will be advantaged by passions for plumbing rather than piano), then A cannot complain that his right to pursue his own end rather than some other is being violated, or that he deserves the liberty to play the piano. A has no ends that rightfully are his, and A deserves no liberty, until the social unit adjudicates what those ends and liberties shall be.

> At this point it is necessary to be clear about the notion of desert. . . . [C]laims are legitimate expectations established by social institutions, and the community is obligated to meet them. But this sense of desert presupposes the existence of the cooperative scheme. (p. 103)

To be sure, Rawls does not advocate brainwashing and corrective neurosurgery in the collective interest. Persons will be allowed to keep the ends that they have along with their distinguishing abilities and character:

> [I]t does not follow that one should eliminate these distinctions. There is another way to deal with them. The basic structure can be arranged so that these contingencies work for the good of the least fortunate. (p. 102)

"It does not follow that one should eliminate these distinctions"—but neither does it follow that one should *not*. It is probably the case that any vast social program of altering men's minds and bodies, shaping ends and abilities to fit a collective design, will be counterproductive. The least well off will have their condition worsened rather than made better. On grounds of efficiency it might be better to leave ends where they lie. But if totalitarian psychoengineering flunks a cost-benefit analysis, that is a fortuitous accident and one that is largely a function of available technology. Rawls can take little comfort from its practical unfeasibility. It would be a strange irony if the philosopher most insistent on the rejection of appeal to that which is morally arbitrary had to rest a claim for noninterference with that which is central to the integrity of project pursuers on the (temporary) absence of handy means to mold men's souls.

It might be objected that Rawls is not vulnerable in this respect because the maximum equal liberty principle rules out any such interference with personality. Since that principle is lexically prior to the difference principle, the latter can never be employed to justify direct social control over persons' ends.

The objection fails. It does not explain why societal meddling with the character a person happens to have counts as a violation of liberty while the exercise of ultimate control over property holdings a person happens to have does not. More crucial, it fails to note that any appeal to the formally derived principles of justice is logically inadmissible in this context. What is now under consideration is Rawls' *informal argument,* intended to make convincing the claim that whatever emerges from behind the veil is an adequate representation of our intuitive sense of justice. It would be blatantly circular to introduce at this point a principle whose moral acceptability is being scrutinized. Why should we subscribe in wide reflective equilibrium to the difference principle? The informal argument is set forth to provide part of the answer. But that argument places the principle of maximum equal liberty in jeopardy. If contingencies can be socially controlled to work for the benefit of the least well off, then the ends that persons contingently have must also be placed in the pot of social assets. In the attempt to render credible one of his two principles, Rawls inadvertently pulls the rug out from under the other.

Rawls has failed to show that social control over property is in any way more justifiable than social control over personality. That failure is not surprising. His argument that property is a social asset is explicitly based on the proposition that natural talents—and all else that is morally arbitrary—are a social asset. It follows directly that there is no domain within which an individual enjoys a privileged moral position such that he and he alone is entitled to control anything—including his own activities. Everything pertaining to persons except their personhood, whatever that could be when abstracted from ends, character, abilities, and relations to material possessions, is thoroughly socialized. Moral space has shrunk to zero. Any liberty rights that persons enjoy are theirs not in virtue of their existence as project pursuers with their own lives to lead, but because the social decision process has created and bestowed those rights. The conclusion is thoroughly illiberal. Individuals, insofar as they are recognized as more than bare egos, are the creation of society rather than its creators. The result is clearly not one that Rawls wants or believes that he has achieved,[25] but it dogs *A Theory of Justice* nonetheless.

Where does Rawls go wrong? Most critically, in his insistence that that which is morally arbitrary is infinitely open to social melioration. A robust liberalism must instead maintain that contingencies become imbued with moral weight once they are intimately attached to the lives that persons *actually live*. If an end, a talent, a material object happens through a chain of circumstance to become mine, then I have a personal stake in it that I have unique reason to protect. Successful civility requires that others acknowledge and respect these personal attachments reciprocally with my like recognition of the individuality of others. That which is initially a surd becomes suffused with moral significance once it enters the projects of a person.

Rawls finds this transformation imcomprehensible:

> It seems to be one of the fixed points of our considered judgments that no one deserves his place in the distribution of native endowments, any more than one deserves one's initial starting place in society. (p. 104)

To the extent that this is "one of the fixed points in our considered judgments" it is because it trades on an ambiguity. Unless one subscribes to a doctrine of karma, it will be uncontroversial that one's *receipt* of native endowments was not conditioned by any antecedent desert. However, once one contingently and nondeservedly *has* those endowments, it is by no means obvious that one does not *deserve* (to keep, use, reap the fruits of, etc.) those endowments. In that sense of 'deserve his place', Rawls seems to have gotten the considered moral judgment backwards. That I happen to have this marvelously healthy left kidney is not the result of any merit I accrued as a zygote or noumenal self. But now that it's mine, I *deserve* it; it may not be taken from me against my wishes; it is not a social asset that can be distributed for the advantage of the least well off. Or if the term 'deserve' seems out of place—it does not to me—then I have a *basic right* to that kidney, a *valid claim* or an *entitlement* that constrains what society may do with the kidney. Surely this fits common morality and the tradition of Anglo-American law far better than does the denial that I deserve the kidney. Neither left kidneys nor material wealth are social assets that may be comandeered in the service of some theory of distributive justice.[26]

Finally, it should be noted that two points made earlier also tell against the Rawlsian argument. First, even if it were the case that no individual could ever deserve anything, it does not follow that what individuals do not deserve is deserved by the collective. If the fact that A *has I* does not confer upon A a moral claim to the use of *I* in A's projects, then the fact that a million Rawlsian contractors *have I* does not entitle them to make a dispensation concerning *I*. The absence of appropriability by individuals does not entail social appropriability; instead it entails that material objects are sucked into a moral vacuum whence they can never emerge as (rightfully owned) property.

Second, unless Rawlsian contractors are conceived to embrace all humanity (a conception that Rawls himself disavows),[27] it is hard to see how the social appropriation of goods can be any less arbitrary from the point of view of justice than is private appropriation. That societies have the members that they do and not some others, that national boundaries mark off a particular allotment of natural resources, that the GNP of the United States will allow for lots of redistribution and the GNP of Chad for little—these facts are all morally arbitrary. They do, however, give rise to considerable inequality among persons in different societies. If inequalities that do not better the condition of the least well off are arbitrary and thus unjustifiable, then the existence of separate sovereign polities cannot be justified. For whom or what then will the Rawlsian theory of justice be a theory of justice?

When Rights Are Wronged

Although rights *must* not be violated, they *will* be. That is the unavoidable accompaniment of social life in an imperfect world, imperfect with respect to the moral character of individuals and with respect to the information that persons have. Even if all persons were maximally conscientious, infringements of rights would still occur as the result of inadvertence. The theory of basic rights must, then, include provisions for response to acts that intrude on moral space.

Such response has two aspects. The first involves expressions of opprobrium to be visited on the transgressor. These are incorporated within the theory of punishment. By no means is it the case that all acts in violation of rights call for punishment. Those which are committed unintentionally and convey no disrespect for persons or for the system of rights need not be taken as jeopardizing the status of the transgressor as a full member of the moral community. Intentional wrongings are a different matter, and in such cases sanctions express the social conviction that disrespect for the rights of others redounds to the impairment of the transgressor's status as a moral claimant.

But whether rights have been violated intentionally or unintentionally, it remains the case that someone has been victimized. His ability to live as a project pursuer has suffered because of an unwarranted act of interference, and he therefore can justifiably demand to be accorded the position that was formerly his. The second aspect of response to the violation of rights centers on the victim rather than the transgressor, and it issues in demands for *compensation* or *rectification*.

There is a shade of difference in meaning between the two terms. The root of 'compensate' is "to weigh," that is, to weigh different things together in order to establish a balance between them. 'Rectify' has the root meaning of "making right." Therefore, 'compensation' carries the connotation of providing something *equivalent* in value to that which has been lost, while 'rectification' has the sense of *restoring precisely* that which was removed. It makes sense to speak of compensating someone who has undergone extreme pain and suffering, but rectification is logically impossible. If A's stolen car is returned to him, then the loss has been rectified, but a requirement that additional monetary damages be paid to A in consideration for the inconvenience and anxiety that the loss of the car occasioned would be a requirement of compensation.

Is it rectification or rather compensation that should be considered the primary avenue of response to an infringement of rights? It is clearly, I believe, the former. Persons' rights are rights to particular performances and are rights over particular items of property. This is a reflection of the fact that individuals assign personal value to their own projects and not to a welfare measure consequent upon their acting in pursuit of those particular projects. What A wishes to realize is specifically E_1, not the attainment of whatever level of utility is associated with the realization of E_1. A will therefore not be rationally indifferent between having the necessary means to go about the pursuit of his project E_1 and having the necessary means to pursue E_2, even if it were somehow demonstrable that the attainment of E_2 by A would have the same welfare measure as does the attainment of E_1 by A. A will not be rationally indifferent between these because he is not obligated to subscribe to an impersonal standard of value in terms of which E_1 and E_2 are commensurable. If value is not thoroughly impersonal, then compensation cannot possess moral adequacy equivalent to that possessed by rectification.

Robert Nozick argues that independents who decline to enter civil society can justifiably be prevented by the state from enforcing their Lockean rights provided that they receive compensation. The form that such compensation should take, recommends Nozick, is rights protection, courtesy of the state.[28]

This argument is doubly defective. It assumes that an infringement of rights can be made good through compensation, the moral balance restored to what it was *ex ante*. No such general assumption is justifiable. Compensation is inevitably a second-best response that comes into play when full rectification is impossible. But in this case there is a morally more adequate alternative: simply letting the independents be.[29]

In addition, the suggestion that suitable compensation can take the form of a grant of citizenship is remarkably insensitive to persons' interests in the projects that they actually have. Presumably, those who are willing to bear the high costs entailed by their reluctance to enter into civil society assign considerable personal value to living as an independent. They will not be indifferent between enforcing their own rights and having those rights enforced by even a high-powered social mechanism. Whatever could count as morally satisfactory compensation cannot be *this!*

Nozick's analysis of prohibition and compensation makes use of an apparatus of indifference curves. It need not be claimed that such devices are useless in moral theory to note that they can disguise morally crucial factors. Figure 6.1 represents two of the infinite number of indifference curves for A with respect to goods G_1 and G_2. Every point on U represents a utility level equal to each other point on U, and every point on U represents a higher utility level than any point on U*. Suppose that A's initial position is x. A then loses a quantity of G_1 sufficient to land him on U* at y. If A then receives $(z - y)$ units of G_2, A lands back on U and, by definition, has regained the initial utility level.

Judgments of compensation will necessarily be framed by some such measure as that diagramatically represented in Figure 6.1. However, the moral adequacy of compensation is a function of the extent to which the presuppositions of Figure 6.1 are realized. It is assumed that G_1 and G_2 are commensurable over the full range through which the indifference curves are drawn and that it is morally indifferent which position on U is achieved by A. Insofar, though, as A does not hold G_1 and G_2 to be commensurable or that A does not care simply about obtaining measure U of utility but rather about bringing about particular outcomes for himself, the indifference curve apparatus cannot be used as a guide to restoring a moral equilibrium.

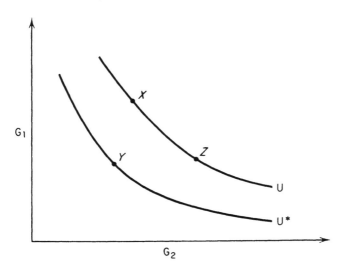

FIGURE 6.1
Indifference Curves for A

When rights are violated, the ability of the victim to pursue his projects is impaired. A morally adequate response will address itself in the first instance to restoring that ability. Rectification makes redress by providing once again the means that were temporarily lost; compensation supplies different means that can be employed in the service of one's projects. Both respond, though with different degrees of adequacy, to a person's interests in the project he actually has. A mode of redress distinct from and morally inferior to either of these is to supply means useful in the realization of ends that the individual does not acknowledge as his own. It would be neither rectification nor compensation to commandeer Ralph Sampson's basketball and to offer him philosophy lessons instead. (Nor would it be if he were first given a pill that caused him to *like* philosophy lessons, thus restoring him to his original indifference curve.)

It can prove beyond the powers of any earthly institution to restore one's lost ability with respect to one's projects. No satisfactory rectification or compensation can be made to the athlete who becomes a paraplegic as the result of an automobile accident. In such a case even the morally best form of redress will be highly unsatisfactory. The awarding of damages will supply means for whatever semblance of the pursuit of one's original projects remains feasible and will also make available means for the pursuit of new projects that one may subsequently develop. Additionally, the awarding of damages symbolizes social respect for the victim's prior moral status as a project pursuer, even if that status cannot be restored. Punitive damages and the award of money to (the estate of) a deceased individual are, at least in part, to be construed as symbolic in this fashion.

"Justice delayed is justice denied." The old adage betokens a recognition of the fact that lives are finite and that, consequently, an extended disruption of one's activities can never be made good in an entirely satisfactory manner. The value of rectification or compensation is inversely proportional to the length of time that passes before such redress is made. The fundamental point underlying the insistence that an encroachment upon rights demands redress is the moral urgency of restoring the victim's full abilities as a project pursuer.

A corollary of this point is that some violations of rights call for no acts of rectification or compensation. If it is impossible to identify which individuals have been victimized or in any way to make amends to them, whether actually or symbolically, then no transfer of property rights is called for. It is undeniably the case that virtually all current holdings of property descend from a historical chain involving the usurpation of rights. It does not follow that those holdings are thereby rendered illegitimate, morally null and void. Nor does it follow that it would be permissible to place all property holdings in a social trust from which they would then be assigned to individuals, but *this time* with scrupulous concern for justice. Any such grand utopian design invokes a mistaken premise: that concern for rights is made manifest through the obliteration of all fruits of rights violations. But that is to dissociate the value of rights from the value that resides in the persons whose rights they are. The evil of transgressions would take on an independent status and would have to be washed away so that the cosmic moral order will be made clean again.

There is no basis in the theory of basic rights for this attitude. According to that theory, the reason why rights matter is because persons have ends that they personally value. No radical upheaval of property rights now can in any degree make redress for rights violations that occurred centuries ago. Just the opposite is the case: a confiscation of property preparatory to bringing about the Brave New World would sin against the rights of contemporary individuals to be secure in the possession of the property they are actually using in the ongoing pursuit of their projects. The consuming urge to remake the world according to some transcendent ideological mandate can acquire no support from the fact that past injustices are causal contributants to current holdings. Those holdings may not be upset unless to do so would

be to reclaim rights wrongfully usurped and to make restoration to the rightful possessors. To do otherwise would be to add yet further depredations to
a sorry history of disrespect for rights.

If all consequences of rights violations must be obliterated, then *we* must
volunteer for annihilation! It is virtually certain that had no right ever been
violated, no currently living human being would have been born. (Is this the
metaphysical counterpart to the theological doctrine of Original Sin?) Perhaps it would have been better *sub specie aeternitatis* had the inhabitants of
the morally untainted possible world come into existence rather than us—an
admission I would make grudgingly, if at all—but that value judgment has
no bearing on what is morally required of actual individuals. Neither the
persons nor property holdings that would have characterized an ideal world
are now actualizable. The option that *is* available to us is to respect the
interest in project pursuit of actual persons by refraining from encroachment
on their property holdings.

The place of rectification and compensation within the theory of basic
rights is not the result of a moral imperative to construct the closest attainable facsimile to the possible world untainted by rights violations. It is instead due to the need to restore to actual individuals to whatever extent is
feasible their capacity for project pursuit. That they have come to have this
capacity, including their property holdings, as the result of factors that are
"morally arbitrary," or even in virtue of morally pernicious antecedents,
does not to any degree lessen this moral necessity.

The Supply of Public Goods

Successful project pursuit requires, in addition to a stock of goods privately
owned and controlled, goods that are *public*. The two defining features of a
public good are (1) that its consumption by one person does not preclude its
like consumption by others and (2) that if the good is made available to one
person, then others are thereby granted access to it. These will be referred
to as the criteria of *nonrivalry* and *nonexcludability*. Both admit of degree.
My viewing of a movie is nonrival with your viewing, but the capacity of
the theater limits the total number of persons who can simultaneously "consume" the movie. Moreover, some seats will offer a better post for observation, thereby affecting the quality of the good consumed. Nonexcludability is also a matter of more or less. It may be technologically possible to
scramble television signals so that only those who possess an unscrambling
device will be able to view a clear picture, but the cost of doing so may be

prohibitive. If so, then access to the signal is, in practical terms, nonexcludable.

The existence of public goods creates the temptation to free ride. Each individual can calculate that whether or not he contributes to the cost of the good will hardly at all affect his subsequent ability to consume the good. Whatever others do, the marginal cost of supplying a unit of the good will exceed the marginal benefit that accrues to oneself. Because these cost considerations obtain generally, purely self-interested individuals will drastically undersupply public goods. Even if individuals take some concern for the welfare of others, unless it is the case that everyone regards a benefit that accrues to someone else as fully equivalent to one that he himself enjoys, public goods will be undersupplied. However, if there were some mechanism that promised to each person that his own contribution to the cost of the good would be matched by equivalent contributions from each other person, then even purely self-interested individuals would find it in their interest to supply the good in question.

Where the number of persons is small, the mechanism can be unanimous agreement. If A and B are the co-occupants of a hot, stuffy office, then it may not be difficult for them to come to an agreement to share in the cost of an air conditioner. Even here, though, there will be a temptation to dissemble. If A can convince B that he, A, delights in heat and humidity, then perhaps B will be induced to assume the full costs of air conditioning—and to pay compensation to A as well!

As the number of persons increases, the transaction costs involved in reaching unanimous agreement are likely to become greater than any benefit consequent upon supply of the good. Arrangements that would make everyone better off will not be achieved. Either public goods will be forgone or else a mechanism that does not require universal voluntary compliance must be invoked. That is, a coercive institutional structure will be required if public goods are to be supplied.[30]

National defense is a paradigmatic public good. It is impossible to supply defense against foreign aggressors to one person without thereby supplying defense to his neighbors. Legal institutions for the protection of rights are also public goods. Each person benefits from the maintenance of the rule of law, but no one can supply those institutions for himself as a private good. Even if access to the system on a case-by-case basis can, to some extent, be denied to those who do not pay for it (for example through court costs), the existence of a legislature, police, and courts will confer positive externalities upon everyone.[31] Unless these goods are supplied, the existence of an order in which rights are respected is impossible. Yet the specter of the free rider once again rears its ugly head: it cannot be presumed that individuals will voluntarily supply morally necessary public goods in sufficient quantities. Therefore, it is morally permissible, or even morally mandatory, that individuals be coerced to pay their fair share of these public goods.

Public goods provision is frequently appealed to as a function that only a coercive state can fulfill and thus as justificatory of the existence of the state. There are, however, two fundamentally different forms that such an argument can take. The first of these maintains that there is a principle of fairness obligating one who is the recipient of benefits conferred by the cooperation of others to contribute one's fair cost share to the provision of those benefits.

> [W]hen a number of persons engage in a mutually advantageous cooperative venture according to rules, and thus restrict their liberty in ways necessary to yield advantages for all, *those who have submitted to these restrictions have a right to a similar acquiescence* on the part of those who have benefited from their submission. We are not to gain from the cooperative labors of others without doing our fair share.[32]

The alleged principle of fairness clashes with individualism. It implies that any group of cooperating persons can ensnare a person within their scheme of activity merely by showering unasked-for benefits upon him.[33] Whatever their projects are, one would be mandatorily enrolled in them and would not be at liberty wholeheartedly to devote oneself to one's own ends.

Project pursuers have reason to resist such involuntary enlistment in the designs of others. Is it necessary to build and reside in a moral fallout shelter that shields one from the gratuitously imposed benefits cast hither and yon by cooperating groups in order to be free from obligations to underwrite their efforts? Apparently—if there exists a right to acquiescence. That there is no such right and that any such scheme of enforced cooperation is profoundly illiberal has been argued throughout this book.

The fact that public goods confer general benefits cannot be taken as a general rationale for the extraction of cost shares. There is a different argument, however, that can be offered in justification of coercive institutions. If individuals *assent* to being coerced in certain respects, or if their rational assent can somehow be inferred, then compulsion by others need not be in violation of the liberty to direct one's own life. Ulysses chained to the mast is the classic example of rationally motivated precommitment to be controlled by others.[34] Or, to borrow an example of J. S. Mill, to restrain by force someone from crossing a bridge that you (but not he) know to be rotted out is not an impermissible infringement of his liberty. It can be deemed that a rational individual would assent to coercion in such circumstances, and therefore that in so acting you are aiding him in his projects rather than making him an adjunct to yours. Of course, you might be wrong: he might be intent on suicide or on undertaking risky action for its own sake. But you might also be mistaken if you failed to intervene, and that likelihood is much greater. In this example the costs of the two mistakes vary: suicide delayed by a few seconds is not suicide denied. That feature, though, will not necessarily characterize otherwise similar examples.

Rational individuals will prefer to live in an order within which the effects of their ignorance are mitigated rather than magnified. Therefore, intervention of the sort noted above is not incompatible with, but instead supports, a regime of rights founded on considerations of practical reason. To generalize the result, institutions that enhance the abilities of individuals to pursue their own projects are justifiable from the perspective of the standards of personal value to which individuals adhere. That is the principle that was invoked in Chapter 4 to derive the rational acceptability of basic rights. Each project pursuer assigns personal value to his own projects and therefore has reason to respect the moral space of others, conditional upon their like respect. Not only is it the case that each person is better off when rights are generally respected than when they are not, but, in addition, each person has reason to act to bring about conditions of general respect for rights.

If everyone else is respecting rights, then I will be made better off if I can violate rights whenever it is to my advantage to do so. That would be to free ride on the morality of others. However, since I recognize that everyone else is in a similar position, I assign personal value to the existence of an institutional structure that will enforce rights and thus impose costs on would-be free riders. There is some amount of my stock of private goods that I would be willing to pay to bring about the creation and maintenance of such institutions rather than go without them in a Hobbesian state of nature. Each other nonfanatical project pursuer can similarly be deemed to find protection of rights within the rule of law rationally preferable to anarchy. Therefore, the coercive extraction of cost shares to supply public goods necessary for the protection of rights is properly responsive to each individual's interest in his own ends. No one can justifiably complain that the existence of such coercive institutions is intended to take him away from the pursuit of his own projects and enlist him in the projects of others. A person who is rationally motivated to assent to being coerced is not being treated as a mere means rather than as an end in himself when such compulsion is brought to bear on him. Contrast this to compulsion based on the principle of fairness, where it is the *assent of others* to a cooperative scheme that is invoked to justify *one's own obligation* to cooperate.

It is obvious that if persons are asked by the tax collector, "Do you agree to be taxed to provide for public institutions?" with the proviso that a negative answer would relieve one from all obligations to contribute, each person could gain by free riding. Whether or not many or most would avail themselves of this opportunity, each person has reason to reject such a voluntaristic device for supplying public goods. Because social decision procedures that encourage free riding motivate persons to act in ways that ultimately make everyone worse off than they might have been, persons have reason to reject the imposition of procedures that elicit such baleful motivations. They will instead rationally and freely prefer the imposition of structures from which they are not at liberty to withdraw their support.

It has been argued that cost shares for public goods necessary to the maintenance of civil society can be coercively extracted from members of that society without rights thereby being violated. But what of public goods not strictly necessary to a civil order but which citizens nonetheless value? May they be provided through a coercive tax mechanism?

The question is surrounded by pitfalls. If the public good is such that individuals in fact assign personal value to its availability, if they actually prefer its supply through coercive means to its absence, and if these two facts are known with a high degree of assurance, then coercive supply of the good evinces respect for persons' individuality. However, to force people to pay for a good whose benefits they judge insufficient to justify public provision is to encroach on moral space. The burden of proof in a liberal society clearly rests on those who propose provision. What is risked is the violation of a moral side constraint, while what may be gained is merely the enhancement of welfare. It is impermissible either intentionally to violate a side constraint or to act negligently in a manner that risks violation of side constraints. Still, it cannot be concluded that the only public goods that may be provided by a liberal society are defense against foreign aggressors and the internal maintenance of the rule of law.

Many of the things commonly referred to as "public goods," however, are clearly inappropriate for provision through state power. Those "goods" which are known to be "bads" for many persons, for example, transfer programs, may not be coercively provided. Items for which private provision is feasible may not be publicly provided even if privatization would lead to suboptimal levels of production. There is no moral requirement that markets function perfectly, and the alternatives to imperfect markets are themselves imperfect. The existence of "market failure" is matched by the phenomenon of "governmental failure."[35] Postal services are an example of a good that can be supplied privately, and they also are eloquent testimony to the reality of governmental failure.

Finally, even if a good otherwise qualified for public provision, persons who are known to disvalue the provision of that good may not be forced to pay any amount for it. It is, unfortunately, the case that individuals' underlying preferences are not open to scientific observation, and that it therefore cannot always be known whether an individual's expression of reluctance to pay for a good betokens genuine disvalue of the good or merely an inclination to take a free ride. However, sometimes it can be known: the person who raises mosquitoes as pets and devotes his life to breeding new strains is to be *believed* if he claims to disvalue a program of insect control. Although his ends are peculiar, they must be afforded respect by a liberal polity.

7

Extending the Moral
Community: Children

Project pursuers enjoy rights in virtue of being project pursuers; that, in essence, was the argument of the preceding six chapters. Shall we then argue that *only* project pursuers enjoy rights, that non–project pursuers lack rights in virtue of their not holding those long-term commitments which so distinctly and decisively shape the lives of those who pursue projects? It is *prima facie* appealing to conclude exactly that. At least three reasons seem to support such an inference.

1. The foregoing argument has had the general form: all those who are characterized by property F (project pursuit) have property G (possession of basic rights). Moreover, it is *because* they have F that they also have G. Had F been lacking, then there would have been no adequate basis to support any inference to G. Therefore, it seems straightforward to conclude that no grounds exist to ascribe G to any beings other than those who have F.

2. The preceding consideration is based entirely on the logical form of the inference from F to G. But we can buttress that with further considerations stemming from the particular natures of F and G. Rights stand athwart unconstrained maximization of impersonal value. It is nonetheless rational to acknowledge the existence of rights because not all value is impersonal; project pursuers are the source of personal value which they have reason to advance independently of the results of an impersonal calculus. But in the absence of personal value, rationality would dictate unconstrained maximization of impersonal value. Those who do not pursue projects cannot be sources of personal value, and so it would seem that all dealings with them can be morally adjudicated entirely on the basis of considerations that do not take *their* distinctive good into account.[1]

3. We carry to the explicit argument for basic rights certain beliefs about the shape that any such argument must have even to be a *contender* for adequacy. One of these that appears robust is the conviction that a grounding for rights must lie in something *internal* to the rights holder rather than in a relation to something external. If I have rights, it is because of something about *me,* not something that resides in the messy world outside. This internalist construal of rights makes them appear more solidly established, less tentative, than would an externalist conception. For if my enjoying rights were a function of being related in a certain way to some other being, then I could lose my status as a rights holder if *that being* were to disappear or undergo alteration even though there was no corresponding change in *me.* To put it another way, my rights would then be *conferred* rather than native.

There does not seem to be any great resistance to holding that *duties* or *obligations* typically have an external source. One can have duties with respect to parents or benefactors *because* that relation obtains. And, of course, the existence of other rights holders thereby entails the obligation to respect their rights.[2] Plausibly, the appeal of an internalist view of rights may be motivated by an individualistic response to the externality of obligation. One is bombarded by claims from without; the fact that one holds rights limits the extent of these claims so that they do not diminish one's moral space to the vanishing point. Were rights also externally derived, then moral space would be in perpetual jeopardy. At any rate, prevalent accounts of rights do almost entirely rest on internalist foundations. A Kantian End in Himself is such in virtue of his *inherent* rationality; *human* rights are, by definition, ascribed to individuals who possess the (internal) property of being human. And project pursuit is likewise a power that firmly resides within the agency of the project pursuer. For internalist theories of rights, beings who possess the relevant characteristics enjoy rights and others do not. If rights by way of project pursuit is internalistic, then only project pursuers have rights.

While these three considerations carry weight, they are not decisive. The argument from logical form is clearly insufficient by itself to show that only project pursuers have rights. That there must be F's in order for there to be G's does not entail that *only* F's are G's. Some beings who lack F can yet be G's by piggybacking on those who are F's. The class of rights holders would then be made up of two importantly different subclasses: those who have rights because they pursue projects and those who have rights for some other reason. This is to offer a *multivalent* rather than a *univalent* account of rights.[3]

Considerations 2 and 3, above, adduce reasons for holding that an adequate account of rights must be univalent. Consideration 2 notes that it is the existence in the world of personal value that lends cogency to ascriptions of rights. Unconstrained maximization is rationally indicated except when it runs up against personal value. Since only project pursuers create personal value, no other beings can properly constrain maximization. The third consideration rejects a multivalent account in which some rights holders piggyback on others because this would be to violate internalism. Only one of the two subclasses of rights holders would possess rights in virtue of their own attributes; the other's rights would be externally derived—and thus not genuinely rights at all. If the moral community is to be expanded beyond project pursuers, these objections must be confronted.

Rights and Social Relations

Is a pure internalism with respect to rights possible even when restricted to those who are project pursuers? If so, then no attributes external to an individual need to be invoked to explain why he holds rights. But the progression to rights of the preceding chapters was not circumscribed in this manner. That individual A holds rights against individual B (or against all other individuals) was held to be due to facts about A—but also due to facts about B. A may have reason to demand freedom from encroachment by B, but this demand is abortive unless it is also the case that B has reason to accede to it. Rights emerged as the mutual and reciprocal demands for minimal forbearance that one has reason to present to all others and to which one has reason to accede when they are presented to oneself. Whether B has reason to acknowledge and respect rights in A is not simply a fact about A but also about B. And it is a fact vital to the progression to basic rights.

A purely internalist theory of basic rights can provide reasons why individuals seek the *protections* that rights afford, but it will fail to generate rights as the means to such protection. It is not only other persons who can imperil one's status as a project pursuer; the unthinking doings of the natural order can also lay one low. A may claim a right to noninterference from B but not from microbes or earthquakes. The latter are incapable of recognizing and responding to A's need for noninterference and so are not the sort of entities that can meaningfully be described as either respecting or failing to respect A's rights. The very concept of *having a right* therefore presupposes relations to others with whom one is involved in complex recognition patterns.

What, then, of the alleged internality of rights? It would be odd if a view that has so persistent a hold on moral convictions were simply and demonstrably absurd. Perhaps, though, like many (most?) philosophical stances, it stems from considerations which are undeniably legitimate but which, when myopically fastened on in isolation from all others, produce doctrines which only a philosopher could bring himself to believe.[4] That some beings are the source of personal value is to note an internal attribute in the absence of which rights do not emerge. "I am special (at least to myself)!" is the implicit claim of each project pursuer, and the recognition by others of this assertion marks the enablement of moral community. Only if there are attributes of project pursuers that set them apart from the other furnishings of the world will there be a basis for acknowledging them as ends in themselves rather than as items to be used in whatever manner happens to be most efficient. Both from the point of view of one who claims rights and one to whom those claims are presented, the attribute *being a project pursuer* is crucial. This much of internalism is true.

Still, being able to claim protection from encroachment and being granted such protection are distinct. When the claim is made against a suitable agent but not respected by it, rights are violated. This is quite obvious. Less obvious, though, is what should be said about the reverse situation. Suppose that A lacks all conception of a good-for-A and thus is unable to advance any claim to its promotion by himself or anyone else. B may nonetheless recognize (or mistakenly take himself to recognize) a good-for-A which B then takes as reason to acknowledge A's status as a rights holder. Otherwise permissible actions will be avoided if they encroach on the territory marked off as protecting the good-for-A. In such a case, B will be recognizing A as a rights holder even though A is unable to recognize himself as one. Two questions present themselves: (1) Can such asymmetrical recognition occur? (2) Are there valid grounds for such recognition? If the answer to both is affirmative, then there are rights holders who are not project pursuers.

The first of these can be summarily answered. It is an evident component of common moral experience that non–project pursuers are routinely regarded as beings with rights. Most obviously this is the case with respect to very young children. Under no reasonable construal can infants be taken to be pursuing projects during their infancy, yet common morality regards them as beings with rights that merit protection. To kill an infant is to commit homicide in the same sense that killing a mature human being is homicide. Of course, common morality may be confused, insupportable, bound up in traditional taboos.[5] But however one appraises the normative issue, it can hardly be questioned as a point of descriptive ethics that rights are routinely ascribed to neonates and other children too young to form and commit themselves to projects.

Nor are children unique in this regard. Among other beings for whom rights are more or less regularly claimed are the severely retarded, senile individuals, comatose persons, fetuses, the dead, and animals. The listing is roughly in descending order of the strength and persistence of such claims, although no attempt is here being made to justify the ascription of rights to any or all of them.[6] It is intended rather to serve as a reminder of how easy and natural it is for us take others besides paradigmatic adult human beings as worthy of respect as rights holders. The reminder may be salutary as an inoculation against philosophical theories that make it seem mysterious how any beings that are not thoroughly rational and autonomous can be held to enjoy the privileged status of *rights holder*. For example, Kantian theories[7] that tie rights to rational agency are unable to assimilate rights ascriptions in these cases as other than gross moral errors. That is to presume too much too quickly. Rationality may be a necessary condition for there to *be* rights without its possession being a necessary condition for someone to *have* rights. That can be so if the correct account of rights is multivalent. Lending serious attention to the diversity of beings on behalf of whom rights ascriptions are made will tend to shake whatever certainty one might have that the correct account *must* be univalent. There is no obvious common denominator among all the beings recognized as rights holders by common morality. And more than three centuries of intense philosophical reflection on the basis of rights has not yielded a univalent account that can assimilate these diverse cases. The game is not thereby decided, but this is perhaps one strike for multivalence.

The prospect of framing an adequate multivalent theory of rights leads directly into the second question. One may choose to treat almost anything *as if* it were a rights holder (corporations, the Great God Pan, petunias in one's garden), either playfully or fetishistically. Such demonstrations, though, are clearly beside the point. If a being is genuinely a rights holder, then privileged treatment for it is *mandatory* rather than optional. If one is at liberty to choose whether to treat a being as if it has rights, then it does not have rights. It might be claimed that "treating as if" accounts for the status enjoyed in law and common morality by children, the retarded, animals, and other non–project pursuers. Out of sentimentality or misguided anthropomorphic projection or even supererogatory kindness, we extend to them courtesies that, strictly speaking, are *owed* only to project pursuers. They thereby come to enjoy (some of) the protections afforded to rights holders, although they themselves possess no basic rights. Were such treatment withdrawn, it would not *wrong them,* although it might render them worse off.

Still, this seems to be an awkward way to explain the shape of common morality. It is by no means apparent that the protections afforded to infants and other relevantly similar beings are conferred in the way that protections of, say, the American flag are conferred. One who misuses the flag may incur legal penalties and be judged morally culpable because the flag is damaged but not because it is wronged. Flags are not the sort of entity to which moral violations can accrue; whatever morally significant harms do occur are attached to those who stand to the flag in some relationship of regard. It is tortuous to attempt to extend the same kind of analysis to maltreatment of babies. Certainly those affectionally tied to an infant are harmed by its maltreatment, but this cannot account without remainder for the judgment that damaging infants is wrong. There is, in addition—the *crucial* addition—the judgment that the baby itself is harmed, and that this harm constitutes wronging the baby. If parents and interested onlookers take offense at the child's maltreatment, that fact is itself to be explained by their conviction that, in the first instance, a wrong has been committed *to the child.* The parent accounts the harm a misfortune to him or herself *because* it is a misfortune of the child. This constitutes, in part, the difference between regarding something as an *object* versus regarding it a being with moral standing.

Why, though, morally speaking, should infants not be regarded as objects, albeit ones that undergo portentous transformations as they mature? A univalent theory of rights will be likely to interpret the passage from infant to adult as a transition from *object* to *person.* But other answers are feasible. Perhaps the transformation process marks not simply the passage of a being from moral neutrality to moral significance but instead *prospectively confers* moral significance on the yet-to-be-transformed. It is unnatural to view adult project pursuers and infants as two distinct kinds of beings. Rather, one notes that all current project pursuers were previously infants and that those who are currently infants are just the kind of being that regularly and predictably develops into project pursuers (although, of course, in any particular case the development may misfire). Nor is maturation the transformation of one thing into another thing but rather the continued progress of one selfsame being. Borrowing Aristotelian language, the process is one of *change* rather than *generation and corruption.*

The pork chop that I eat for lunch eventually becomes (part of) me. Events that befell the chop before I ingested it might redound to the eventual harm or benefit of me. For example, had the cook laced it with arsenic prior to serving it, I would have suffered harm. However, to inject poison into the pork chop is not to inject poison into me even though the chop begins to be transformed into me when I eat it.

Contrast the Case of the Poisoned Pork Chop with that of administering to an infant a very slow-acting poison, one that does not begin to take effect for thirty years or so. It is the adult, we might say, who suffers from this act and not the child. More accurate, though, would be to describe the case as one in which *that person* experiences pain, spasms, nausea, etc., during his adult years because he is *that person* who was poisoned thirty years prior. It is not that two histories intersect but that one continues. This is represented by the temporal ascriptions that one will offer in relating the sequence of events. Jones (the baby) is poisoned; thirty years later, Jones (the adult) suffers pain. Evidently someone has been harmed, but who? Should we say that it is Baby Jones? No, because he passes through his infancy unaffected by the dose. Then Adult Jones? But no harmful act was committed any time during Jones' adult years. Perhaps, though, it is Adult Jones who is harmed, but through a prolonged causal process that begins with the dose of thirty years before. That also seems questionable. Harms cannot be free-floating evils but rather must attach to some particular individual or individuals. One could not say that an act harmful to Adult Jones takes place with the administration of the poison, since there does not (yet) exist the subject of the harm. However, neither does the act harmful to Adult Jones occur subsequently. So it does not occur at any time! This analysis is unlikely to prove comforting to Jones writhing in his sickbed. It is *he* who is now suffering because of a wrongful act done to *him* three decades earlier.

This is not intended as a demonstration that it is strictly contradictory to take Baby Jones as an individual numerically distinct from the Adult Jones who appears some years later. It does, however, point to the awkwardness of such a stance. Substantial revision of our language and moral ascriptions would be necessitated. For example, the slow poisoning case would have to be described as similar to planting a time bomb scheduled to injure only future people, not anyone who now exists. If that act merits condemnation, it is because it *will* cause injury, not because it *has* generated a harm to someone. Individuals reflecting on their careers will have to learn to begin the story at a later stage—or to regard the early chapters as prefaces which are properly about other beings but which relate events having significant consequences for themselves. Perhaps it would be possible to bring about such a conceptual reformation, but it would be neither easy nor natural. And for what end? The practical concerns one has for oneself and other individuals would simply have to be expressed in the language of distant causation *affecting* those persons rather than in terms of what is directly *done to them*.

Even though nothing one now does can alter the past, assignments of value or disvalue to past events will often serve as reasons for acting in certain ways in the present. Practices of punishment and reward, expressions of gratitude or reproach, fidelity to contractual obligations one has assumed: each represents a shadow cast by past occurrences into the present. No doubt there are often also future-directed reasons for engaging in these activities. Punishing the guilty will deter other wrongful performances, living up to contractual obligations will render one a suitable candidate for further dealings, and so on. Nonetheless, it is a losing game to attempt to reduce each of these to a calculated strategy for enhancing future value. Threatening punishment now will succeed as a deterrent only if it is made credible to potential transgressors that their wrongful acts will subsequently be regarded as providing reason for responses to what then will be past. Thus, although the past cannot be changed, value judgments about past occurrences can be practical.

Each project pursuer has reason to value past events conducive to his current success as a project pursuer.[8] Is this judgment practical? If it is, then that fact will provide a basis for ascribing rights to prospective project pursuers. It is clear that nothing one now performs with respect to prospective project pursuers can affect the manner in which one was treated as a prospective project pursuer.[9] If moral reckoning is entirely confined to egoistic calculation, then reflection on what was of value to all current project pursuers will have no implications concerning what ought to be done to prospective project pursuers. It is not necessary, though, to climb into the egoist's Procrustean bed. As was argued in Chapter 4, the recognition by A that some state of affairs constitutes value-for-B can itself have motivational force for A. A has reason to promote the occurrence of that state of affairs because of the value it holds out to B irrespective of whether A has independent reason to value it. Of course, this reason can be outweighed by other concerns that A has, but even when outweighed it remains a positive value-for-A.

Value-for-B will have motivational force for A only if certain conditions obtain. First, B must be recognizable by A as a distinct being for whom circumstances can be of more or less value. Second, it must be the case that A is capable of being moved by that recognition. If A is totally disengaged from the prospects of success or failure of B-type entities, then value transmission is stymied. Both of these conditions are amply satisfied in characteristic relationships between mature project pursuers and young children. Children are, after all, just the sort of being one once was oneself. One who damaged the child I once was has damaged *me*. One who can identify with a past childhood stage as incorporating events that happened to oneself and that carry value for oneself thereby evidences the cognitive ability to pick out at least one prospective project pursuer as a distinct being for whom value can obtain. Barring an onslaught of solipsism, the recognition of childhood stages of other (actual or prospective) project pursuers as containing value-for-them directly follows. No more is required for the satisfaction of the first condition.

The second condition is more complicated. One cannot proceed directly from the first-person case because the recognition of value-for-oneself in past childhood episodes will convey no motivation at all to generate that value for one who disbelieves in backward causation. Nonetheless, as was argued above, judgments of value referring to the past are practical insofar as they provide reason in the present to respond to that value. It is plausible to maintain as a necessary truth applying to all beings capable of exercising practical reason that judgments they make about value in the past have motivational force for them in the present. For suppose that this were not so. Then the judgment that one event or agent produced value-for-oneself and that some other had produced disvalue-for-oneself would not constitute a reason to respond differentially between the two. Recognizing someone as one's benefactor and another as having done one injury would in no way enter into the determination of responses made to their acts. But, then, in what sense can it be said that one has ascribed *value* to their acts? Value-in-the-past would be radically disjoint from value-in-the-present or value-in-the-future, recognition of which provides one reason to promote or thwart, welcome or decry, certain outcomes. It would be a "value" that is not valued. Such motivationally inert judgments would be judgments of value only in the sense that, counterfactually, *were* such an event or performance producible in the future, then one *would* have reason to value/disvalue its occurrence. But what one would, counterfactually, value is, necessarily, what one does not actually value. Therefore, one incapable of being motivated by value-in-the-past is also incapable of judging there to be value-in-the-past.

Whether or not the above argument is valid, it is uncontroversial to observe that typical adult human beings regularly do evaluatively judge of the past and frame their current responses accordingly. It is difficult to think of any significant patterns of activity which do not incorporate performances stemming from reflective judgments of value. The past is not dead to us, either as the reservoir of causal factors that intrude on the present or as the reservoir of values that are taken to be bases for subsequent response. Thus, it is evident that we are the sorts of beings that satisfy the second condition, and it is at least arguable that this represents a fact necessarily true of any being capable of judging value in the past.

I want now to show that the preceding observations both help explain why common morality takes children to be rights holders and provides justification for this classification. Common morality ascribes rights to the child because it recognizes rights in the adult it will become and to which it is numerically identical. To damage an infant is to damage the project pursuer that it will be. Indeed, what counts as damage or benefit for an infant is determined by what will likely further or diminish its eventual success in living as a project pursuer. To deprive it of food or shelter or mental stimulation does it harm.

However, to deny the child wine with dinner or the liberty to engage in sexual relations does it no harm even though such restrictions on adults would be harms to them.

Children have rights (against adults) if and only if there are goods-for-the-child that others have reason to acknowledge and respect. There are goods-for-the-child because it is identical to the being that will eventually come to have ends that can be advanced or retarded by what is done to it during its earliest years. Do others have reason to take the good-for-the-child as meriting respect? It certainly seems that is the case, and for the same reasons that call for respecting the good of adult project pursuers. The child is identifiable as a distinct individual upon whom one can act for better or ill. True, there is little the child can do to retaliate against those jeopardizing its well-being. But that will also often characterize dealings between project pursuers. Some are weaker and more vulnerable than others, and they will be unable to secure their claims to moral space against the encroachments of those determined to live as predators. Rights are not necessarily self-enforcing. Hobbesian egoists will not be deterred from aggression—except by deterrence. However, contra (the spirit of) Hobbes, the argument of the preceding chapters did not attempt to derive a pacific order from a base of atomistic individuals incapable of motivation from any source other than their own calculated perceptions of self-interest. If others are viewed purely instrumentally as dangerous obstacles to what one wants for oneself, then characteristically moral motivations for action, including respect for rights, could not emerge. Moral conceptions are practical only if the recognition of others as having a good directly motivates one to promote that good.

That is not to say, implausibly, that enforcement is irrelevant to moral activity. Agents with their own ends to pursue will lack sufficient motivation to defer to the ends of others unless such deference is compatible with their own ability to live as project pursuers. If enforcement is intermittent or breaks down entirely, the Law of the Jungle reemerges in all its unpleasantness. (About that, Hobbes is to be *believed!*) One's own projects have *first* call on one's efforts: that is what it is for the projects to be one's own. But they need not have *exclusive* call, and a stable moral order provides the necessary backdrop for hearing and responding to the calls emanating from others.

The weak are not excluded from a regime of rights and, to some extent, weakness will generate especially stringent moral demands. Someone who is unable to secure his or her own good without the constant solicitude of others is one whose welfare entirely depends on their being morally motivated to provide the needed assistance. It is not merely that others must refrain from egregious encroachments so that the weak individual can get along with his activities. Rather, they have to be more like active partners than silent partners, and active partnership entails explicit attention to the requirements of the one unable to fend for himself. It is this kind of consideration that explains why common morality regards as especially despicable injustices visited on those who are most vulnerable: the very old, those mentally or physically infirm, and, of course, small children. They cannot be expected to defend themselves, and so they *must* (a moral "must") be defended by others. Every violation of rights represents a moral failure, but the failure is most pronounced when the victims are those who must be protected by morally motivated others if they are to be protected at all.

It is, then, not merely sentimental regard for the very young that places them within the moral community. They rather assume their proper position there as distinct and identifiable beings with ends that will be expressed in project pursuit. Although that project pursuit has not yet begun, they are numerically identical to the project pursuer that will emerge. A harm to one is a harm to the other.

This may seem to entail paradoxical results. To chop off the left arm of a baby will be accounted a violation of its rights. Mutilation now impedes successful project pursuit later. But to kill the infant will not have that consequence. There will simply *never be* any project pursuer identical to the child that was killed; no being will ever come to have ends that were blocked by that homicidal act. So, in what sense can killing an infant be adjudged a violation of its rights? Not from the perspective of the adult who never is and so cannot be the subject of good or ill, but neither from that of the infant, because its perspective contains no ends to which it has committed itself. Shall we then assert that the aggrieved party is not any *actual* being (child or adult) who is impermissibly harmed, but rather the *potential* project pursuer that never comes into existence because of the killing? That would be to embrace too rich a metaphysical diet. Moral claimancy would be expanded to include not only actual persons but also possible ones. Every sperm and egg that never had the fortune to be united into a zygote and then to grow into adulthood would be the repository of harm done to it. If no actual individual can be identified as the one wronged, then the rights of no one have been violated. Must it therefore be concluded that to injure a child who subsequently becomes a project pursuer is morally impermissible, but that to kill that child is not a rights violation?

No such paradoxical result is indicated. There is an aggrieved party in cases of infanticide, and it is, of course, the child itself. The nature of the harm is that it precludes, totally and irrevocably, all project pursuit by that individual. The activities blocked are prospective, but the being whose activities they are is, at the time of harm, existent. This, then, need not and should not be construed as the infliction of injury on some possible but never-to-be-actualized person. The infant has, during his infancy, an interest in developing into a full-fledged pursuer of projects. He is, admittedly, incapable of *taking an interest* in having a future of a certain sort, but others can recognize that good-for-the-child and act appropriately to protect it.

Is it mysterious to posit the existence of future-directed interests, the blocking of which are accounted as harms, even though the individual in question lacks any such present-directed interests? It can be made to *seem* so by language that bifurcates individuals into person-stages who somehow inherit concerns from each other. But a firm grip on the continued identity over time of persons will prevent the infiltration of metaphysical perplexities. In the case of the infant, one must not be tempted to regard it as numerically distinct from the project pursuer it becomes. For if one does, then it indeed does become enigmatic how the good for some *other* being who may or may not eventually emerge (the adult) can refract back through time to count as establishing that a current harm has been done to this different being, the infant.

It is not only children who can be the subject of this kind of conundrum. Suppose that Betty has a summer home at the shore. On January 5 Alphonse the Arsonist visits it, leaving behind only a pile of smoking cinders. Betty has no interest in living in or otherwise using the house during the winter, but would have been pleasantly enjoying herself on the beach in July had Alphonse not applied the torch. It would be absurd to deny that Betty's interest in the use of the house has been harmed. But the interest of *which* Betty has been infringed: January-Betty, who, by hypothesis, has no current interest in the house, or July-Betty, who does not yet exist? To accept the question in this form is to take the first step down the slippery slope. *Betty* is harmed by the arson when it takes place because she is the selfsame person who would have been enjoying the house six months hence. The interests of July-Betty are the interests of January-Betty in a full and straightforward sense. That would be so even if Betty were psychologically incapable on January 5 of regretting an inconvenience whose effect would not be experienced until July. In that case the harm would not be *felt* (as a harm) until later, and it might not even be felt at all: being a resilient person, she has turned her attentions away from the beach and to the mountains. Nonetheless, to damage the person-she-would-have-been is to damage her; they are the same.[10]

The fact that children do not pursue projects is no bar to their holding rights. But it does affect the shape of the rights they enjoy. For project pursuers, rights are primarily protections against the encroachment of others on the moral space they need in order to advance their own ends. Very young children are incapable of formulating and consistently acting on ends of their own. However, children clearly require far more positive assistance from others than do paradigmatic project pursuers. We are all born naked and defenseless, needing the constant attention of others if we are to survive. Unless the infant is granted this level of care, all the other protections that rights can afford become otiose. Therefore, the rights that can sensibly be recognized in children are the obverse of those in adults. The latter are beneficiaries of noninterference, with rights to positive provision becoming effective only in the event that agents are unable to supply for themselves minimum levels of goods necessary for living as project pursuers, and if no other individual charitably volunteers to make good that lack. For children, though, rights are essentially welfare rights. They need food, shelter, emotional and intellectual stimulation, and they must have these from others. Liberties are beside the point. Freedom from injury *is* a component of their good, but what counts as injury is a function of considerations of the child's long-term welfare. What would be assault if performed on an adult is simply the protection of a rambunctious toddler from himself.

Is it antithetical to the spirit of liberalism to recognize extensive welfare rights in one important class of individuals? The argument of Chapter 5 recognizes liberty as a *sui generis* good for project pursuers. It is needed by all, is needed from all, and is a good which agents cannot supply for themselves but must receive from others. Welfare goods usually have only the first of these three qualities: each individual needs at least a minimum quota of welfare goods to live as a project pursuer, but from where those goods shall come is not determined by the nature of the goods themselves. Because each person has a primary interest in advancing those ends which are *his*, each has reason to supply for himself those welfare goods which are instrumental to success in achieving his own ends. Liberty and welfare goods *are* asymmetrical in rights theory, as classical liberalism recognized. It is only if agents are unable to supply their own welfare goods through cooperative activity, and if no individual or group volunteers the provision of those goods, that the conditional right to minimum levels of subsistence becomes operative.

What can be expected to be atypical for project pursuers is the norm for children. They do not require liberty but must be constant beneficiaries of care from others in order to prosper. Respect for them as distinct rights holders can take no form other than the recognition of what they require as imposing obligations on others. And what children need are welfare goods. If their care were morally optional, usually forthcoming from concerned adults but not demanded from any, then children could be highly regarded accoutrements of the moral community, but they would not be rights holders. Their well-being as prospective project pursuers could be entirely disregarded by anyone who chose to do so. They would then, at most, be instrumental to the ends of others but would not be ends in themselves, loci of moral force that others are not free to ignore.

The Family

A reasonable liberalism will recognize different patterns of rights in children than in adults because children *do* differ in morally relevant respects from paradigmatic adult project pursuers. Children will eventually come to have projects of their own for which they will require noninterference, but they do not have them yet. The wherewithal to achieve that state can be claimed for them as a matter of right. But on whom the onus of providing their support should fail is open to various solutions. It is not necessary that everyone contribute equally or at all to the welfare of the child for that welfare to be realized. It is consonant with respect for children's rights to have primary responsibility for their care localized in some agency less inclusive than the whole society. And, of course, in almost every society past or present of which we have knowledge, the major protectors of children are families.

Explanation of the ubiquity of the family may be attempted by biology, sociology, psychology, or history; it is not uniquely or even primarily a task for moral philosophy. An a priori demonstration of the moral necessity of the family is not credible. Parents can be the primary agency through which most or all of the welfare goods of the child are provided, but alternative social instrumentalities for securing the child's well-being are certainly possible and, to a greater or lesser extent, observable in practice. With respect to children's rights, as elsewhere, the theory of basic rights underdetermines the shape of moral and legal rights. Nonetheless, reflection on the motivational structures that underlie rights-respecting behavior yields certain insights concerning why it may be especially appropriate that primary responsibility for the succor of the child be vested in its parents and, to a lesser extent, in the extended family. At least three considerations merit some attention.

First, it is the progenitive act of the parents that is causally responsible for the existence of the child and so for any weal or woe that falls to it. Causal responsibility is not, in general, identical to moral responsibility, but it is often the precondition for ascribing to an individual moral responsibility for outcomes that eventuate. That someone brought about a particular state of affairs ties that person uniquely to its occurrence. Further attention to whether the agent acted intentionally or unintentionally, wittingly or unwittingly, will precede a full assessment of whether he can be held blameworthy or praiseworthy for what transpired. But even when causal efficacy is unaccompanied by the other conditions necessary for ascription of what we might call *complete moral responsibility,* an agent will not be indifferent to the fact that he is the one who brought about some portentous state of affairs.

Consider someone who is involved in an accident for which he is not at fault, perhaps a motorist who strikes and kills a child who has darted into the road. We will regard it as inappropriate legally to penalize the driver, and properly so, but we would also see some impropriety in the driver being totally unmoved by the fact that *he* was the one behind the wheel when the accident occurred. A fitting emotional reaction will incorporate regret, and not simply the generalized regret that anyone might feel at the loss of life, but grief at being the one who struck the child and caused its death. We will attempt to console the driver, urge him not to punish himself, and so on, but we would not suggest that the driver rationally ought to be detached from the fact that it was he who killed the child. It is equally the case that one who has brought about some momentous good can appropriately take delight in that fact, regard the production of the good as also being a good-for-him, even though the serendipitous result was unforeseen and unintended.

Greek tragedy often revolves around causal responsibility divorced from foresight or intention. The protagonist is enmeshed in a sequence of events which redounds to his doom although he lacks complete moral responsibility for their occurrence. Oedipus is pitiable because he kills his father and sleeps with his mother although he intends no such results. Even if there exists some flaw in his character which leads to the denouement, Oedipus' tragedy lies not there but in what he has caused to transpire.

These reactions should not be dismissed as irrational. That brought about through one's own actions is imprinted with one's agency. It is through causing things to happen that persons have a bearing on the world, in a sense make the world their own. Because agents have a stake in molding outer reality to the form of inner commitment, they will naturally come to regard what they have caused to obtain as having a special claim on their attention. To be sure, the connection is tighter when one has deliberately and intentionally produced an outcome, but bare causal responsibility itself establishes a metaphysical relation whose affective corollary is distinctive attachment to that which is one's own product.

Producing children makes them one's own. That is so whether or not conception of the child was desired and intended. No other individuals stand toward it in the same causal relation as the parents. The good of the child may be recognized by anyone as calling out for some appropriate response, but that there exists any good-for-the-child at all is the parents' responsibility. If it is mandatory that someone provide welfare goods for the child, the parents are the natural candidates to do so.

A second consideration is that having children is often an integral component of persons' projects. Liberalism dictates official neutrality among the projects to which individuals might come to commit themselves, but a polity can be liberal and yet recognize that patterns of attachment widespread within the community create a legitimate demand for the creation of social structures within which these attachments can achieve fitting expression. For many individuals, the attachments that are most forceful and ripe with meaning are not to abstract ideas or to artifacts of one's creation or to large-scale social and political movements but to particular persons. Love for another makes that person's good one's own. Friendship expands the domain of that which is valued for its own sake and holds out prospects of worthwhile activity on behalf of the friend. And having children in whom one invests one's devotion is to undertake a commitment that spans generations and creates personal value for the parent that transcends his or her own span of life. Whether from inarticulate biological promptings or from rational reflection, the urge to create a family is remarkably constant over times and places of human activity. Few people can expect to produce a literary or artistic monument, redirect the life of a nation, garner honor and glory that lives after them. But it is open to almost everyone to stake a claim to long-term significance through having and raising a child. (And not being able to conceive a child is often regarded as a personal tragedy.) Clearly, this opportunity is much prized. Vesting primary responsibility for care of the child in its parents and, secondarily, in the extended family is a rational social response to this characteristic human urge.

Third, regard for someone as a rights holder is grounded in the recognizability of that being as a distinct individual. It is not *personhood* which calls for respect but rather distinct persons. Between these two conceptions there is a sharp divide, one separating an ethic in which individualism is valued from an ethic subscribing entirely to an impersonal standard of value. An abstract ideal requiring the enhancement of personhood or humanity as a whole could, with justification, dictate sacrificing one individual for the sake of the collectivity. People would be cogs in the vast machine, components of the End to be Advanced and not Ends in Themselves. An epistemological prerequisite for valuing particular persons is the ability to identify and reidentify them as distinct individuals. That is, A can recognize and respond to value-for-B only if A is able to pick out the distinct individual that is B. And when A does so over time, A is not identifying numerically distinct person-stages that are assigned the ambiguous name 'B' but is rather responding to a person with a continuous history. The possibility of ongoing social relations with individuals who are perceived to be self-identical over time is a necessary foundation for according them rights. Of course, it need not be the case that A have persistent contact with or even any contact at all to be motivated to regard B as someone with rights. The point is instead that B must be *capable* of being recognized over time as the selfsame being in order to be taken as a repository of personal value in whom rights reside.

An extension of the point is that the establishment of networks of social relationships among persons provides the raw material from which moral community is fashioned. We are able to be motivated by the value resident in distinct persons because they stand to us in relations that mark them off from other persons, relations that provide distinguishing characteristics by means of which each is recognized as *this* particular being. Intimate association provides the firmest possible epistemological basis for appreciation of individuality. For most of us, it is within the family that the earliest and also the most enduring patterns of intimate association are established. The newborn child is not merely *some* anonymous potential project pursuer but, to its parents, is a human being eminently distinguishable from all others. Anyone born into a family is, from the beginning, enmeshed in at least one associational network that socially constitutes it as a distinct, identifiable individual. As the child matures, the range of associations in which it is a part will also grow. Moral community is, we might say, the product of the complex and multiply overlapping relationships in which persons stand to each other and are recognized as distinct individuals. The seedbed of this community is the family.

Again, this should not be taken as an a priori demonstration of the moral obligatoriness of family structures. Surely one can imaginatively construct alternative devices for the protection and socialization of children. This task will hold special appeal to those who wish to promote some radically revised moral order in which the ties that uniquely bind near kin are replaced by others more to the reformer's vision. The *locus classicus* of such moral engineering is Plato's design for communal incubation of future Guardians in *Republic V*. It is even possible that the design will actually succeed in creating institutions through which persons come to be regarded by others as valuable in their distinctness. Possible but not terribly likely; unintended and undesired consequences of innovation frequently dominate those that were sought.

Opposition to the family and attempts to replace it are not, however, usually prompted by the desire to invent a more efficient device through which personal value might come to be recognized. Would-be reconstructors of the social order are typically inspired by a vision of the Good, the True, and the Beautiful. They are in thrall to value, but it is thoroughly *impersonal* value. Grand utopian designs leave little room for particular attachments and idiosyncratic projects; these merely get in the way of the overarching goal. One devoted to his own controlling ends and to specially valued persons as repositories of those ends is less suitable putty to be molded for the sake of an externally imposed conception of the good. For impersonal value to be enthroned, personal value must go—and with it the family as a fount of distinctive attachment to particular others.

If the above seems too speculative, confirmation can be secured by examining the acts and tracts of archetypal creators of The New Moral Order. From Plato to Mao to the Reverend Moon, they have attempted to relocate primary loyalties from the home to the collective enterprise.[11] Whether or not the family is strictly necessary as the foundation for a liberal, individualistic order, it is palpably clear that attacks on the family typically bespeak antagonism to liberal diversity. By no means do strong and persistent family structures guarantee the flourishing of a liberal order; commitment to the individual value of persons within the family can be accompanied by general disregard for individuality outside of it. But in the absence of the family as a nucleus of recognition patterns, it is unlikely that there is much hope for a rights-respecting moral community.

If the preceding observations are valid, why is it that liberal theorists have little to say about the moral significance of families? To take two outstanding contemporary examples, John Rawls' *A Theory of Justices* and Robert Nozick's *Anarchy, State, and Utopia* barely advert to familial ties. Rawls invokes familial relationships as a device to deal with the problem of principles of justice across generations, and for Nozick the affectional ties that hold between parents and children are treated as preferences among other preferences that individuals are at liberty to act on in a liberal order. In neither case is the family of central moral concern. By way of contrast, the *individual actor*, the *polity*, and the demands they may or may not place on each other receive constant attention. Such fixation on microanalysis and macroanalysis, with intermediate structures receiving only passing concern, is typical of contemporary moral theory[12] and has characterized most work on rights since Hobbes.

A theory of rights (or, more generally, of moral standing) that is both *internalist* and *univalent* will find children and the family inconvenient subjects. For such a theory, if children have rights at all, then they do so for the same reason that adults have rights. Exactly what this reason might be is best left unspecified, though theorists may glide over analytical difficulties by speaking of *human* rights, thus implying that the domain over which basic rights are enjoyed is, in some unproblematic way, the class of all biologically human beings. If one refrains from probing too deeply into how this might be justified,[13] one can move briskly ahead to develop implications concerning the normative requirements of a just political order. Individuals—almost exclusively normal, unimpaired adults—are featured as the bearers of rights; the state is featured as the vehicle by means of which rights are enforced. It may be recognized that persons form families, but that is not a morally fecund fact.

Nozick, as has often been noted, begins with rights bearers already on the scene. Presumably, children are included. But why it is that either adults or children have the rights that he claims on their behalf is nowhere clarified. They may (and, if acting as rational maximizers, will) form states, and these states may (but probably won't) respect the rights that were on stage when the curtain opened. How these *dramatis personae* may permissibly interact is the theme of the remainder of the story. Rawls devotes far more attention to foundational concerns. From an Original Position of starkly limited individuating information, parties contract to recognize two principles of justice that define the rights of all. Once the two principles are established, individuals emerge from behind the veil of ignorance and engage in political activity that must be in accord with the previously derived requirements of justice. The rights-generating process that goes on in the Original Position does not, of course, invoke familial ties, because the Rawlsian contractors are hypothesized as being without any social relations whatsoever, and even without any attachments to ends that they can recognize as their own. When persons emerge from behind the veil, many will discover that they hold attachments to family members and, within the requirements of justice, they are at liberty to advance the welfare of kin. The Rawlsian state recognizes that liberty right, but *familial or other social relations play no part at all in the grounding of rights.*

Rawls and Nozick are, as best one can ascertain from their work, committed to rights that are internalist and univalent. They invoke as guiding lights from the past, respectively, Kant and Locke. It is unsurprising that a Kantian theory hold to an unswerving view of moral status as vested in rational agency. Locke, though, pays rather more attention to the peculiar status of children than do most other liberal theorists. However, Locke's concern is addressed to the question of when children can claim emancipation from parental control, not to how children can reasonably be considered rights holders during their childhood.[14] Children's rights rest on precisely the same ground as those of adults: creation by a God who endows them with rights. What needs to be settled is only the practical question of when individuals can be deemed to have come to such an age as to make the exercise of their God-given rights feasible. Nozick does not take up Locke's theological grounding of rights, but neither does he offer any substitute. (Where he touches on foundational issues, it is Kant rather than Locke who comes to the fore. See *Anarchy, State, and Utopia*, pp. 48–51.)

Children and the family take on particular moral significance when univalent internalism is abandoned. Project pursuers have rights, but so too do beings who are not yet (or once were: see Chapter 8) project pursuers. That is because they are related to actual project pursuers in bonds of recognition that make their good a concern for others. Families are central to the moral domain because it is within the family that these bonds are initiated. Respect within the family for the individuality of each of its members is the precursor of a rights-regarding moral community. That is not to say that the social order is or can be the family writ large. The special ties among parent and child, sibling and sibling, set apart particular others as objects of *focused* concern, while the undifferentiated relation of citizen to citizen entails no particularized regard. However, the person whose concerns are not my concerns, who is a stranger to me, is yet someone whom I can recognize as being enmeshed in *some* networks of particularized affection with other persons who in turn are socially bound to yet others who . . . when taken together make up the moral community of which I too am part. New human beings are enrolled in this overlapping system of social relations through becoming an object of focused concern to some prior members. In the vast majority of cases, and not merely due to some cultural accident, the initiation occurs within families.

Children, Families, and the State

That the *primary* responsibility for the nurturing of the child ought to reside within the family does not, however, entail that *exclusive* responsibility lies therein. The rights of the child impose correlative obligations on everyone, at least in the negative sense of not doing damage to a potential generator of personal value. Just as no one may assault or kill an adult, no one may assault or kill a child. But general obligations to children go beyond the avoidance of doing them harm. There are also positive performances that can be claimed for the child as a matter of right. The exact form they will take in any given setting is a function of particular circumstances and can differ widely among cultures. They can, though, at a level of considerable abstraction, be divided into two major subareas: obligatory action on behalf of families so that parents can reasonably expect to be able to function as primary providers, and obligations to undertake direct support of children when families are unable to assume that responsibility.

It should not be assumed that action in support of the family must involve positive provision, such as welfare payments to augment the resources of indigent parents. While welfare payments may be called for as a matter of right in unusual circumstances, the characteristic form taken by rights affecting the family is, as with other liberal rights, negative. What parents can demand from all others is a generous quantity of noninterference. It is an infringement of the legitimate claims of parents when either private individuals or agencies of the state intrude on parental liberties to transfer resources to children, educate them in a manner deemed suitable, inculcate religious or moral principles, choose a place of residence for the family, or to engage in other, similar practices with respect to the child's upbringing.

Does that mean that parents enjoy complete *carte blanche* in their relations to their own children? No such conclusion is supportable. It is one thing to assert that parents properly should be afforded wide discretion in pursuing their own conception of what will advance the child's good, quite another to maintain that this discretion is unlimited. Families do not enjoy some mystical status that renders them untouchable; it is, in the first instance, concern for the child's good and who is best situated to act to attain it that underlies the privileged status of the family. Parents no more than anyone else are at liberty to inflict harms on the child. Political institutions are certainly entitled to prohibit flatly abusive treatment and to enforce vigorously those laws protecting children.

There can be legitimate differences of opinion concerning what counts as action directly inimical to the welfare of the child and thus prohibitable in spite of the parents' wishes. Such questions cannot be settled in advance by philosophical analysis. They await empirical determinations and will properly be dealt with differently by different polities. What the theory of basic rights can tell us is that legal structures bearing on the parent-child relation must be framed with the idea of guaranteeing to the child the opportunity to realize *some* good, not with the aim of extending a social imprimatur to one particular pattern of upbringing. For example, laws requiring that infants be secured in child restraint seats while being transported in automobiles are a reasonable exercise of state powers. Hurtling through a windshield at forty miles per hour can prove remarkably dampening to all one's prospects of future project pursuit. Although requiring parents to purchase and use a child restraint seat ties up resources that they might have wished to use for some other, more highly valued purpose, the amount is small.

On the other hand, an outright prohibition on driving with children would be excessive. Even if risk to the child were thereby lowered, it would be at the cost of extensive interference with the ability of the family to give effect to its preferred way of life. For somewhat different reasons, a requirement that all children be given at least three years of violin lessons would be an illegitimate encroachment of the state into the private domain. It may well be arguable that almost all children are benefited by an early and prolonged introduction to music, but that does not suffice to justify mandating such provision. That is in part because the opportunity cost of violin lessons is considerable and, even more important, because deprivation of musical education does not seriously impinge on the child's prospective ability to live as a successful project pursuer. Obviously it renders certain projects less likely of attainment, but no one has a claim to be afforded the means to become a concert violinist, however splendid such an outcome might be.

Consider a genuinely difficult case. Laws requiring that children be inoculated against dangerous infectious diseases stand on a generally firm foundation. In the vast majority of cases their enforcement will provide substantial benefit to the child while negligibly impinging on parents' ability to direct the child's upbringing. However, for some people the stakes will be considerably higher. Their religious beliefs prohibit such medical intervention, and the liberty to act in accord with their religious lights is a chief component of the good for them. Should inoculation of children be compulsory in such circumstances? Idealogues of one stripe or another will be quick to answer, but the rest of us will find the problem perplexing. (This is perhaps a case in which the sensitive legislator will take a *very* hard look at data such as morbidity statistics before offering a considered judgment.) What should be noted, though, is *why* this rests uneasily at the borderline of permissible state intrusions. On the one side, there exists a risk of severe harm to the child's ability ever to attain the status of project pursuer. On the other side lie projects that will be severely compromised by governmental intrusion. It is too much to hope that events will be so kind as never to throw up this kind of dilemma or that studied casuistry will always unravel these tangles smoothly. However, attention to the principles *on both sides* that generate moral conundrums will yield whatever degree of harmony is attainable between the general requirements of civil society and the private agendas of families.

When the child's welfare requirements can be met in several alternative ways, it is *prima facie* suspect for the state to mandate one particular path or to place substantial stumbling blocks in front of all but one. Even if officials believe, with some justification, that one option is preferable to another, they are not entitled to impose their preferences on families. To put it slightly differently, it may not permissibly be required of parents that they provide their children with the *best* upbringing that can be afforded them (as determined by whomever is currently enthroned in the seat of expertise), only that the upbringing be *adequate* to prepare the child to live as an independent project pursuer. For if some particular standard of the proper exercise of parental authority is given official sanction, personal value is crushed. A socially imposed impersonal standard of value impermissibly coerces those who see their ends lying elsewhere.

It follows that a state-established system of primary education raises serious issues of improper encroachment. It does so in two ways. First, through setting norms of school attendance incumbent on all, the state removes from the domain of private decision judgments concerning the extent of schooling that one's child should have. (I deliberately speak of "schooling" rather than "education" to emphasize the obvious but often elided point that governmental regulation can bring about the presence of young bodies in the classroom with far greater assurance than it can any subsequent inculcation of knowledge.) This is a real cost even if it is believed that among the welfare goods children require to develop as independent project pursuers is a minimum level of basic education. For example, if the avoidance of too much "worldliness" is a component of the projects of a family, mandatory school attendance will be a threat. There is, therefore, a strong presumption against any official requirement of school attendance. The presumption can be overridden by a social determination that education is a crucial requisite of successful living as a project pursuer, but the onus is on the side of those favoring coercive interference with family determinations. Also, the greater the term of school attendance required, the more dubious become prospects of justification. It may be true that more education is (usually) better than less, but what is *better* for the child is not the same as what is *needed*. Only judgments of the latter sort suffice to support coercive enforcement.

Second, even to the extent that state-mandated school attendance can be justified, it does not follow that the state rightfully can require or differentially encourage attendance in state-sponsored schools. Education lacks qualities of nonrivalry and nonexcludability that would make it a public good. It therefore is amenable to supply either via the market or through political undertakings. Thus, were it otherwise a matter of indifference whether schools are to be private or public enterprises, there is a presumption in favor of the former.

But it is *not* otherwise a matter of indifference. If education is monopolized by the state, then the manner in which it is supplied will be determined through political processes and be imposed on all consumers. They will be faced with a "take it or leave it" choice (or, if school attendance is mandatory, a "take it or take it" choice). Public monopolies may or may not tend to be as predatory as private monopolies, but they are equally inimical to consumer choice. The maintenance of a liberal order is incompatible with imposed homogeneity. If a state education monopoly produces a product that is not uniformly desired by all citizens, then it quite directly impinges on their freedom to secure desired goods through voluntary exchange. (And if the product is, quite implausibly, universally desired, then state provision would *still* be unjustified because that variety of educational services would also have been demanded and supplied on the market.)

In the real world it is obviously the case that no one educational package satisfies all. Views differ both as to *what* ought to be taught and *how* it should be taught. Will discipline resemble that of a Marine boot camp or a Woodstock love-in? Should the study of human sexuality be a component of the curriculum, and, if so, from what perspective should it be taught? Are secular studies to be mixed with religious devotions? Should values be explicitly taught, implicitly shape the form in which instruction is given, or excluded to the maximum possible extent—and *whose* values should be included/excluded? Is it the job of the school to inculcate patriotism (jingoism)? Will textbooks be scrutinized for tinges of racism, sexism, ageism, socialism, secular humanism, or whatever else may be the prevailing bogey? These and numerous other questions of pedagogy necessarily confront the formulator of educational policy. They cannot be ducked; in one way or another they will be decided, even if through inadvertance. The issues at stake are not trivial and, predictably, some individuals will be pleased and others outraged. If diversity of educational services is disallowed, then citizens face two alternatives: coerce or be coerced. Educational elites and others who exercise disproportionate political influence will tend to have their own preferences written into public policy. But even if decisions concerning what is to be taught, by whom, and how are made entirely democratically, the result is the dispossession of minorities by the majority.

This outcome is thoroughly unjustifiable—and avoidable. How one's children are to be educated is likely to matter very much to parents. A liberal society will lend maximal effect to parental desires by avoiding curtailment of choice. Each family should, as a matter of basic rights, be at liberty to secure through market transactions the sort of educational package that it prefers and that educational entrepreneurs can be induced to provide. If it is judged that the financial means available to some families are insufficient to allow them to provide a minimally adequate education for their children, and if private eleemosynary institutions will not or cannot supplement their resources, then it is preferable that the state provide parents with the *means* to secure the education of their own children rather than usurp parental discretion by direct provision of educational services. Either cash grants or vouchers exchangeable for educational services can be utilized to this end. While payments are made *to* the parents, they are *for* the child, and are in response to the child's right to the positive provision of needed welfare goods.[15]

It may be objected that just as the state system of public education might leave some consumers dissatisfied, so too might alternatives available in the market. A family of freethinkers may live in an area in which the only primary schooling is provided by Evangelical Christians. An adherent to the tenets of classical liberalism may find, to his chagrin, that the only teachers offering their wares at a price he can afford are socialists. Each will find it impossible to provide the child with the sort of education that is maximally desired, even with an education that is judged remotely satisfactory. Therefore, the objection concludes, market provision of educational services no more guarantees that individual preferences will be satisfied than does supply through governmental institutions.

The objection misfires, and does so on several grounds. First, while market arrangements do not *ensure* that there will be diversity of offerings, at least they do not *preclude* diversity. Second, if there does exist strong demand for a certain kind of educational program as expressed by the willingness of consumers to pay for it, then there is a direct financial inducement for purveyors of educational services to supply it. The stronger the demand, the greater the incentive. Democratic political determinations are also sensitive to the demands of the electorate, but with a difference. It is the desires of *majorities* (or of diverse interest groups that can be forged into a majority) that motivate politicians in a democracy to supply a collective good. And since each citizen has one and only one vote, majoritarian determinations are insensitive to the *strength* of citizens' preferences. Thus, there is a much greater tendency for minority educational preferences to be satisfied through market exchange than through political processes.

Third, and most important, even when product availability on the market is judged unsatisfactory by a consumer, that does not represent an infringement of liberty. If one wishes to secure for one's child an education that emphasizes the classics and petroleum geology, teachers all of whom are Methodist Swarthmore graduates between the ages of thirty and forty-seven, and at a school no more than ten miles distant from one's home, it is likely that the search will be no more successful than Ponce de León's. But that such a preference remains unsatisfied in no way goes to show that liberty is compromised. The individual is free to contract with others on whatever terms to which he is able to persuade them to agree. If no entrepreneur will agree to supply the requisite number of Swarthmore Methodists at the maximum price the consumer is willing to pay, that is a corresponding exercise of *their* liberty. *Liberty* to secure some good G should not be confused with the *ability* or *power* to get G or with the *sufficient conditions* for securing G. Coercive hindrance of voluntary cooperative activity does violate liberty, though, and that is what the state does when it erects a privileged system of education. So, although neither market provision nor political provision ensures satisfaction for all, the market affords liberty to enter into satisfactory contractual arrangements while politics does not.

A second objection: it may be conceded that mandating attendance of all children in state-sponsored schools violates the rights of parents. But neither the United States nor other Western democracies places such a demand on citizens. Rather, political institutions supply schools, but so, too, do private parties. (These non-state schools may even receive subsidies from public coffers.) Parents can choose to avail themselves of public education or else contract with privately run schools. Doing the latter will usually involve greater expense, but it is nonetheless an option that persons are at liberty to select for their children. Thus, it is incorrect to speak of a state *monopoly* on primary education or to allege that there is an impermissible restriction on the *liberty* of persons to secure alternative educational services.

It is true that supplying public schools while allowing private schools also to operate is a lesser restriction of liberty than would be supplying schools while simultaneously forbidding all others to do so. But it is by no means innocent. If the state secured its resources entirely through the contributions of a grateful citizenry, or if state enterprises earned their own way in free and fair competition with other would-be providers, then the existence of government-run schools would be innocuous from the perspective of liberty (though its economic rationale would be mysterious). But, of course, public education does not work that way. It is funded through tax money and afforded other legal advantages not similarly available to private schools. (Land on which schools are built can be acquired through eminent domain; private schools can be required to provide instructional programs equivalent to those of state schools; etc.) Thus, the state does not exercise studied neutrality among the myriad possible alternative modes of education.

Suppose that individuals were free to join and worship in the church of their choice, but that, alongside the various private religious denominations, there was one officially recognized by the state as the Public Church System (perhaps justified on the grounds that its services would, unlike the others, be made available equally to rich and poor at no direct cost). All are taxed to erect Public Church buildings in every community, pay the salaries of Public Church ministers, deacons, janitors, groundskeepers, and accountants, purchase vestments, provide bus transportation to daily services, sponsor Public Church softball teams and Theological Disputation clubs, buy picnic tables for Public Church socials, and otherwise endow various Public Church programs. Those of other religious persuasions may provide alternative religious services, but they will have to do so with the resources that remain to them after paying their full share to fund the Public Church. Would this arrangement be consonant with liberal freedom of religion?

In fact, the analogy does not go far enough. Suppose additionally that people were not at liberty to participate in some religion or none but were legally required to join a church. They could either join the Public Church at no cost (beyond what is already extracted through taxation) or join some other church, at additional expense. Suppose also that each nonestablished church had only limited discretion to set its own ritual and dogma because it had to comply with requirements issued by State Boards of Transcendental Illumination, all of whose appointed officials were communicants of the Public Church. Anyone who believes that individuals are morally entitled to untrammeled exercise of religious freedom will find the scenario uncongenial and will regard as grotesque parody any claim that it represents the enshrinement of religious freedom. On what basis, then, can the equivalent hamstringing of individuals' ability to educate their children as they see fit be regarded as consistent with liberal basic rights?

The familiarity of state-sponsored systems of public education should not be allowed to disguise their basically illiberal cast. Although it is true that schooling in the United States and other Western democracies has not usually been subverted to blatantly propagandistic ends as it often has in severely authoritarian societies, the potential for gross abuse is there. More directly to the point, the *actuality* of conformity imposed from above is scarcely deniable.

Only a privatized educational regime that makes way for diversity is consistent with respect for liberal pluralism. But may the state properly require minimal standards of curricular adequacy for schools? In theory, the answer seems to be yes. If children need education to develop as project pursuers, then they need *adequate* education, and the state can demand it on their behalf. But the theoretical propriety of mandatory standards does not translate unproblematically into a political imperative. First, it must be shown that suggested standards are objectively justified by the interest of the child as a prospective project pursuer and are not instead covertly intended to favor certain classes of projects over others. Second, even if there does exist an objective basis for formulating neutral educational standards, what is the assurance that governmental agencies will issue edicts on that basis rather than on more quotidian political grounds? That impartiality is *possible* does not make it *likely*. Third, before calling for a governmental solution, it should be demonstrated that there is indeed a problem. Do we have reason to believe that parents are generally indifferent to the quality of their children's education? That they are inept consumers of educational wares? Even if parents will *sometimes* do a poor job of securing educational services for their children, is it reasonable to believe that governmental bureaucracies will do so outstandingly *better* that coercive enforcement of standards becomes indicated? There does not exist a track record of parental choice in a totally free educational market to engender either confidence or caution, but we *do* have information on how well public schools have fared in upholding rigorous standards. The record is . . . mixed. If the alternatives available were vesting choice in fallible parents or in an omniscient and perfectly benevolent governmental bureaucracy, the case for coercion would be easy— or, at least, easier. But, of course, *both* are fallible, *both* occasionally evince malice, bigotry, and ignorance. A chief difference between them, though, is that when the state fails, it imposes that failure on everyone. Mandatory state educational standards pose threats to the rights of children and families; so, too, does the absence of such standards. Between the two, the former will usually be the greater threat.

The foregoing excursus on state-sponsored primary education is intended to afford descriptive content to the assertion that there exists a general obligation to refrain from interference with parental provision of welfare goods to children. It also mentioned in passing direct state provision of the means to obtain welfare goods—educational vouchers—when the family is unable to secure welfare goods for the child with its own resources. This acknowledgment of the legitimacy of *some* compulsory transfer of wealth among persons is not an abandonment of classical liberalism. Note that:

1. The obligations on others to respect the family's privileged status with respect to the child are, for the most part, negative. Neither private parties nor state institutions may act so as to interfere with parents' ability to provide as they see fit for their own children unless parental action or inaction threatens the basic right of the child to an upbringing that will fit him to develop as a project pursuer.

2. Positive obligations toward the child entirely rest, in the first instance, on the parents. They *must* provide for the child if they are able to do so. Duties of provision devolve to those outside the family only if it is the case that parents are unable (not "unwilling") to supply minimally adequate welfare for the child and if no private party voluntarily agrees to supplement the family's resources through charitable contributions. That is, all general positive obligations are conditional, and there is no good reason to believe that they will regularly come into play.

What of families that fail to provide adequate support for the child although able to do so? It was argued previously that having and raising children is, for many individuals, a vital component of their projects. All have an obligation not to impede the success of such projects. Nonetheless, it rests on project pursuers themselves to undertake actions in their powers to realize the ends to which they commit themselves. If raising a child is one of those ends, then the responsibility is theirs to supply to whatever extent they are able the conditions necessary for its achievement. No one else is obligated to carry this particular burden for them.

Two different rights claims must be distinguished. The first is the claim of the child to necessary welfare goods; the second is the claim of parents to be allowed the opportunity to establish families. The former is not canceled by improvident parental actions, and the latter is not untouchable. The desire to raise children is one project among many to which individuals come to commit themselves, and they may no more enlist unwilling others in its service than they can in alternative pursuits. Parents have first claim to direct the upbringing of their children; but should they neglect to tend to the child's welfare, then they have, through their own actions, forfeited that claim. Biological family units are not sacrosanct within the theory of basic rights, and children are not material possessions to be used or discarded as the "owner" sees fit. If others are willing and able to provide for the child those goods that its parents are not, then the responsibility for the child's upbringing is justifiably transferable to them. The child's rights take pride of place; the rights of parents to form families are dependent. Only insofar as parents adequately provide for their children do they retain a continuing right to direct their upbringing.

General obligations of direct support are thus genuine—but sharply limited. They extend only to that which parents are unable to supply. Also, provision extends only to that which is minimally adequate to ensure the child opportunity to develop as an independent project pursuer. There is no general social duty to ensure to each child resources more or less equivalent to those enjoyed by all other children. It may be generally beneficial to the child to have a home computer or six weeks at summer camp, but there is no social duty that these be supplied to each child. (Nor is there any bar to the charitable provision of these by philanthroically inclined private parties.)

"Everyone should have an equal place on the starting line!" Yes—if it's a race that's being run. But the metaphor is thoroughly inapposite. A race features a course that all competitors must run and is zero-sum: if A wins, then B does not. Liberal rights theory *denies* that there is any one Grand Racetrack on which we are all necessarily bidden to run, *denies* that there is a Social Referee duly authorized to place all the participants in their proper starting positions, *denies* that outcomes are zero-sum. Rather, individuals assume for themselves the course they elect to run and take charge of providing for themselves the resources they require. Because projects are infinitely various, A's success does not necessarily entail B's failure. Both may succeed on their own terms—or both may fail. All that one can claim as a matter of right are minimally adequate conditions to live as a project pursuer, including, most importantly, noninterference.[16]

Upbringing and Autonomy

Material well-being is not the only, or even the most significant, requisite for development into a project pursuer. The ability to direct one's efforts toward certain ends that one has assumed as one's own and to value achievable outcomes in terms of the commitments that are central to one's identity as an active being are the essence of project pursuit. One who is psychologically debilitated, unable to form long-term attachments to ends that are distinctively his own, is thereby rendered unfit to live as a project pursuer.

This suggests that there is at least a latent tension between the desire of parents to further *their* own projects and the value for the child of developing as an individual able to pursue *his* own ends. Few parents will consider it a glorious success to have produced after years of upbringing an adult *tabula rasa*. Rather, their efforts will characteristically incorporate attempts to instill in the child a preferred volitional makeup: religious beliefs of a certain sort, abiding loyalties to kin and country, political convictions, moral codes, love of knowledge (or love of athletic prowess, or love of entrepreneurial zeal, or . . .), and a host of other attitudes, dispositions, and beliefs. The potentiality for conflict is apparent. The more successful the parents are in molding the child to their own preferred pattern, the less scope there is for the child to strike out in a direction that he has autonomously chosen.

Suppose that a group of adults goes off into the wilderness to establish a community where they can be true to the Word of their God. Years go by and children are born to them. The new generation is sedulously raised to be witnesses to this Word. Corrupting influences such as cinemas, saloons, the collected works of the Marquis de Sade, philosophy departments, automobiles and MasterCards are not permitted within the environs of the community. The children hear one voice and learn to intone it themselves. In due course they come to represent with full fidelity the beliefs and attitudes of their forebears. Children are then born to them, and the process of inculcation is repeated.

Is this a morally permissible scenario? If we say that it is not, we thereby deny to this community of faith entitlement to give effect to that which most profoundly matters to them. Even if *we* believe that they are doing damage to their children, *they* assuredly do not. Rather, they believe that those children are being provided a maximally uplifting and rewarding life. Nothing is being imposed on the young that their seniors have not fully and voluntarily assumed for themselves. By what right can our conception of personal value impose itself on others who view things dramatically differently? On the other hand, if the community is left entirely free to follow its own lights, are they not being granted *carte blanche* to turn out evaluational clones of themselves, beings who lack the vital freedom of self-determination?[17]

It is important to be clear about what is *not* at stake here. First, this does not represent a quandary about determinism. If the thesis of causal determinism is true, then *all* persons are products of external influences acting on them. Whether one's upbringing is lax or strict, pluralistic or single-minded, it is one of the causal contributants that make one what one becomes. Some causal effects are deliberately aimed at and achieved, while others are unintended and unpredicted. All, though, partake of the same causal necessity. If there is some special moral problem attached to the scenario sketched out above, it is not a function of general determinism. That is not to deny that the truth or falsity of causal determinism matters in some way for moral theory. It is instead to affirm that *how* outcomes are caused also matters.

Second, it is important to avoid being taken in by an ideal of *autonomy* as the exercise of choice completely unconditioned by any factor external to one's faculty of practical reason. It would be hard to overstate the importance that contemporary moral philosophy assigns to autonomy, both within the Anglo-American analytic tradition and in Continental philosophy. Each is rooted in nineteenth-century Romanticism's attraction to complete and unconstrained self-realization and, ultimately, in the moral psychology of Kant. But, as has been noted more than once above, Kantian moral choice is not exercised by persons enmeshed in the tugs and pulls of the ordinary world around them but by pure noumenal egos whose volitions transcend causal determination. When the Kantian metaphysic is stripped away (and perhaps even when it is not), nothing can be made of the idea of totally unconditioned choice. Instead, the ideal of autonomy is, more often than not, covertly used to oppose influences that the *theorist* happens to disfavor. Marxists find the constraints of capitalistic means of production fearfully inimical to the realization of the autonomous self; atheists express disdain for the lockstep mentality of believers. Each professes an idealogy that will burst the chains asunder.

In Chapter 3 a contrast was offered between *autonomy* as an ideal and the personal value inherent in living as an *independent project pursuer*. It was argued there that autonomy, in its extreme form, is not a necessary condition for being a project pursuer, is very likely not possible of attainment at all, and is not worth having even if it is attainable. A project pursuer is not a *Luftmensch,* motivationally dissassociated from all conditions not of his own making. I shall not repeat those arguments here but rather assume that if children born into the religious commune are impermissibly harmed, it is through being rendered unable to pursue projects of their own and not because their autonomy is infringed in some other way.

The theoretical issue that has been broached is extraordinarily thorny. For that reason, we might well be thankful that human nature is obdurate. Children persist in turning out differently than their parents intended and predicted. From Plato to B. F. Skinner, designs for fashioning young lives according to blueprint have persistently foundered. Not totally, of course, but strategies of rearing the young confront enough uncertainty and intractability within the raw material to make the art of parenting a continuing adventure.

Still, the theoretical question remains. And it is not entirely theoretical. Even if the technology of molding children has not (yet?) been perfected, it would be foolish to deny that intense efforts to shape the young are often consequential. Groups such as the Amish enjoy considerable success in walling themselves off for generation upon generation from the intrusions of the modernity that surrounds them. In providing for their own continuity as a distinctive way of life, are they ceding their wills and those of their children to the visions of a defunct dreamer?

There are two importantly different ways in which one can be involved in projects. One can act for the sake of one's *own* projects or be dispatched to work for the projects of *another.* The slave acts to advance projects, but he does so under compulsion to secure ends that are not his own. That is what it is to be a slave. The obsequious or servile person is not under compulsion and so is not a slave. He is, nonetheless, slavish. That is because the ends he (voluntarily) acts on are not his own. They are picked up from others as one might piece together a wardrobe from the Salvation Army store.

The thought needs to be made more precise. There is a sense in which the servile person *does* act on his own ends. Though not originally of his own conception, the ends become his when he recognizes them as calling for his own attention because they have been adopted by someone else. But that is not sufficient to explain what constitutes servility or why servility is a vice. For we all inherit ends from others and, contra the fervent champions of autonomy, it is good that we do so. Were that not the case, we would find our way barred to the formation of projects that essentially make the good of another a component of one's own good. And, as was formerly argued, the ability to be motivated by the personal value of others is a necessary condition for moral community. A regime of rights would otherwise be unattainable.

So the servile person is not servile because he takes some of his volitional bearings from others. Rather, it is *excessive* fealty to the pursuits of others that is vicious. But clarifying what is meant by 'excessive' is what is at issue. To hold that servility is a vice does not commit one to the proposition that selfishness is a virtue.[18] Altruism of almost any degree is thoroughly compatible with being one's own man or woman, with being no one's lackey. At least that is true of *principled* altruism: concern and activity for the sake of (some) others that is motivated by a firm and abiding conception of the value that inheres in them. Altruism of this sort is the *confident* expression of a self that is fully formed and guided by its own standard of personal value. Rather than being demeaning, it is admirable.

The servile man is not admirable. We do not recognize in him principled commitment to valuational standards that impel him to recognize and advance value in others. Rather, he is one who takes on the ends of others because he has none of his own. This trait can hardly be confused with altruism; the servile individual is just as prone to find himself saddled with inherited misanthropic beliefs and attitudes as with any others. As much as anyone can be who is not subject to coercion, he is an instrument for the ends of others and not an end in and for himself. Indeed, the servile man is very much like the Indiscriminate Evaluator introduced in Chapter 2. Like the latter, his various activities over time do not add up to the shape of an intelligible *life*. His doings lack a center. They are instead disjointed episodes of acting on behalf of one end and then another, none more than superficially his own. There is, though, basis for distinguishing between servility and indiscriminate evaluation. The activities of the Indiscriminate Evaluator make no reference to projects and are unexplained by them. In contrast, the actions of the servile man *are* understandable as flowing from projects, but they are not the projects of the agent himself. The projects that move him are external. The analogy to the slave can again be invoked: the slave's life can be a perfectly coherent pattern of acting to achieve ends, but they are the ends of the master and not those of the slave.

One who is thoroughly servile is not a project pursuer. Children have the right to be raised to live as project pursuers. Thus, an upbringing calculated to induce servility, to make the child no more than a slavish auxilliary to the pursuits of the parents (or of the Community of Faith, of the Worker's State, of the enlightened reign of Philosopher Kings) stands in violation of rights. Whether a form of child rearing is permissible or not does not rest on how regularly it succeeds in instilling in the child desired attitudes and values. For if the enterprise is such a total failure that the child is left attitudeless and valueless, and thus can only be moved to action by the projects of others, then the child has been severely harmed. On the other hand, if the child comes to subscribe almost entirely to the ends held by the parents but does so through taking on those ends as projects of his or her own which now shape a life that is recognizably coherent on its own terms, then the child's rightful claim to live as a project pursuer has been satisfied. Observers may decry what is, from their own perspective, the malodorousness of *that* kind of project—as observers will—but no complaint can legitimately be raised from the point of view of the child.

Might it be said that contentment with such a life evinces false consciousness? Well, of course it can be *said,* but what is the conception of *veridical* consciousness to which false consciousness stands opposed? Such a judgment will typically presuppose an impersonal standard of value to which, allegedly, all "fully realized human beings" subscribe. If they do not subscribe, that stands as proof of their being in a muddle from which they need extrication. Marxists characteristically advance a judgment of this kind and, unsurprisingly, the fully realized humanity they present in shining contrast can be seen to have stepped out of the pages of the young Marx. Similarly, evangelists of the One True Faith find unbelief to be not merely an intellectual flaw but, far more seriously, symptomatic of a diseased soul that must be brought to salvation through the exercise of an external agency if it is to be saved at all. To state the obvious, these views are illiberal.

A more promising line is to evaluate an individual's projects from his own perspective or, rather, what his perspective would be had he been the beneficiary of exposure to different beliefs, attitudes, circumstances, and so on. This seems not so blatantly illiberal because it does not oppose impersonal value to personal value. Instead, it opposes *counterfactual* personal valuation to actual personal valuation. From the agent's "own" (give or take a few hypothetical conditions) subjective state, his actual projects can be critically evaluated and found wanting.[19]

Let it be granted that each of us could have turned out differently, that what we now loathe we could have come to love and that which now attracts us could have been an object of repulsion. That is to say: projects could have been very different. Also grant that, from the perspective of what could have been our projects, current projects appear unworthy. What follows? Nothing, I think, unless it can be established that the alternative hypothetical perspective is substantially superior to the actual one. And that will be extremely difficult to do while holding on to liberalism. That A holds B's projects in distaste does not warrant the conclusion that A may be coercively interfered with for the sake of B's lustrous ends. What, then, could justify the inference that if Would-Have-Been-B can be shown to disapprove of Actual-B's projects, steps can be taken on behalf of Would-Have-Been-B to stymie Actual-B's pursuits? At least the A who abhors B and B's ends partakes of reality. If the disdain of actual persons cannot justify coercive intrusions into lives, how can hypothetical disapproval do so?[20]

Appeal to the valuations of the hypothetical self as against those of the actual self will often sneak in reference to a preferred standard of impersonal value. The projects of Would-Have-Been-B rank more highly than those of Actual-B, and so B is dispossessed—in favor of himself! The appearance of crediting the individual's own subjective preferences gives way to the illiberal canceling of personal value by impersonal value. The conclusion reached is similar to that arrived at by Idealists of the nineteenth century who professed to distinguish a "Real Will" from the "Empirical Will," pride of place going, of course, to the former.[21] An alternative attempt to justify setting aside the individual's actual goals for those he would have had can be assayed by attempting to spell out in neutral terms those conditions maximally conducive to the formation of a fully rational and mentally healthy self. The (actual or hypothetical) judgments of such a maximally rational and mentally healthy individual can then be set against those of less well-favored persons. The enterprise is daunting and, precisely because personal value is incommensurable among individuals, one I judge incapable of successful completion.[22] What may represent itself as being such a neutral inquiry is far more likely to be a hypostatization of the personal values of the theoretician.[23]

This is, as should be apparent, an extremely difficult area within moral theory. What one says is integrally bound up with metaphysical quandaries concerning the identity of the self as an active being over time and with fine discriminations concerning when persons are acting on their own projects and when they are tools, even willing tools, of another. Caution is indicated. With that proviso made explicit, certain conclusions nonetheless seem warranted.

First, the burden of proof for interference with familial attempts to inculcate strong loyalties in children is a heavy one, and it properly rests on those who propose interference. They must do more than offer evidence that the parents intend to raise a child who will subscribe to parental projects. Such evidence is, by itself, *no justification whatsoever* for interference. Rather, what must be demonstrated is that the upbringing envisioned poses a substantial degree of risk to the child's ability to develop into an independent (not "autonomous") project pursuer. It is not *which* ends the child will come to value that is crucial or *how strongly* they will be held. Rather, the relevant question is: *whose* ends will they be?

Second, projects to which adults may permissibly commit themselves are also projects which adults may permissibly act to inculcate in their children. Widespread disapproval of some way of life does not entitle the state to use its coercive powers to prevent new generations from entering into it.

Third, while the state is entitled to prevent parents from rendering their children servile instruments of others, proscriptive action carries clear potentiality for abuse. Especially if it is the case that the way of life into which children are being inducted is distasteful to oneself, it will be tempting to draw the conclusion, ''No one could possibly be drawn into *that* mode of living except through manipulation—or worse!'' If those who come of age nonetheless adhere to the disfavored way of life and deny that their evaluative faculties have been damaged, that will only count as further evidence of the sorry state to which they have been lowered. As a practical matter, then, respect for the integrity of persons living within families dictates that coercive action be tightly constrained by rigorous standards of proof. Here, as so often elsewhere with judgments about what civility demands, no great precision seems achievable. We can only hope that men and women of practical wisdom will judge for the particular case how law can best reflect the basic rights of persons.

8

At the Margin

Whatever difficulties there are in developing an account of the rights possessed by paradigmatic project pursuers—and they are many—only multiply when gaze is shifted to beings that bear *some* affinity to project pursuers yet differ from them in significant ways. Are these marginal beings to be counted as in or out? And if they are, in some ways, members of the moral community, is it a full, unrestricted membership that they possess, or are they less-than-maximal members?

A theory of basic rights can be adequate even if it fails to settle all such issues with respect to all such beings. One possibility that needs to be confronted is that there simply is no one correct answer to some of these queries. Whether beings of a certain sort possess rights may be undetermined by moral theory. Finer and finer analyses will yield diminishing—and, eventually, no—returns. The upshot will be that under one set of social conditions it is reasonable or even mandatory to accord rights to beings of that kind while in another setting there is no good basis for taking them to possess rights. (And in an intermediate setting the reasons for according rights are exactly balanced by reasons for denying rights!)

Philosophers often put theories to the test through devising ingenious thought experiments. "Yes, the account seems to do reasonably well with standard, everyday examples, but what would we say about————if things were significantly different?" Proscriptions against torturing the innocent are *generally* reliable guides to conduct, but suppose that the only way to avert World War III were to torture a young child; should we not then torture? If the world contained not four but forty billion people, what then would we say about the sanctity of human life? Suppose that baby seeds floated through the air everywhere, sprouting wherever they chanced to fall; could we then say that uprooting a developing human embryo is wrong?[1] What we are led to say about torture, the sanctity of human life, and abortion in these imagined circumstances is taken to have significant implications for moral life in the world as it is.

What many of these virtuoso philosophical conjurings presuppose is that moral principles, and most especially principles grounding basic rights, must be true across all possible worlds to be true in any. Their status is like that of mathematical truths. It is this appraisal of the logical status of moral judgments that is being denied. Because morality is to a considerable extent a function of contingent social phenomena, thought experiments have limited utility within normative ethics. Moral demarcations not only fail to characterize all possible worlds; they have limited currency even in the actual world.[2]

The prospect is messier than what theorists prefer to contemplate. It cannot arise under an internalist construal of rights. For internalist theory, a being either has or does not have the crucial property that confers rights. It is like the mark of Cain, conferring moral untouchability on whoever displays it. The task of the theorist is to state as precisely as he can what the rights-conferring property is, in the process offering a justification why it is *that* property and not some other which is portentous, and then to apply his analytical microscope to the job of close observation of candidates for rights to see whether they truly wear the rights-conferring badge. There will be little or no room for indeterminacy to rear its unattractive head; either a being has the crucial property or it does not. Rights—or their lack—follow directly.

With the abandonment of internalism, matters become much less cut-and-dried. The case for inclusion will now rest on (1) who the prior members of the moral community are and (2) in what social relations to those prior members the candidate stands. Because social relations take different forms in different settings, membership in the moral community can properly differ across cultures. That is not to abandon the field to moral nihilism or to embrace an extreme form of relativism. Plausibly, there are constants or near-constants characterizing something like the full range of human sociality. The status of children as components of families within which complex and deep-seated recognition patterns emerge seems to be very close to constant, and it underlies much of the discussion of the previous chapter. Other such morally fecund regularities might present themselves. But we ought to be prepared for the real possibility that they will *not*, and that importantly different parsings out of maximal moral claimancy will be indicated for different societies. Project pursuers will always (subject only to satisfaction of minimal conditions for the possibility of successful sociality as developed in

Chapter 4) count as rights holders, and children very nearly always. Other potential claimants, though, may fall within the fuzzy zone and, if they do, that should not automatically be accounted a defect of the theory that places them there.

That is not to say that the theory of basic rights can wash its hands of cases near the margin. Theory need not settle once and for all precisely who the rights holders are and the nature of the rights they enjoy. It should, however, provide explanation of why the genuinely problematic cases are problematic and sketch out the kinds of conditions that make for inclusion within the moral community and those that would indicate exclusion. Multivalent rights theories are liable to be far more successful at handling this task than are univalent, internalistic accounts of rights. The latter are notoriously ungainly when called upon to advance beyond consideration of paradigmatic rights holders. Moral distinctions among different classes of beings that fail to fit the paradigm are often tenuous, with a whiff of the ad hoc to them. For example, if high-level rationality is proffered as the internalist property that carries with it rights, assignment of different moral status to neonates, fetuses, and animals is problematic. The slight degree to which they might differ in rational attainment is palpably insufficient to justify placing them in different moral categories, and gradations in degree that do obtain are as likely as not to point in the wrong direction. For example, two-month-old puppies display ratiuonal activity of a substantially higher order than do human infants of the same age. The theorist is then faced with the dilemma of either lying in the Procrustean bed he himself has fashioned or walling off recalcitrant cases from the purview of the theory. Deeply grounded ethical intuitions are sacrificed to logical rigor or else rigor is sacrificed to intuitions. Neither course satisfies.

A multivalent theory *can* do justice both to rigor and to intuition. It faces, though, a different hurdle: breaking the grip of the conviction that an acceptable theory of rights must be internalist and univalent. Preceding stages of the argument, and especially Chapter 7, aim at loosening the hold of univalent internalism. That is accomplished in part by showing that there is nothing in the logic of moral concepts that inextricably commits us to such a structure. But another and complementary way of breaking its grip on one's philosophical convictions is through applying the proposed multivalent account to those cases which univalent rights theories find most intractable. If multivalence gives us a noticeably better run for our money than does univalent internalism in speaking persuasively concerning nonparadigmatic potential moral claimants, that fact itself renders the lure of the latter more resistible.

This chapter looks at several classes of beings residing near the moral margin. Its aim is not to be exhaustive, either in the sense of discussing all nonparadigmatic claimants that are of interest to moral philosophy or in providing a comprehensive treatment of any one of them. Analyses will be brief—though doubtless not nearly brief enough for those who regard the whole approach as fundamentally wrongheaded! The controlling idea is not to provide a comprehensive account of, say, the moral status of fetuses but rather to indicate the line of direction afforded to ethical inquiry by a view of rights that takes its bearings from the centrality of project pursuit yet declines the embrace of univalence. If the ramifications that are sketched out here seem at all promising, that will render the theoretical foundations on which they rest more acceptable. Admittedly, I would not be *dismayed* if readers find themselves swept away by the power of the arguments of this chapter, convinced that problems about the status of fetuses, mentally defective adults, and so on have actually been *solved*. My realistic hopes, though, are a good bit more modest than that. It will be satisfactory if the discussion here, though far from complete, is seen as following in a reasonable manner from the ground that has been plowed previously, and if it retrospectively confers enhanced credibility on the premises from which it is developed.

Fetuses[3]

All project pursuers were formerly children, and all children were formerly fetuses. Children were shown to be proper bearers of rights because they are numerically identical to the project pursuers that they become. Does it not follow, on precisely the same grounds, that fetuses are rights holders?

The question is not merely academic. On it hangs the moral permissibility of abortion, and no other policy issue has so fully engaged the attention and the passions of both ethicists and laypersons. When moral philosophers shucked off the grip of logical positivism and decided en masse that it was not only seemly but indeed salutary to turn their craft to the resolution of quandaries in normative ethics, abortion became the subject of a stream of philosophical essays and monographs that has not yet abated.[4] Any expectations that the concerted efforts of philosophers would resolve the abortion debate have, by now, been disappointed. That is not to deny that contributions have been at a generally high level; the quality of the discussion conducted in philosophical forums has certainly far exceeded that found on the editorial pages of the nation's newspapers or in the U.S. Congress. The intractability of the dispute, though, may itself be philosophically significant. It indicates that facts about the fetus pull in two directions, making determination of its moral status problematic.

Rather than coming to the abortion dispute with a thesis in hand and ready to be wielded against all naysayers, it may be profitable to begin by acknowledging that fetuses are neither clearly in nor clearly out of the moral community, and then to consider whence their marginal status derives. By proceeding in this manner we are forewarned against presupposing that abortion *must* be morally equivalent to infanticide or that it *must* be equivalent to contraception. For whatever it's worth, neither of these extremes has much currency outside the academy. Those marching under the Pro Choice banner do not extend their call for freely available abortion to a demand that unwanted infants also be subject to medical termination; the slogan "Every child a wanted child!" implicitly segregates born children from the unborn. But it is also the case that those who style themselves Pro Life refrain from including within proposed Human Life Amendments to the Constitution an article ensuring to each sperm a fighting chance to impregnate an ovum. (True, the opposed camps darkly warn that the *next* step will be calls for infanticide on demand/a ban on contraception. That, though, is politics.) One need not equate *vox populi* with *vox dei* to regard it as a significant moral datum that the ordinary moral consciousness is prone to take fetuses as constituting a distinctive class.

Questions about the status of the fetus are often phrased as revolving around the issue of "when human life begins." That, though, is a thoroughly misleading locution. It seems to locate the dispute in some imperfectly understood corner of the biological sciences. The U.S. Supreme Court contributed mightily to misunderstanding in its seminal *Roe* v. *Wade* decision. Justice Blackmun, writing for the majority, confuses more matters than one would believe possible in so limited a space when he contends, "We need not resolve the difficult question of when life begins. When those trained in the respective disciplines of medicine, philosophy, and theology are unable to arrive at any consensus, the judiciary, at this point in the development of man's knowledge, is not in a position to speculate as to the answer."[5] Although there are numerous quandaries about fetuses, their biological status is the least of them. And what biology reveals is that the fetus is, from conception on, a distinct human individual. It is *human* in that it possesses the genetic endowment of a human being and not some other species, *distinct* in that its genotype is unique to itself and not that of either parent, and it is an *individual* in that, unlike germ cells, it possesses a full complement of genetic material. Finally, it is *living,* as opposed to dead or inert, else the abortion quandary would be moot. In short, the question of when human life has its beginning is not, contra the Supreme Court, a riddle that has perplexed sages and ages; biology provides us as good information as we need to assert that each individual human life begins at conception.

It would not be at all surprising if many biologists took issue with this statement. They would do so, however, not in their capacity as experts in the life sciences but as citizens concerned to advance their own conception of morality. If fetuses are living members of the human species, the case for a permissive abortion policy is not so easily made. Those who support freely available abortion are inclined to match their policy preference with a view of the fetus that emphasizes its moral inconsequentiality. No indictment is intended; they are merely speaking the prevailing argot. The question of when human life begins has become so thoroughly blurred in public discourse with issues of whether and when fetuses become rights holders that one requires the services of a cryptographer to determine when 'human life' means human life rather than some other thing. Confusion of what should remain distinct realms of discourse is endemic. Nonetheless, one can assert with confidence that there would be no controversy about whether fetuses are biologically human were it not for the apprehension that answers immediately become the property of the abortion disputants. If there is any doubt on this score, consider the following questions. Is there some fundamental biological datum contested by the proabortion and antiabortion camps? Is it claimed by any party to the dispute that a crucial piece of evidence is missing which, when it comes to hand, will settle the issue of whether fetuses are members of species *Homo sapiens?* Negative answers indicate that the abortion controversy is not generated by scientific uncertainty.

It is not the biological status of the fetus that is in doubt but rather its *moral* status. Fetuses are members of the human species, but does this membership carry with it *rights?* The question is summarily answered by those internalist theories holding that all and only biologically human beings are rights holders. The very ease with which it settles this issue, however, gives one pause. All the characteristics that separate zygotes from adult project pursuers are held to be morally irrelevant; the simple humanity of each is the only factor allowed to count for anything. This is intuitively implausible. We find ourselves genuinely troubled about what treatment is permissible toward marginal moral claimants such as the permanently comatose, animals—and fetuses. It is because they differ in morally compelling ways from the paradigm of adult project pursuers that we encounter difficulty in saying what claims can justifiably be made on their behalf. The internalist theory of *human* rights will brook no such dilemmas: if it is biologically human, then it is in the protected zone; otherwise it is out. At the very least, this is question-begging.

Whether biological humanity is a *sufficient condition* for being a rights holder is disputable. So, too, is whether it is a *necessary condition.* Our acquaintance with full-fledged project pursuers is restricted to human beings, but this could change. A close encounter of the third kind might come our way, bringing to our attention a nonhuman race of project pursuers whose various attainments match or even exceed our own. Would it be acceptable to maintain that these are just so much meat on the hoof, available for use by human beings? Suppose that those beings also subscribed to internalism but one holding that all and only XYZens have rights; by means of what argument could they properly be shown that humanity and not XYZity is the morally crucial property such that *they* are expendable and *we* are not? None comes readily to mind. On both prudential *and* moral grounds, a *modus vivendi* seems indicated. Or suppose, optimistically, that we do not blast ourselves into extinction but are allowed to evolve in peace for several million years, in the process adding a chromosome or two and tripling average IQ. *Homo sapiens* has been supplanted by *Homo super sapiens*—have rights disappeared along the way?[6]

It is equally misplaced to deny to fetuses all moral protections on the grounds that they exhibit none of the intellectual attainments that characterize project pursuers. For this too is to presuppose an internalistic analysis, albeit one of a different stripe. It locates moral standing in the ability to exercise rational agency. Whether one is a human being, an XYZen or a *Homo super sapiens* is unimportant; what counts from the moral point of view is the ability to attain and act from suitably elevated conceptual states. This genus of internalism is not species-specific but represents a pure meritocracy of the mind. Different theorists will propose more or less exacting admission standards for entry into the moral community. A relatively "open admissions" policy grants membership to all who possess sentience. Bentham, for example, applies the moral calculus to all organisms responsive to pleasure and averse to pain. Others propose Ivy League admission requirements: to be a member of the moral community is to have the ability to comprehend and be motivated by moral reasons for action. And, of course, there exist positions intermediate between these. For convenience we shall speak of all these views as "Kantian," not thereby intending specific reference to Kant's own distinctive ethic. To the best of my knowledge, no Kantian theorist has proposed standards so stringent that he himself was unable to meet them—surely a convenient result!

There are several curious features of Kantian theories that deserve mention. First, elevation of intellectual attainment obviously admits of degree. Nonetheless, almost all such theories stake out some benchmark above which all qualifiers are equally and fully deserving of moral respect. This is inherently suspect, made more so by the fact that different theorists place the benchmark at different levels. Would it not be more in keeping with the spirit of moral meritocracy to recognize degrees of rank? Philodendrons and slugs might fail to qualify for any moral protection at all, but fetuses would get a little bit, dogs a little more, and chimpanzees, dolphins, and toddlers more still. Used-car salesmen qualify—barely—for noncommissioned officer status, while ranking far above them are bankers, engineers, and poets. Commanders in chief of the moral community are, of course, the Philosopher Kings. The possibilities for novel moral architecture fascinate, and distinguished philosophical forebears can be cited. Plato builds his utopia on a tripartite division of the citizenry; Aristotle freely claims higher status for men than women, Greek than barbarian, practitioner of the contemplative life than man of affairs. Why is this an avenue virtually unexplored in contemporary moral philosophy?

Schematisms incorporating continuous gradation of moral status arise from an impersonal standard of value. One's place in the moral continuum reflects one's score according to that standard. Because all value is rendered commensurable, assignments of differential standing follow. Rights, on the other hand, reflect personal value. Rights holders are not those who score equally well on some moral achievement test, but rather are sources of personal value incommensurable with the personal value of others. Kantian theories cannot both make moral standing an increasing function of degree of rational attainment and also arrive at rights. Thus, they seek to locate some one benchmark above which all qualify equally for moral respect. A continuous function ranging over degrees of impersonal value is interpreted such that it generates a cutoff point for the recognition of personal value. The result is theoretically precarious.

A second feature of Kantian theories that deserves mention is their fixity of vision. They are blind to all potential factors of moral significance other than the one dimension they recognize as conferring moral status. If very different kinds of beings are similar in their degree of intellectual attainment, then they are moral indiscernibles. Human children who cannot match the accomplishments of the household pet merit no higher status than that pet. Advanced fetuses and neonates differ only slightly in their capabilities and so will be on a moral par. Wherever the benchmark is set, the result will be morally revisionary. Abortion and infanticide become morally equivalent acts, either both permissible or both impermissible—and to the same degree. Killing a very young child is no greater a moral offense than killing a deer, though it may be classified as a lesser offense or no offense at all. Plainly, our moral intuitions do not run along the same lines as do these Kantian theories.

"All the worse for intuitions!" a Kantian might say. However, his dismissal of the deliverances of common morality rests on an exceedingly shaky foundation. If some particular Kantian theory of morality possessed a high degree of warrant such that to give it up would leave moral philosophy in a state of disrepair, then conflicts with even very strong and deep-seated moral intuitions could justifiably be resolved by junking the latter. Such is not the case. Where the crucial benchmark for moral significance lies and what renders it of such abiding significance are disputed by Kantian theorists amongst themselves. No one of these theoretical constructions carries a stamp of unquestionable moral authority, and, as has been seen, the commitment to univalent internalism is itself eminently disputable. When one finds oneself holding inconsistent beliefs, it is rational to conserve those which are most well confirmed and closest to the core of one's belief structure and to dispense with beliefs further toward the periphery.[7] Moral theories are tested in the first instance by how well they fit and systematically account for strongly held pretheoretical beliefs. Kantian theories fare badly when put to this test. We might then better exclaim, "All the worse for Kantianism!"

Abandoning internalism makes it possible to explain the marginal status of fetuses. Each human career begins with conception. Just as each adult was formerly a child, each child was a fetus. There is a good for the fetus, and it is, of course, to develop into a being that generates personal value through the projects it comes to undertake. Each of us has reason to value the circumstance that our good was not terminated by abortion. Indeed, the valuational perspective of the fetus is precisely the same as that of the infant. There is no need to develop a novel argument here; Chapter 7's discussion of the good-for-the-child is directly transformable, *mutatis mutandis,* into one about the good-for-the-fetus.

Can we then immediately conclude that fetuses have rights on just the same basis that children have rights? That would be too quick. The progression to rights has two distinct stages. One involves the determination that the putative rights holder indeed has a good for which the ascription of rights is fitting recognition. Both fetuses and very young children satisfy this condition. The second stage involves showing that those who are in a position to act on the being in question, for good or ill, have reason to acknowledge it as an individual meriting their respect. It is at this second stage that fetuses and children diverge.

To value particular human beings as individuals is not the same as assigning value to humanity. A general appreciation of humanity, howsoever it happens to manifest itself, entails no commitment to the welfare of any particular human being. A utilitarian who construes the ultimate imperative as "Maximize human happiness!" will freely sacrifice the happiness of one person for an incremental gain elsewhere. No individual's good is allowed to count for anything except insofar as it is a component of the totality. Because utilitarian morality takes all value to be impersonal, utilitarianism makes no room for individualism. It values humanity but not individuals. In contrast, the theory of rights that has been developed above assigns primary value to individuals. Because it is particular persons who generate personal value, they are afforded moral space within which they are at liberty to develop a life according to their own lights. One who recognizes the individuality of those with whom he transacts has reason to forbear in his dealings with them subject to reciprocal forbearance from them.

Recognition of individuality epistemically rests on the ability to identify and reidentify a being at different times as the selfsame individual, one carrying out a connected life. Birth marks a quantum leap forward in the identifiability of human beings. One's self-identity as the individual one is does not commence with birth—it spans the progression from conception through death—but participation in social relations that constitute one a recognizable individual for others takes a dramatic turn at birth. Before that event one exists in relative anonymity. That *some* fetus is being carried is evident, but distinguishing information that marks it off as *this* particular being characterized by *these* specific features is largely lacking. Should the fetus be instantaneously annihilated and another substituted in its place, the event would be entirely unperceived as the loss of a distinct individual. To the extent that the fetus does participate in any vestigial social relationship, it is with the mother. It is her body that responds to the events of pregnancy and it is she who feels its movements after the onset of quickening. In keeping with the uniqueness of the relationship between mother and fetus, proponents of a permissive abortion policy uniformly locate in the mother final discretion concerning whether to carry to term or to abort. Others beside the mother may have an interest in the generation of a new member of the moral community with whom they will then stand in some significant relation, but only she can claim to have already begun the establishment of such a relation.

Birth is the transition from anonymity to public standing. Within hours the infant is viewed and handled by several people. It is bathed, diapered, clothed, fed, cuddled, and sheltered. Its sex, height, and weight are determined and communicated to interested grandparents, aunts, uncles, and friends. Epic debates commence: "Does he have brother Albert's nose?" "Are we *really* sure we want to name her after great aunt Agatha?" "Is it not transparently clear that she favors the mother's/is the spitting image of the father's side of the family?" Footprints are recorded and officially filed along with other individuating data; social service and medical organizations stand ready to offer assistance; the newspaper prints a birth announcement; three hundred exciting mail offers from insurance salesmen, photographers, magazines, multinational diaper and baby formula conglomerates, encyclopedia publishers, and real estate agents flood the mailbox; the IRS duly bestows a tax deduction.

Each of these identificatory events is, in itself, trivial. And even in their entirety they constitute no more than limited entry into the realm of social relations. It is nonetheless an epochal step. Thenceforward the establishment of significant relationships to others will proceed steadily as the child becomes aware of and learns to interact with persons in its environment. Its maturation inside the womb has been gradual, and its subsequent development will also be gradual. But birth marks an abrupt alteration, not in some internal property but with respect to external relationships. It is the single great discontinuity that breaks what is otherwise a smooth curve. Therefore, it stands out as the indicated demarcation point constituting inception of membership in the moral community. Fastening instead on some other point would be arbitrary in comparison.

It is clear that both law and common morality do recognize birth as a pivotal moral event. Although abortion has historically been regarded in some quarters as an offense, it is almost invariably accounted a *different* offense than infanticide. Inheritance in common law is conditional on live birth. Funerals are conducted for deceased infants but not for fetuses that miscarry. The list of moral and legal distinguishing features can be extended indefinitely. The preceding discussion of identifiability and reidentifiability as the epistemic basis for moral recognition provides the analytical foundation on which law and common morality rest.

Many ethical theorists, however, will not be satisfied. How, they will ask, can a minor change in *location* constitute a being as a full-fledged moral personality? There is precious little that a neonate can *do* which a fetus cannot, and even less that it can do which a puppy cannot. Is it not a philosophical *scandal* to hitch one's star to a *prejudice* or *taboo* resident in common morality?[8]

By this point it should be evident to the reader that such criticism rests on an implicit commitment to internalism in the theory of rights. From that perspective, birth truly is no more than a morally trivial event. Infants can do some things that fetuses cannot: breathe, nurse, holler their various displeasures to the world. But these are too slight to bear any theoretical weight at all. Thus, internalists almost without exception ignore birth as a morally compelling event. Instead they focus on the attainment of characteristics proper to the fetus or child: conception, inception of brain waves, capacity to experience pain, viability; or, subsequent to birth, reflective self-awareness, the ability to be motivated by moral reasons. If moral considerability were simply a possession of the being that enjoys it, some one of these accountings would be acceptable. But, contra the internalist, moral standing essentially makes reference to the rational motivation of others to recognize and respond to the one who has it. We must ask not merely what the fetus or child can do but what those who transact with it can do. The answer that has been suggested is: they can identify the neonate as a distinctive being and can reidentify it as the selfsame being throughout its career.[9]

It can be objected that attention to the existence of social relationships will leave some legitimate moral claimants defenseless. Not everyone lives the life of a contented Rotarian enmeshed in social dealings. The hermit who has absented himself from the company and concern of others becomes, on this analysis, fair game for them. Or a woman might isolate herself before giving birth to her child. If no one else has contact with the newborn, if she herself carefully refrains from examining it or establishing any emotional bond to it, will it not then lack the moral protections routinely afforded other children? Suppose that Aryans sedulously refrain from establishing any civic ties with Jews; may they then carry out extermination policies untroubled by moral compunctions?

The objection incorporates several confusions. First, being enmeshed within a network of social relationships was invoked to explain why *non–project pursuers* can merit the status of rights holder. In the context of the multivalent theory of rights that has been presented, they piggyback on those who do pursue projects. If the hermit is himself a project pursuer, no such piggybacking is required to explain why he has rights. Second, it has not been maintained that one is obligated to respect the rights only of those with whom one is oneself socially related. Being a participant in *some network of social relationships* suffices to constitute one a being with an individual good that can be acknowledged by others. A third and related point is that it was not argued that *actual recognition* by others as a distinctive individual is required for initiation into the moral community. Rather, it is the *recognizability* of a being that renders it a proper object for the respect of others. Should the mother choose to avert her eyes from the child, or the Aryans from the Jews, they do not gain immunity from the obligation to acknowledge the rights of the one they choose not to see.

A fourth consideration runs theoretically deeper. Some children will be born to widespread recognition and others will receive scant attention from anyone. Some fetuses are minutely inspected before birth via amniocentesis, sonograms, and other modern medical techniques. All sorts of information about them can be in hand before they are born. Nevertheless, no attention was paid to differences in amount of individuating information available with respect to particular fetuses and infants. The argument was conducted in terms of the broad categories *fetuses* and *children*. An alternative strategy should be to argue that it is the availability of individuating information on a case-by-case basis that renders a being a member of the moral community. If some particular child is scantily known, then it is out; if some particular fetus has achieved recognition, then it is in.

The difference between the two strategies is similar to the divide separating *act* utilitarianism from *rule* utilitarianism. The former emphasizes the particularity of each occasion for choice and insists that moral determinations should be as fine-grained as is achievable. The latter emphasizes generalizable features of choice situations and holds that moral determinations should be predicated on the acceptability of rules that prescribe for an indefinite range of cases. While a theoretical debate exists concerning whether the rules of a maximally optimific rule utilitarianism turn out to be as act-specific as the prescriptions of act utilitarianism,[10] it seems apparent that any rule utilitarianism that can be practiced by agents such as us would incorporate only a limited number of distinct rules and would frame its injunctions in terms of familiar classifications.

It is impossible without very lengthy digression to begin to argue the case for a *rule-* or *principle*-specific view of morality as opposed to one that is *act*-specific. Briefly, I have taken it for granted in this essay that an acceptable moral theory must be of the former sort. That is based on the belief that whatever else morality may be, it is necessarily *practical*. Agents of ordinary intelligence and sensitivity must be able to *learn* what it is that they should do and be capable of *applying* what they have learned to most, if not all, occasions for moral choice. It follows that criteria bearing on action must not be multiplied beyond necessity and that the terms of moral discourse should be those which agents customarily employ to appraise their world. Actors cannot be supposed obligated to judge the suitability of their intended actions by reference to concepts which are not available to them.[11]

We have inherited a conceptual lexicon in which *fetuses* and *infants* are readily distinguished. It is evident that we can and do learn to apply principles via which they are located in distinct classes. The argument of this section has built on that conceptual resource and has maintained that infants by and large stand in vastly more individuating social relationships than do fetuses. Therefore, it is reasonable *as a general policy* to recognize in infants but not in fetuses full standing as rights holders. That in peculiar circumstances some fetuses are better known than some infants does not trouble this result. Pervasive features of our moral experience are portentous even if they fall short of being strictly universal. It is not only in this chapter that appeal has been made to the moral significance of regularities that are less than absolute. For example, project pursuers were characterized as holding long-term commitments that shape the range of outcomes that can be of value to them. As generalizations go, this one is reasonably sturdy. However, even usually resolute pursuers of projects occasionally waver, they fall into black funks that devour possibilities for accruing value, they entertain— and sometimes succumb to—perverse fantasies of violating that which they hold sacred and worshiping the profane. All of these variabilities within human experience can be admitted without rendering dubious in any way the general policy of affording to project pursuers moral space within which they are at liberty to seek personal value.

It may be questioned how *deep* a moral gulf it is that separates the born from the unborn. It seems to be a thoroughly contingent matter that fetuses lack the publicity of infants. Imagine the following scenario: a few millenia of random mutations produces the species-wide trait of females with transparent tummies and uteri and with hatchback doors that can be opened to provide instant access. It becomes common for parents to view their little blastocytes and to invite friends in who do likewise and politely mouth pleasantries about its exquisite cell structure and the firmness of its grip on the uterine wall. When the fetus is a bit older it can safely be taken out and played with for up to an hour at a time. Mother and father have a grand time cradling it, bouncing it gently, and listening to its faint gurgles. Its final physical separation from the mother does not occur until birth, but it has been part of a large number of social encounters prior to that event. Does it not follow, according to the argument of this section, that those future fetuses are proper bearers of rights even though they are otherwise exactly like present fetuses? If so, this seems to violate the formal moral principle that equals are to be treated equally, and to violate it in a circumstance in which the stakes are, literally, life and death.

The excursus into science fiction has been presented as an objection to the claim that the possession of rights can be a function of social relations. However, it is quite benign. I have not argued that a being who is a rights holder will similarly be a rights holder in any and every possible world in which it might exist. That sort of essentialism about rights was explicitly denied. Rather, the moral standing of a being was located in *both* its own native endowments *and* in the social setting in which it finds itself. That fetuses in some possible world might merit recognition as rights holders does not show that they merit that status in the actual world. The hypothesized changes are quite plausibly significant enough to justify taking a different stance toward fetuses. No formal principle of treating equals equally is thereby violated. Or, rather, the allegation that it is violated presupposes an internalistic analysis of what can count as a morally relevant difference. Fetuses that can take brief vacations from the womb *are* different from those that cannot, even if they are anatomically and psychologically the same.

It is too much to hope, though, that we can prescribe sagaciously for a world such as that sketched out above; it is difficult enough to take accurate moral bearings in the one in which we live. Speculation about the status of visible and transportable fetuses is just that: speculation. Without fully fleshed-out knowledge of the circumstances confronted by a society, we do best to refrain from gifting it with a decalogue. No scantily sketched thought experiment can provide that flesh; even gifted novelists find difficult the task of creating a credible world. (To the extent that novelists are able to do so, they can claim the title of moral instructor every bit as legitimately as can the most abstruse moral philosophers.) Moral theories are best tested by the convictions we bring to bear on vistas with which we have some acquaintance; elaborate counterfactual hypotheses are more apt to be misleading than insightful.

The foregoing argument has offered an account of why abortion is a genuinely difficult moral issue by locating that difficulty in the marginal status of the fetus. The fetus is biologically human from conception on, but it lacks the identifiability and reidentifiability that characterize full members of the moral community. For that reason it is inappropriate to equate abortion with homicide, but it is also a mistake to equate abortion with contraception. Abortion is the termination of human life, and it will be judged culpable by those who assign impersonal value to human life as such. There do not exist sufficient grounds, however, to judge it to be the violation of an individual's right to life.

Defective Human Beings

It is no misfortune of the child (or fetus) that it lacks the capacity to entertain and pursue projects. In due time it will develop that capacity, and the child's present good is a function of its status as a prospective project pursuer. Were one condemned, however, to remain a child throughout one's existence, or to grow in bulk without simultaneously growing in the capacity to conceptualize ends and to act for their sake, it would be a personal misfortune of the utmost gravity. Unfortunately, this is no counterfactual hypothesis; millions of human beings are born with starkly limited endowments rendering them unable ever to assume the status of project pursuer. Other persons begin life intact but, through disease or accident, are lowered below the threshold at which project pursuit is possible. Both prospects are bad, but they are bad in different ways and may pose different implications concerning morally indicated treatment of the individual so afflicted. For example, a person in the grip of Alzheimer's disease or permanently comatose will have a career as a project pursuer behind him. The commitments he has undertaken will leave traces that postdate his own effective agency. Therefore, it is advisable to consider separately (1) individuals who never are able to assume the status of project pursuer and (2) those who relinquish that status prior to their death.

In a sense, the person who is born with severe and irreparable mental defects is the moral obverse of the fetus. By that I mean that fetuses are, in general, prospective pursuers of projects and thus possess a corresponding good of their own. However, they lack the publicity that would constitute them recognizable individuals for others. Severely impaired persons, on the other hand, are permanently blocked from project pursuit but possess publicity that renders them possible objects of concern. As children, they are born into families that give them a name, a reservoir of affection that they can tap, and a network of social relations of which they immediately are a part. Despite lacking the potentialities of other children, they are beneficiaries of widespread attitudes and moral principles directed at the welfare of the young. Because children enjoy the protection of rights, so, too, I shall argue, do those who are permanently childlike.

This may seem like special pleading or an unthinking moral conservatism. After all, the preceding chapter argued for the ascription of rights to children on the grounds that they are the selfsame beings as the project pursuers they become. Those who will never be able to undertake projects of their own fall outside the ambit of that argument. They do not need liberty to attain their good, and whatever need they have for welfare goods is like that of animals, to survive here and now, and not as a prerequisite for the development of independent moral agency. Their inclusion in the human species is not in doubt, but biological humanity is neither a necessary nor a sufficient condition for holding rights. What justification can there be, then, for expanding the moral community beyond current and prospective project pursuers?

An opponent of acknowledging rights in the severely defective need not deny to them moral protection *similar* to that which rights afford. Such protection, though, will be justified on the basis of the sentimental regard that we tend to have for beings of our own kind. It is not easy for parents and other kin emotionally to disown children who have entered their lives. Though unable to assume projects of their own, these children are nonetheless encompassed within the projects of others who will freely offer their love and care, sacrificing other interests for the sake of the one who will never be able to look after his or her own interests. It would be thoughtless to maintain that beings who are the repositories of such involvement should be afforded no protection. Thus, law and common morality will affirm a duty not to injure these beings gratuitously and to assist them to secure whatever good they can enjoy. However, such recognition is not afforded them in their own right but rather insofar as they are adjuncts to the projects of others. They are more like pets than like beings morally considerable in themselves. Injury to a pet damages not only it but also, and more significantly, the interests of its owners. We may choose, out of squeamishness or regard for the family, not to speak of defective human beings with the same language we apply to pets or possessions, employing instead terms whose primary application is to those with independent moral standing. Even if this becomes a customary linguistic practice, that should not be allowed to disguise the gulf between an intact and a defective being. The former is protected because it has its own life to lead, while the latter is safeguarded because of the likelihood it will figure as a positive value in the lives of others.

The strategy of according to defective human beings the semblance of moral standing while withholding the genuine article may have some initial plausibility but it is not the only course one can take, nor is it the one that best accords with a considered view of the purpose of moral categorization. Against it I wish to argue that children born with severe mental and physical defects have rights in the same sense as do those born unimpaired, and that is because they are equally *children*. It was argued in the previous section that moral standing is not parceled out on a case-by-case basis (and who would be charged with doing the parceling out?) but is instead the property of all those who are members of a class of morally considerable beings. If moral principles that confer rights on young human beings do so on the basis of their belonging to the class of children and not, say, on grounds of boasting an IQ no more than two standard deviations below average, then even severely defective children will be accorded the status of rights holder.

It requires no prodigy of moral invention to construct the principles of identification and regard that embrace the class of children as such: the principles already exist and are persistently employed in our cognitions of the beings that inhabit our world. Children are the ones who wear children's clothes, read children's literature, contract diseases of childhood (and are sometimes treated in children's hospitals); according to some reports, they are the ones to be seen and not heard and are what we must become again to enter the Kingdom of Heaven. Our attitudes, practices, and institutions predispose us to identify indifferently beings of vastly different attainments and potentialities as children. Therefore, it is eminently natural—considerably more natural than what will be mandated by any revisionistic proposal—to frame moral principles, including judgments concerning rights, such that they make reference to *children* rather than to some less commonly invoked class. Although it is the case that rights are ascribed to children in the first instance because they tend by and large to develop into project pursuers, those who will never enjoy that good fortune are nonetheless protected by the same umbrella that covers those who will. We might say that, just as prospective project pursuers piggyback on the recognition of actual project pursuers, so, too, do impaired children piggyback on those who are unimpaired.

It will be objected that, as a justification for according rights to the severely deficient, this is blatantly circular. Because distinguishable cases are customarily lumped together it is maintained that they are properly treated as equals. Is this not the tyranny of the status quo masquerading as a moral argument? It is the presentation of a piece of *descriptive* ethics as carrying *normative* weight. Even if it suffices to *explain* why we in fact tend to regard all children as rights holders, it does not *justify* that result. To accomplish the justificatory task it would first have to be shown that habitual patterns of categorizing the world in terms of children and others are themselves well motivated. And that is precisely what the critic denies.

There is some point to this objection, but it presupposes unrealistically demanding standards for moral argument. In morality as elsewhere, we must start from where we are. The conceptual resources individuals deploy to comprehend their world also set the parameters of their moral discourse. Modes of comprehension need not partake of the alleged a priori necessity of Kantian categories to carry moral significance. That we are prone to identify beings as children and not in some other way *could have been* otherwise—although one should not underestimate how far-reaching the resultant alteration in customary patterns of life would be. However, well-entrenched classificatory practices are a kind of intellectual capital that we squander at our peril. Moral reformers may argue that we ought to train ourselves to shed traditional moral categories and think instead in terms of intact and impaired. Even if such reformation could be carried out, it is doubtful that it would produce lovelier moral vistas.

Mental deficiency admits of an infinity of degree, occurs along many dimensions, can be counterbalanced by the possession of special talents, occasionally vanishes spontaneously or is successfully treated, and is difficult to measure with any exactitude. These factors should give the would-be reformer pause. How deficient must an individual be to merit exclusion from the moral community, to be more properly appraised as a *thing* than as a *person?* Because there is no sharp dividing line separating the defective from the whole (is not each of us defective in *some* regard?), whatever answer is given will appear arbitrary, most especially to those who have invested their love and care in a child deemed to fall just on the other side of the line. Qualifiers and nonqualifiers will resemble each other closely; perhaps trained psychometricians will be able to produce reasonably reliable tests for distinguishing between the sheep and the goats, though even the best tests will leave considerable room for error. But such arcane considerations of metrology show how far the idea of reform has gone off the tracks. Morality is not an esoteric craft whose performance is restricted to a coterie of specialists. Successful sociality requires that the vast majority of persons be capable of applying moral principles to the bulk of the cases they encounter in which the significant interests of other persons are at stake. It must, then, be possible to recognize with a very high degree of success those beings who are morally considerable. A moral geometry that indulges in fine distinctions of inclusion and exclusion may present itself engagingly in a casuistical text, but it will be a disaster in practice.

Beyond the problem of moral identification is that of moral motivation. The same ingenious bureaucrats who give us Social Security numbers, passports, draft registration cards, driver's licenses, and ZIP codes could perhaps devise a mechanism for certifying who is to count as a rights holder and who is not, visibly distinguishing the two classes. (Requiring those who fall short to wear a yellow badge has precedent, but not one that is terribly attractive.) What reason, though, would one have to take *their* accounting as definitive? In many ways those protected and those who are not would appear indistinguishable, and each is the son or daughter of men and women who tend to bear considerable affection for their own. Whatever might be decreed by the moral mandarins would appear artificial and strained, and compliance with the imposed classification would not come easily.

Against the considerable liabilities attaching to the proposed revisionary schema are the attractions of customary practice. Human beings, adults and children, are readily picked out. If they are the ones accorded unique moral standing, the range of application of moral principles is transparent: rights holders are just those who are born of other rights holders. This is to build on natural reserves of motivational energy rather than to work against them. To enter into a biologically constituted network of interpersonal relationships is simultaneously to enter into the moral community. Parents need not fear that their children will fail the entrance exam, and no high priesthood of psychometricians will be entitled to turn thumbs up or thumbs down. For these reasons it seems clear that the dictates of common morality concerning who is to count as a being with full moral standing are considerably more *practical* than the revisionary suggestion that moral status be tied tightly to the demonstrated intellective capacity of individuals. This is not a surprising result. Common morality is not sacrosanct. Its dictates are often obscure, it changes over time, and it may be confused, inconsistent, or inarticulate. But it also encapsulates the experience and wisdom of generations of men and women who were not afforded the luxury of speculating freely from their armchairs about the grounds of moral obligation. In any *practiced* morality tensions are likely to bubble to the surface, where they will then be resolved or at least confronted. Rationalistic constructions will also incorporate tensions, but those very likely will lie latent until and unless a society is bold or foolhardy enough to impose the theorist's vision on itself. The case for moral conservatism is a strong one, and it is made more attractive still when juxtaposed against the checkered history of grand utopian experimentation.

That mentally deficient persons have rights does not entail that they are to be treated exactly like project pursuers, any more than it is the case that children should be treated on all fours with adults. Full and equal *consideration* is not the same as identical *treatment*. Those who are impaired will have less need of liberty than do others but will have a correspondingly greater need for the provision of welfare goods. This should not be exaggerated. Even those severely handicapped may still be able to achieve goods through action, and in order to do so they require liberty. A low IQ is not a felony calling for confinement; awkwardness in the pursuit of ends does not mean that the attempt should never have been made in the first place. It will be tempting, especially for those whose concerns run deepest, to safeguard the impaired from possible failure by wrapping them in a cocoon that snuffs out all room for enterprise as it protects. But a being who can conceive for himself a good achievable through action, however limited, and who can act over time to bring about its realization is harmed if prevented from pursuing it.

Still, impaired persons will require more care, both as children and as adults, then those more generously endowed. It is not inconsistent with liberalism that others be obliged to provide them with welfare goods sufficient to enable them to attain that measure of value consistent with their condition. Or, rather, there is no inconsistency so long as the obligation does not become onerous enough to interfere with the ability of others to pursue their own projects. It is not only altruistic concern for those born to impairment that motivates the establishment and support of social mechanisms for those unable to advance their own good. Each of us is vulnerable to the ravages of age, disease, and accident. One who was formerly a resolute pursuer of his own ends may find himself cut off from further activity. Such an individual will still have a good achievable through action, but it will then be the actions of others that are crucial. Each person therefore has a self-interested reason to support social arrangements that secure the welfare of those unable to tend to their own well-being.[12]

It should be noted that not all social arrangements for securing the welfare of the disabled involve coercive extraction of resources. If minimally adequate support for those born impaired is forthcoming through voluntary channels, there is no room for the state to sponsor its own programs even if it believes it can do more and better. And in this area there is a decisive difference between those who eventually lose the capacity to direct their own affairs and those who never possessed that capacity. The former, but not the latter, had an opportunity to look to their own future well-being. Insurance policies that guarantee adequate health care and income in the event of disability enable individuals prospectively to arrange for their own subsequent care. Each person has primary responsibility to secure the ends that are his own, and if he is able to do so, then no one else can properly be obliged to do so in his stead. One may choose to gamble on one's own continued vitality or on the willingness of others to assume the burden of care—but gambles can be lost. It is illegitimate coercively to extract assistance on behalf of those who had the opportunity to provide for their own care but elected not to do so.[13]

One distinction between those who are born impaired and those who are brought low late in life is that the latter, but not the former, have had the opportunity to make provision for possible disability. Another distinguishing feature is that the latter will typically be involved in projects whose objects of concern continue to exist beyond the effective agency of the individuals in question. Therefore, it should not be assumed that respect for them as project pursuers ceases when their capacity for agency does. One's good is affected by subsequent events that bear on the success or failure of undertakings that have been cut off in mid-course. For example, one whose life is largely directed by concern for the welfare of his or her family will not be indifferent to what is likely to befall them once he or she is unable to act any longer on their behalf. It is true that, at that time, one may be incapable of comprehending and being moved by their circumstances. However, it is a plain fact of experience that individuals can and do take a current interest in temporally distant outcomes, and there is no reason to subscribe to a narrow psychological egoism that would hold persons unable to value states of affairs that they do not themselves experience. Individuals can be benefited or harmed by events of which they have no awareness, and so, for example, the breaking of a promise will typically be a moral violation even if the promisee never learns of the breach. (And it is specifically a violation of the *promisee's* right to fulfillment.) In general, performances that are A's due as a matter of right remain such after A's effective agency has ceased.[14]

Because persons have interests that outlast their power to advance them, they have reason to support the maintenance of structures designed to extend their powers to affect future happenings. Insurance provisions have already been noted. Similar in motivation are so-called living wills, documents indicating one's current preferences concerning the provision and withholding of medical intervention should various contingencies emerge when one is no longer able to express or even entertain preferences concerning treatment. The case for taking these documents to be binding on others is often expressed in terms of the value to the individual of "death with dignity," but this is a highly misleading formulation. Whether one's dignity is enhanced or retarded by an extended period of lying inert in a hospital bed with a multitude of tubes sticking out of one's body need not be decided by licensed Aestheticians of Morbidity. Rather, the justification of the living will is that it renders individuals better able to impose their preferences on the world, whatever direction those preferences might take. If I care not a jot for dignity but want very much to keep breathing as long as possible, a living will affords me the opportunity to give effect to that preference. (A respiration aspiration?) The general point is that project pursuers have reason to value the capacity to enter into contractual arrangements that will be enforced on their behalf once they no longer can act to determine outcomes. Appropriate legal structures are required if this is to be the case, and such structures are morally required by respect for basic rights. This is the political corollary of individuals' interest in extending the reach of their agency.

I have argued that even profound disability does not disqualify persons from membership as rights holders in the moral community. They are entitled to the full regard and respect of others, and this will likely include the provision of welfare goods. It does not follow, though, that allowing the impaired to die violates their rights. When a competent person elects not to receive life-extending treatment, it is clear that he stands within his rights; the violation would be if others unilaterally overrule his decision and coercively impose unwanted measures. Severe mental deficiency eliminates the power to give genuine consent, but, as in the case of a living will, a person can prospectively consent to the withholding of treatment. Matters are not as simple in the case of an individual who never possesses the capacity to direct his own affairs, for example, an infant born with major mental and physical handicaps. Due in large measure to advances in medical technology, it is possible to sustain indefinitely lives such as these. What is in question, though, is whether the existence of the technology provides the moral imperative for its use. Because the infant will never be in a position to consent to the termination of its own life, must it be kept alive as long as possible?

The answer, I believe, is a qualified no. To have rights is to possess a good that others are not at liberty to disregard, but a longer life is not necessarily one blessed with a greater measure of value. If it can be in some-

one's rational self-interest to bring about *his own* death, then it will also be
in the interest of that person that others act to bring about his death.[15] Choosing
the death of another is morally riskier than choosing death for oneself, but
that is because it is choosing for another, not specifically because of the
nature of the outcome that is chosen. Opting to preserve someone in a painful, precarious, and prospectless life is also risky. To choose unwisely for
oneself is a *misfortune*, but to impose an unwise choice on someone else is
a *violation*. There is, though, no way to shed the risk. One charged to act
on behalf of another may move decisively on a conception of the other's
good or he may dither endlessly. In one case the choice is made deliberately, in the other, by default; it has nonetheless been made. If it is in the
interest of an individual unable to choose for himself to die, then it is also
in his interest to have death chosen for him. His authorized guardian is
entitled—or, rather, obligated—to bring about his death if there is a morally
permissible avenue for doing so.

The preceding sentence raises two questions: (1) Who is it that ought to
act as caretaker for the incompetent person? (2) By what means may the
death of someone permissibly be brought about? Both raise complex moral
issues that deserve extended attention. It would be out of place to enter full
bore into that discussion here, but perhaps the following brief remarks will
be suggestive.

1. It was argued in the preceding chapter that custody of children is properly vested in the immediate family. Many of the considerations adduced
there apply also to guardianship of the severely impaired. Kin will generally
possess a greater measure of concern than do others. Moreover, stricken
children, spouses, or parents who no longer entertain (or never entertained)
projects of their own will retain a place in the projects of family members.
Love for another or even just the onerous conviction that the burden for care
properly rests on oneself ties one's own success or failure as an agent to
one's efforts in advancing the good of the ward. It is an injury to individuals' ability to conduct their own lives if state institutions refuse to acknowledge the special relationships that enter into and shape their projects.

Again, the right to act on behalf of the family member is not a blank
check. It is contingent on the ability and willingness to act for that person's
good, and where either is demonstrably absent, political intervention is called
for. But the burden of proof should rest on the state to justify its intrusion.
Reasonable persons may differ in their conception of what is required to
secure the minimal good that remains to one *in extremis,* and appeal to an
impersonal standard of value to which all must give heed is illicit. That
which is accounted gross malfeasance is prohibitable, but judgments that

can reasonably be construed as motivated by concern for the interests of the ward should not be coercively overruled.

2. Killing an individual and allowing a person to die are equivalent from a consequential perspective, and both may be prompted either by base motives or by noble ones. Some would argue that this renders them morally indistinguishable actions such that if one is to be accounted permissible in a given set of circumstances, so, too, is the other.[16] That is too quick. Letting someone die is intentionally to refrain from intervening, whether to generate a good or an ill, while killing is an act of intervention that causes death. The distinction is central to the rights theory of classical liberalism. Liberal rights are predominantly claims to noninterference. Refraining from conferring a benefit on someone may be greatly detrimental to the person's well-being, as much so as would be the infliction of a profound harm, but there is no general obligation to extend aid to others. And paternalistic intervention to confer an unwanted benefit is also an impermissible violation of moral space, not because it engenders any specific harm but because it is unbidden interference. Because killing, unlike letting die, involves interference with the course of an individual's life, one has a basic right not to be killed by others but not a right that others provide whatever is needed to keep one alive.

Consent renders licit what would otherwise be in violation of rights. To assault someone with your fists is impermissible—unless that person has agreed to step into a boxing ring with you. Similarly, someone who finds life intolerable torture and judges that he would be better off dead may rightfully kill himself or request that service from someone else. Should the other party comply, he has violated no rights. Of course, he may, out of moral scruples or from some other reason, choose not to comply with the request, but liberty not to kill is simply an instance of the general liberty not to be enlisted in the projects of others against one's will. A person is not wronged if his request to be killed is not honored—but neither is he wronged if the request *is* honored. Legal prohibition against even consensual homicide may yet be justified on grounds that the competence of one who assents to his own killing will often be questionable or because it will be impossibly burdensome on judges and juries to separate consensual homicides from murder—but not because consensual killing violates the rights of the one killed. I say that legal prohibition *may* be justified; it is more likely that selectively allowing individuals in certain delimited circumstances to contract to be killed will impugn no legitimate purpose of the law. A terminally ill hospital patient suffering excruciating pain can rationally request that his life be terminated, and compliance not only reduces suffering but additionally provides the patient with enhanced capacity for self-determination. Voluntary active euthanasia is not inconsistent with the primacy of individualism but rather complements it.

The case is more difficult when consent cannot be forthcoming. It may not be detrimental to the welfare of a gravely handicapped individual to be killed; it may even be to his detriment *not* to be killed. Nonetheless, it is at least arguable that others are not at liberty to cause the death of one who has not consented to being killed. That means that an otherwise optimific result is blocked by a moral prohibition, but that kind of eventuality is part and parcel of the existence of rights that stand as side constraints on value maximization. Whether killing not preceded by consent of the victim (or, rather, "victim") can be rightful is a difficult question that I shall not attempt to settle here. Instead I conclude with a cautious judgment: it is permissible to allow a severely deficient individual to die even if the individual has not requested his own death provided that desire for the person's death is motivated by genuine concern for the individual's good; it is less certain that beneficent killing of an individual who has not given prior consent is morally permissible.

Rights of the Dead

In some respects it seems altogether plausible to maintain that the dead have rights and thus that certain acts which would count as violating the rights of an individual were he living similarly count as violating his rights should he happen to be dead. For example, many promises retain their force even if the promisee dies prior to the time stipulated for fulfillment. Those that do not will be promises in which the continued life of the promisee is presupposed by the terms of the promise. A's promise to B to show B the collection of colorful slides that A took at the latest meeting of the American Philosophical Association dies with B because dead men view no slides. But A's promise to make the slides available to B's daughter is not similarly canceled by B's death, although of course it would be by the death of the daughter. It is not simply a wrong to the daughter if the latter promise is not kept but a wrong to B himself, and therefore it is B's right that is violated by nonfulfillment. Similarly, B is harmed by slanderous accusations made about him after his demise and can be benefited by posthumous honors that he receives.

On the other hand, when viewed in a certain way, it seems absurd to attribute harms and benefits to the dead or to regard them as beings who have rights that can be either respected or violated. A corpse that lies moldering in the ground is simply not the sort of being to whom good or ill can befall, any more than a venetian blind can be the beneficiary of good or bad tidings. Whatever the corpse (or its predecessor) once was, it is now merely an inert hunk of matter thoroughly removed from the realm of moral signif- icance. A dilemma confronts those who would attribute rights to the dead. Saying that the deceased Jones now possesses rights means one of two things: either that Jones the corpse is a rights holder or that Jones the living and breathing person possesses rights that survive his own demise. The former represents a moral confusion about what sort of being can have rights, and the latter seems to incorporate a logical confusion. Jones the living human being no longer exists once Jones has died, and so to attribute continued rights to *that* being is to ascribe properties to something nonexistent. In either case, the criticism runs, it is palpably absurd to attribute rights to the dead.

I wish to maintain that it makes good sense to speak of the dead as having rights and, further, that considerations previously adduced entail that this is a morally sound result. The argument involves two stages: giving reasons for believing that the interests of persons that ground their claims to rights while they are alive are not extinguished by their death, and confronting the charge that it is nonsensical to conceive of the dead as rights holders. Al- though the second of these is logically prior—if we *cannot* meaningfully ascribe rights to the dead, then there is no moral case to be made for the *justifiability* of doing so—it is more natural to proceed in the reverse direc- tion. Logical puzzles about how the dead can be subjects of moral attribu- tion become pressing only if there is some reason in the first place to think of the deceased as leaving behind them claims that others are obligated to respect. It is once we are convinced that there are such claims that the question of who the holder of the claims could possibly be presents itself as a vexing conundrum.

It is because individuals have projects that assign value to states of affairs extending beyond their own conscious experience that they can have inter- ests surviving their own death. We want the world to be a certain way—and act to bring about that result. Death cuts short the ability to act, but that for which one has acted survives the death of the actor and is affected for better or worse by the doings of others. If one of A's directive ends is to bring about E, then A has reason to value circumstances conducive to the reali- zation of E and reason to disvalue that which hinders the realization of E. Whether these occur during A's life or after it has ended is immaterial to their value-for-A. Of course, A will be unable to *experience* value or dis- value that eventuates subsequent to his death, but *existence* of value and *awareness* of value are distinct matters. It is not only after one is dead that valued outcomes materialize of which one is not aware. I am writing in the hope that readers will find the arguments of this book challenging and stimulating, perhaps even persuasive. Should you be one who does, I would be grateful if you would drop me a note so informing me. However, even if you choose not to write and I never become aware of your opinion, it is still of positive value to me that you find these pages to be of some interest. I want the appreciation of readers and not just the knowledge of their appreciation—though I wouldn't mind having that too. Should the appreciation not be forthcoming until after my death, it would nonetheless be a value for me, though not one that I would be able to experience.

Desires that embrace happenings subsequent to one's death are not restricted to aspiring authors but are a universal datum of human experience. Only a handful of misanthropes would be indifferent to whether the planet explodes five minutes after their heart ceases beating. Most of us have a vague preference for the welfare of other human beings and more intense and sharply focused preferences for the welfare of particular individuals to whom one stands in relations of regard and affection. It would be an instance of gross practical incoherence to work to advance the interests of a loved one, to place the interests of that person at the center of one's projects, yet to assign no value to how that person's life may go after one's own is ended. Someone whose concerns were so delimited by his own mortality could not accurately be described, or describe himself, as valuing the good of the other but would rather be one who values *presenting himself* as cherishing the good of that person or who values *experiencing* the other's joys. Admittedly, there is room for deception—and for self-deception—in an accounting of a person's fundamental valuations, but one could hardly deceive oneself or anyone else concerning what it is that is genuinely valued unless that which is *incorrectly* believed to be a source of motivation is something that *could* actually command a person's loyalties.

Egoistic hedonism, though, would have it that deception is ubiquitous. Each person, it maintains, is unable to value anything other than his or her own subjective state of consciousness. That a theory so contrary to ordinary experience and so often the subject of philosophical refutation persistently reasserts itself may seem mysterious, but it underlies much of the opposition to the claim that there can be value for the dead. Egoistic hedonism trades on the close association between valuing an outcome and taking pleasure in the realization of that outcome. If A values end E, then A's desire for E is satisfied when E comes to obtain, and A typically is pleased when he comes to know that E has been achieved. Because the pleasure of satisfaction typically follows the fulfillment of desire, there is temptation to claim that it is the anticipation of pleasure that moves one to act. Nonetheless, it is a mistake to equate satisfaction of a desire with the feeling of satisfaction and also mistaken to hold that what A *really* values is the feeling of pleasure produced by knowledge that E obtains. A desire is satisfied if that which is the object of the desire should come about, but there is no necessary connection between satisfaction of a *desire* and satisfaction of the *agent*. One who gets what he wanted may feel satisfied by the result, but he may also feel disappointment, satiation, zeal to get on with the pursuit of other ends, or may experience no significant emotions at all. We would not predicate the term 'satisfied' of both desires and agents were it not the case that they usually go together, but it should not be thought that wanting a desire to be satisfied is to want the feeling of satisfaction. There is no phenomenological difference between feeling satisfied when one *knows* that E obtains and feeling satisfied because one *mistakenly believes* that E obtains. If what A cares about is E, then A will disvalue being led to believe that E obtains when it does not, and A will assign positive value to the state of affairs: E obtaining but A believing that E does not obtain. In general, pleasurable feelings of satisfaction are of little moment to agents, else we would value pleasant delusions; what we care deeply about is the realization of the ends for which we act and not the feelings that may accompany their realization.

Some of the agent's ends necessarily die when he does: those which involve having experiences and performing actions. Their irreversible termination is what makes death an evil,[17] but death does not eliminate all value that can accrue to an individual. For one who values only his own states of consciousness death is the great misfortune, and no posthumous events can add or detract from the total of value that the individual accrued during his life. But, as was noted by Aristotle, the tally of a life can continue to mount after the life itself has ended:

> Must no one at all, then, be called happy while he lives; must we, as Solon says, see the end? Even if we are to lay down this doctrine, is it also the case that a man *is* happy when he is *dead?* Or is not this quite absurd, especially for us who say that happiness is an activity? But if we do not call the dead man happy, and if Solon does not mean this, but that one can then safely *call* a man blessed as being at last beyond evils and misfortunes, this also affords matter for discussion; for both evil and good are thought to exist for a dead man, as much as for one who is alive but not aware of them; e.g. honours and dishonours and the good or bad fortunes of children and in general of descendants.[18]

Honor or dishonor and the fortunes of children are common objects of concern, do not make essential reference to the ability to have experiences, and so can be affected to an agent's benefit or detriment after he has died. Indeed, there is even a sense in which the agent himself can exert an efficacy that postdates his own demise: not as a ghostly substance casting spells on a world he has left, but through actions he took while still alive that continue to bear fruit when he no longer exists.

Project pursuers have reason to act while they are alive to bring about states of affairs that will continue to generate value for them when they are dead. In part this is a natural consequence of other-directed activity, requiring no special provision for posthumous dispositions. A parent who locates a substantial component of personal value for him or herself in having and raising children whose good is thereby the good of the parent will, while alive, accrue benefits and harms as the children fare well or ill and will continue to reap those values after death. The success or failure of the parent's projects will depend on how things work out for the children. That is Aristotle's point. A further consequence is that the parent has reason to act to bring about specific performances conducive to the good of the children to be carried out upon the parent's death. Arrangements for insurance payments, guardianship of minor children, and disposition of property in the parent's estate are familiar examples of such arrangements. Because these tend to generate good for surviving children, they also redound to the parent's tally of achievement. Consider what we would be inclined to say about a parent who was thoroughly devoted to his or her child's welfare, lavished affection on the child, dutifully read Dr. Spock from cover to cover, visited the pediatrician, dentist, piano teacher, and PTA at regular intervals—but neglected to make provision for the child's upbringing in the event of his or her untimely death. Should the child then suffer an Oliver Twist–like fate, we would say that it was a misfortune to the child but also that it represented a severe (and probably culpable) failure on the part of the parent. *Both* lives have been diminished in value.

It follows that individuals have reason to secure results contingent on their own death and thus have subsidiary reason to support institutional structures guaranteeing that posthumous dispositions will in fact be carried out according to the wishes of the deceased. This is not a strictly universal desideratum of project pursuers: volitional solipsists with no ends beyond their own subjective states of consciousness have no stake in what transpires after their careers as recipients of experience have ended. Such total self-absorption, though, must be uncommon, else successful sociality would be impossible. In any stable polity it will be in the interest of the vast majority of project pursuers that they be legally enabled to enter into contractual arrangements that will be deemed valid and enforceable in the event of their death. One is harmed if one's last will and testament is not honored and also if the society's legal framework does not vest individuals with the power to author a binding and legally enforceable will. If the collectivity assumes for itself power to dispose of the assets of deceased persons in whatever way best accords with the social goals incorporated in the current Five Year Plan, if the wishes of the deceased have only the force that political authorities choose to give them, then individualism has suffered a blow. Because individuals have a basic right to the enjoyment of liberty, they have the right to exercise liberty with respect to posthumous determinations.

The ability of each of us to affect the world is starkly limited. Our careers as active beings are short, our causal powers minute, our most resolute efforts at the mercy of an uncaring natural order and the limited sympathies of other human beings. Reflection on one's finitude generates the Tragic Sense of Life, and when such reflection is coupled with despair at how little the universe knows or responds to one's feeble attempt to act on it, a sense of the absurdity of human existence naturally presents itself. It is easy to wallow in such seas of pessimism when contemplating the vastness of *it* and the relative inconsequentiality of the *I* that peers out on the world. As active beings, though, we necessarily overcome, or at least set aside, despair. To act for the sake of an end is to assign value to its realization and thus to presuppose that one's existence as an active being is suffused with the power to create value: if not value for the universe, then personal value for oneself. Recognition of the limits imposed by finitude may, when one abandons oneself to reflection, give all action the appearance of being empty and meaningless, but it cannot appear that way to the agent as he acts, else, like Oblomov, he would be paralyzed from undertaking any initiative whatsoever. Koheleth preached that all was vanity—but that did not stop him from writing a book! Awareness of limitation *does,* however, have practical significance for active beings such as ourselves; it provides reason to push against the constraints that bound our efficacy and so to extend the borders, if only by a hair.

Inevitable and inescapable death is the great constraint. It can be confronted by denial of its ultimate reality, envisioning instead a sea of eternity in which we perpetually float. Even if its waves wash away almost everything that we care about in this life, *we* nonetheless endure as beings with a good. An alternative to the denial of death, or, in some versions, a complement to the denial that death is, in every sense, the termination of the self, is to recognize that death does constrain our ability to accrue value, but that it does not mark the furthest outpost to which value for the self can reach. By committing ourselves to ends that outlive the self we create stores of value that also outlive the self. Social devices that extend causal efficacy beyond the perimeter of mortality enhance the individual's abiiity to maintain a grip on the world. Of course, that grip is profoundly loosened by death, and it eventually diminishes to nothingness. Like a projectile that has attained escape velocity, we leave our home behind but remain within the pull of its gravitational attraction for some time. That attraction steadily diminishes, and eventually we are entirely separated from its ability to affect us for good or ill. With characteristic acuity, Aristotle notes both that good and evil can befall the dead, but also that this susceptibility, like life itself, is temporary.

It is therefore rational to ascribe rights to the dead on essentially the same grounds that support rights for living project pursuers. There is indeed a unique poignancy that attaches to posthumous performances called for by deathbed promises or a last will and testament; if compliance is not forthcoming, there will be no opportunity for the individual to recoup his losses by seeking value elsewhere. Reverence for the final declaration of one who has died is not merely some superstitious residue of belief in spirits or shades who watch over the living, but rather rests on an accurate recognition of the injury that death does to the pursuit of value and on a concomitant unwillingness to magnify that injury through treating the dead as if they were simply moral nonentities.[19]

But if the dead are not strictly nonentities, what, then, are they? If death's reality is not denied, if death is seen as the final and irrevocable termination of an individual's existence, to whom could one possibly be attributing rights in claiming them for the dead? This is the logical challenge that confronts the intuitively appealing claim that respect is owed to the dead. Respect must be for someone or something, and it may appear that, once the individual has died, there is no plausible candidate. It is nonsensical to suppose that corpses are the sort of thing that can have interests or rights. To attribute rights to one who has died must be to attribute them to the antemortem[20] person he once was. ". . . person he once was"; the phrase expresses the crux of the difficulty. One who was *once* a person is *no longer* a person and thus is not a potential repository of *current* harms and benefits. Indeed, one who was once a person is no longer anything at all; he has simply ceased to be. Left behind are his "remains," but the decaying body is not identical to the antemortem person whose body it was. If there is no subject who has rights, then there simply can be no rights.

What I wish to maintain is that there "is" a subject of rights, though the one whose rights they are "is" no more. The seeming inconsistency is due to the grammatical usage in which the present tense is employed to refer timelessly to an entity. 4 plus 7 *is* 11; the copula is used to express a timeless proposition rather than one taking specific account of present circumstances. My grandfathers *are* Louis Lomasky and Benjamin Feinberg; though neither lives, I am not thereby rendered grandfatherless in the atemporal sense—though, to my sorrow, I *have* (present tense) no grandfather. Similarly, there are things that I did last Thursday even though those activities and that day have passed from current existence. Reference does not become impossible when the referent of a term ceases to exist; the proposition $F(a)$ succeeds in referring if a is/was/will be, and '$F(a)$' is true if, timelessly, F is a property of a. It is timelessly true of A that A has end E and it also is timelessly true that wrongful thwartings of E count as violating the rights of A. Of course, the existence of every individual has a temporal span and every rights violation is datable, but there is no logical necessity that the times overlap. It is true of my grandfathers that I have recently written about them, but the time at which I wrote was not within the span of either of their lives.

It may seem that posthumous rights violations invoke the ungainly specter of backwards causation. If I now break a promise made to my grandfather, then I violate his right to my performance. But since the right attaches to the antemortem person that previously existed, I have brought about an outcome for someone in the past. Is this not to claim the remarkable ability to reach back through time and cause alterations to the welfare of residents of the past?

The charge is mistaken. There is no reaching back through time, or at least none that is metaphysically dubious. To remember an event is, metaphorically, to reach back into the past, but it is not to *cause* any past event. Does one not cause the event to be (an event that is) remembered? Yes, but the event's being remembered is something that takes place in the present. Similarly, to bring about an outcome for a past person is not to bring about a past outcome. To generalize: one can at time t cause it to become the case that property F characterize the no longer existent entity a, in which case it is timelessly true that: $F(a)$ at t. But it is at t that one has caused F to characterize a.

In an otherwise impeccable analysis of the sense in which the dead have interests and can suffer harms, Joel Feinberg retreats from the paradox of backwards causation only to thrust himself into the equally paradoxical result that one is in "a harmed condition" before the harm occurred. Feinberg writes:

> An event occurs after Smith's death that causes something to happen at that time. So far, so good; no paradox. Now, in virtue of the thing that was caused to happen at that time it is true that Smith was in a harmed condition before he died. It does not suddenly "become true" that the antemortem Smith was harmed.

Rather it becomes apparent to us for the first time that it was true all along—
that from the time Smith invested enough in his cause to make it one of his
interests, he was playing a losing game.[21]

This does not have even the *feel* of a correct analysis. Suppose that the
event that "causes something to happen" is a false and malicious defamatory utterance about Smith's alleged secret life and that what happens is that
Smith's reputation plummets. Feinberg would have it that the deliverance of
the utterance is not what makes it become true then that the antemortem
Smith was harmed; it rather enables us to know that "Smith was in a harmed
condition all along." But that would render the significance of the utterance
purely epistemic; it provides us knowledge of a circumstance that already
was in effect. On what basis, then, could we possibly condemn the utterance? It has caused the scales to fall from our eyes, letting us in on the fact
that poor Smith had lived out his life in a harmed condition of which he and
we were altogether ignorant. However, providing conditions in which persons come to know that a harm obtained is not to be guilty of causing the
harm, nor is it otherwise generally wrongful. Those who care for Smith may
be grieved to be made aware of the harmed condition that characterized his
life, but even if causing them grief is a wrong done by the utterance, it is
not a wrong done to Smith, who, for better or worse, is beyond *that* kind
of harm.

Feinberg confuses timeless truth with "being true all along." It is not
true all along, that is, from some stipulated beginning and at every subsequent moment up until the present, that 4 plus 7 is 11. It is timelessly true
that the defamatory utterance constitutes a harm for Smith, but it does not
follow that if the utterance is made in 1984, then Smith is in a harmed
condition in 1953, is in a harmed condition in 1954, is in a harmed condition . . . when he dies in 1979, and remains in a harmed condition thenceforward. I find it hard to understand what it can be for the dead to "be in a
harmed condition," just as I find it hard to understand what it might be to
"be in a remembered condition." We do not typically use the locution of
someone "being in a ——— condition" to express such relational facts.
Perhaps Feinberg uses 'is in a harmed condition' simply to mean "is harmed."
But in that case Smith is not harmed until the utterance is made (nor is he
remembered until the memory occurs), and it is consistent with the harm
not preceding the utterance that the utterance *is*—timelessly—a harm to Smith.

It can therefore be claimed, quite unparadoxically, that harms (or "the
condition of being harmed") come to be when the harmful event does and
that the occurrences of harmful events are not just the visible signs of previously existing harms but are rather the causally potent instruments through

which harms are generated. Reference to the dead is a semantic mine field that always threatens to explode the unwary, and it is doubtlessly the case that there remain potentially damaging devices that this section has not defused. Whatever the logical pitfalls that remain, it seems unlikely that any are unavoidable. We can, then, with some confidence, continue to attribute to the dead interests, harms, and rights.

Animals

The case for recognizing rights in animals as developed by contemporary moral philosophers[22] characteristically features two prongs. The first is an elucidation of properties possessed by animals, especially the higher animals, that make for moral significance. Animals are sentient, having the capacity to experience pleasure and pain. They are intelligent, manifesting the capacity to learn from experience. They have interests, at least interests in not suffering and in not being killed, and arguably an interest in reproducing and in living an unfettered life within their natural habitat. Animals have desires that can either be satisfied or frustrated. Some seem to be able to develop attachments to others of their species or to persons. They respond to kindness. The indicated conclusion is that animals rise to levels approaching those of human beings.

The second prong is to show that human beings can fall to a level no higher than that of animals, or, rather, they not only can fall to but are born to such a level. An infant lacks even the capacity of a puppy to experience, to advance its interests, and to understand its world. Severe mental deficiency can result in lifelong intelligence inferior to that of chimpanzees. Human beings are laid low by disease and senescence. Even if it is admitted that human beings on average outdo all other animals along every morally relevant dimension, the defender of animal rights takes it to be a significant fact that there is considerable overlap between humans and animals.

The conclusion that animals ought to be recognized as rights holders can next be sought along either of two paths, which I shall call the *radical* and the *conservative* approaches. The radical approach attempts to identify some one property or combination of properties P as necessary and sufficient for having rights. This approach involves doing rights theory from the bottom up: one first makes the case that unique moral significance attaches to P and then proceeds straightforwardly to carry out a census among potential rights claimants to determine which of them are characterized by P. The approach is radical because it does not allow itself to be distracted by pretheoretical intuitions concerning who the bona fide rights holders are. If some beings typically taken to enjoy rights find themselves cast into the moral wilderness, this is a salutary bit of conceptual housecleaning that will replace old taboos and superstitions with rationally grounded requirements for entrance into the moral community. So, if P is the ability to experience pleasure and pain, members of all vertebrate and several invertebrate species will be accorded the status of rights holder, as will children and advanced fetuses. Comatose human beings, however, will not. If instead P is awareness of one's self as a continuing subject of experience, fewer animals will be recognized as having rights. However, neither infants nor many severely impaired adult human beings will be accounted as rights holders. Whether the proposed boundary of the moral community is relatively inclusive or relatively exclusive, it will take a shape significantly at odds with customary moral intuitions.

The conservative approach declines to assume the burden of directly challenging pretheoretical intuitions. Rather, it will take these as given and attempt to show that any consistent rendering of the principles of inclusion underlying conventional morality will allow animals in as rights holders. Infants, the senile, the profoundly retarded have rights; now compare them to the higher animals. It will be found that animals score no lower, and probably a good bit higher, along almost any plausible dimension of moral significance. This is to do rights theory from the top down. The conservative approach attends most strongly to the second prong of the case for animal rights, while the radical approach emphasizes the first prong. Within the conservative brief it can be left quite open what the ultimate ground of rights might be, but whatever it is, one excludes animals only at the peril of being logically forced to exclude human claimants. Even if it at first seems strange to recognize animals as entitled to the respect due to rights holders, that perception can be overcome by attention to other cases in which the standing of moral claimants has been recognized only after a long struggle to broaden the sensitivities of those who would recommend exclusion. Analogies to racist and sexist denigration are commonly invoked: just as blacks were formerly enslaved and deprived of acknowledgment as full-fledged persons, just as women were virtual slaves to males convinced of the superiority of the masculine to the feminine, so, too, are animals victims of a persistent ''speciesism'' that refuses to recognize them as morally considerable beings. The process of expanding moral vision to overcome prejudices based on race and sex has not been completed; similar expansion to take in animals has barely begun. Evolution to an adequately synoptic moral consciousness will not be complete, though, until *all* barriers standing in the way of regard and respect for every morally considerable being have been obliterated.

Both strategies fail to establish a convincing case, and why this is so becomes clear when their presuppositions are uncovered. The radical approach tacitly assumes an *internalist* basis for rights. Sentience, reflective self-awareness, or the capacity to entertain and act on behalf of desires are qualities a thing either has or lacks in its own right. Pick the morally central property and award the laurel wreath to those who exemplify it! The bold theorist will be daunted neither by conflicting views as to what that property is nor by the deep-seated moral intuitions that must be cast aside to make way for radical reconstruction. This construal of the form that an adequate theory of rights must take was criticized at some length in the preceding chapter, and it would be tiresome to rehash those arguments here. Most proponents of the conservative approach also are internalists, but to the extent they refrain from committing themselves to one favored conception of the provenance of rights they are able to skirt the issue of what the ultimate root of rights might be. For the conservative, whatever it is that constitutes human adults and children as worthy of moral consideration will also confer protection on animals. The presupposition standing behind this position is *univalence;* all beings that have rights do so for essentially the same reason, whatever that reason might be. (That is not to deny that radicals also tend to subscribe to univalence; internalism and univalence typically go hand in hand.) Once it is denied, though, that there is any one feature in virtue of which all rights holders are such, the conservative approach collapses. Project pursuers have rights in virtue of being generators of personal value. Children are not project pursuers but have rights because they are prospective project pursuers with individual goods that are a function of the projects they will, in the natural course of things, come to hold. Defective human beings may be unable ever to pursue projects but have rights because they are embedded in rich networks of social relationships with others of their kind and because moral principles applying to persons in general also apply to them. The dead have rights because their erstwhile project pursuit leaves behind significant interests that can be advanced or retarded by others. Moreover, each of these is readily identifiable and reidentifiable by others as a distinct individual with a good of his or her own. The theory of rights that puts forth these disparate nominations for candidacy as a rights holder takes project pursuit as a fundamental datum grounding the existence of rights but rejects both internalism and univalence.

On each of the criteria listed above animals fail to qualify for membership into the moral community. No animal is a project pursuer, a prospective project pursuer, or an erstwhile project pursuer. Nor is any animal a defective or impaired member of a class of beings that ordinarily develop into project pursuers: a mature and intact dog does not *fall short* of being a person; it is rather a fully developed representative of its own kind. The denial of rights to animals is thoroughly *dis*analogous to the denial of rights to blacks, women, and other oft-discriminated-against classes of human beings. Withholding rights from any such class of persons is to violate their legitimate claim to live as project pursuers, to raise their children in peace and security, and so on; the same cannot be said on behalf of animals.

That is not to maintain that there is *nothing* to be said on behalf of animals. To deny that a dog has rights is not to say that it is morally inconsequential in every respect, that to pour gasoline on the dog and ignite it is on a par with burning a pile of leaves. The proponent of animal rights is not mistaken in taking sentience, possession of desires, and self-awareness to be morally consequential characteristics; the mistake is in supposing that they establish the existence of rights. That one ought not cause suffering to a beast (unless as a necessary accompaniment to securing some great good or averting a great evil) does not rest on a prior acknowledgment of it as a rights holder. Suffering is an evil in itself for whatever or whoever undergoes it; that is sufficient reason for its being wrong to cause an animal needless suffering. The willful production of suffering is wrong whether or not it is the violation of rights. A gratuitously insulting remark made to or in the hearing of another person is a wrong committed to that person even if the speaker acts within his right of free speech and violates no right of the one to whom reference is made. A rich man who lights his cigar with a $100 bill rather than giving the money to his neighbor who is poor does what he wishes with property that is his by right, but he nonetheless acts unspeakably. Rights establish moral constraints that *must not* be violated, but one who never violates a right might nonetheless show himself to be thoroughly wicked. To *do what is right* and to *do what is demanded by rights* should not be conflated. It is no paradox to assert that we have the right to do what is wrong.

The transition from asserting of a being that it is not morally inconsequential to claiming for it rights has become all too easily bridged in recent years and is part and parcel of the inflation of rights-talk that was decried in Chapter 1. It is feared by those with a case to make that unless moral claims are phrased in extravagant and grandiloquent terms, they will be ignored. If that is so, the apprehension has the nature of a self-fulfilling prophecy. An incessant barrage of nonnegotiable demands tends to drown out modestly voiced calls for attention. Whether the burgeoning animal rights movement is more cause or more effect of rights-talk inflation I do not know. It is apparent, however, that injunctions against cruelty to animals have been giving way to demands for acknowledgment of rights in animals. It seems unlikely that this shift has been occasioned by any new understanding of the capacity of animals to feel or to have interests, or that it is the result of any breakthrough in the theory of rights. Rather, it is moral escalation pure and simple—and it is uncalled for.

That which can legitimately be said on behalf of animals requires no resort to rights. Animals can experience pain, and so inflicting pain on them is wrong. Moreover, it is not a free-floating wrong (to society at large, to the Form of the Good) but rather is a wrong to *them*. Cruelty to animals is not vicious because it hardens the heart of the perpetrator or because it offends the sensibilities of those who care for animals, although it may have those bad effects too; it is wrong because it injures the animal to no good purpose. Persons who are heedless of the welfare of animals are properly condemnable although they violate no rights. Because there are goods and evils for animals, a person of even modest moral attainment will be one who secures for them benefits when these are easily obtainable and avoids doing them harm except when avoidance is excessively costly. This is not very different from what morality dictates with respect to other human beings. The major difference is that some harms and, very occasionally, some denials of benefits to human beings are rights violations, while no such action done to an animal violates its rights.[23]

This may satisfy the proponent of "animal rights" but not the proponent of animal *rights*. The former is one who has adopted the current fashion of phrasing moral injunctions whenever possible in the language of rights. What he or she wants, though, is to draw attention to the moral considerability of animals and will be content if that considerability is acknowledged by the rest of us. The latter, however, will find any moral acknowledgment short of the recognition of rights insufficient. He or she will make much of the fact that doing harm to animals was above labeled a moral violation *unless* avoidance was excessively costly. This clearly falls short of an absolute or even near-absolute proscription against harming animals. What the dyed-in-the-wool (no pun intended) proponent of animal rights declares is that one may *never* intentionally do harm to an animal (with rights), or may never do so unless it would be permissible to harm a human being in similar circumstances. For example, if it is impermissible (i.e., not merely wrong but a violation of rights) to use a nonconsenting person as subject of a medical experiment testing the efficacy of a new drug, one may not do so with an animal. If it is impermissible to kill and eat your next-door neighbor, it is impermissible to kill and eat a deer. Only this strong line is properly referred to as a doctrine of animal *rights*.

Against this maximal claim there are at least three things that should be said. First, many of those concerned to advance the welfare of animals are not proponents of animal *rights*—the language they employ notwithstanding. For even when "rights" are claimed on behalf of animals, it is clear that often they are not intended to function with the stringency of the rights enjoyed by persons. "One may not inflict *needless* suffering on animals"; "The *gratuitous* causing of pain to an animal is wrong"; "Baby seals should not be slaughtered to satisfy the *vanity* of women who wish to wear stylish furs"; "The confinement that animals suffer on modern factory farms is *inhumane.*" Each of these expresses a moderate claim on behalf of animals, not the maximal demands we would surely raise on behalf of human beings. One may not inflict pain on another person needlessly or gratuitously, but one also may not do so in the service of an attractive end. People may not be slaughtered or kept in involuntary confinement—period. (Well, almost "period." Qualifications for capital punishment or judicial incarceration are duly noted but will not further detain us.) It would be outrageous to come out merely against the employment of painful and fear-engendering butchering techniques on other persons, not because persons lack an interest in avoiding uncomfortable conscious states but because such a stance does not go nearly far enough in stating the inviolability of genuine rights holders. The fact that defenses of animals are typically qualified in ways that would be grotesquely inappropriate if it were persons' interests that were at stake indicates that much of the proanimals movement is characterized imprecisely when described as a movement for animal *rights*.

Second, if animals were recognized as rights holders, a good number of the actions that decent people take on behalf of animals would be moral violations. Recall that rights operate as side constraints precluding otherwise optimific opportunities for value maximization. One may not kill one person to confiscate organs that can be used to save three others even if the utilitarian calculus indicates that total utility is thereby increased. Persons who manifest a desire to continue living may not be killed even though they are in constant pain and though impartial spectators judge that the suffering person would be better off dead. If such side constraints are extended to animals, the result will be that some paths to maximum human well-being will be blocked, but also blocked will be paths to maximum *animal* welfare and maximum *total* (human and animal) welfare. It will be judged impermissible to kill tens of thousands of animals in labaratory experiments for the sake of saving a few hundred human lives, but also impermissible to kill a few hundred animals in order to save tens of thousands of human lives or that number of animal lives. Thinning out a herd of deer will be forbidden even when the result is that many more deer die a painful death from starvation during the winter than would have been felled by the hunter's gun. One could no more euthanatize one's old dog than one's old grandfather. (Actually less so; the grandfather can give consent to his own death while the dog is unable to consent and probably is incapable of entertaining or expressing through its actions a desire to die rather than remain in suffering.) Spaying or neutering animals would partake of the same moral odiousness that stains the "eugenic" sterilizations perpetrated on blacks and the feebleminded earlier in this century; and so on. These results run counter to concern for animal welfare. Do their advocates *really* prefer for animals such an outcome? Because project pursuers generate personal value incommensurable with the personal value generated by others, there is reason to recognize side constraints operative in interactions among human beings. What, though, could conceivably serve as the rationale for imposing side constraints on dealings with animals?

Third, once it has been conceded that animals have moral standing, the impetus to claim for them rights is largely defused. That they are valuable beings to whom good and ill can befall is freely acknowledged and, as stated above, that is at least a substantial component of what is urged by animals' advocates. Standard arguments for animal rights erroneously presuppose that rights are internalistic and univalent. With that prop removed, it becomes extremely problematic how the case for animal rights can get off the ground. It may be that the argument admits of refurbishing or redirection along novel lines, but until demonstration is in hand, we do well to draw the line against rights inflation at the boundary separating the human species from others.

9

Beyond Basic Rights

Rights occupy a strategic position within the overall structure of moral theory, responding as they do to the fundamental separateness of persons and their projects and to the incommensurability of personal value among individuals. However, fidelity to the demands of rights is by no means the whole of what makes for moral rightness—an action can be in accord with rights but yet be manifestly *wrong*—so the theory of rights finds its place within deontic theory of what we ought and ought not to do. Deontology is in turn embedded in axiology, the study of what (actions or states of affairs) has *value*. That is, respect for rights is a subclass of the right, and the Theory of the Right is incomplete unless accompanied by the Theory of the Good.

Modern moral philosophy has shown itself to be much more comfortable with the right than with the good. To the extent that morality is conceived to be a decision procedure for adjudicating the disparate claims of contending individuals to secure what they want (Chapter 3), moral theory is deemed to succeed if it identifies rules or principles for adjudication of interpersonal clashes of interest and desire to which all can (or, stronger still, *must*) rationally assent. The flip side of this conception is that it is not the business of moral philosophy to tell individuals where their good lies or what they *ought* to desire (beyond the harmony that observance of moral rules affords each of us). Individuals bring desires to their social life, and where they acquire these desires or what the objects of their desires might be is up to them. The function of morality is to regulate behavioral expressions of antecedently existent desires so that as many desires of as many persons as possible, or those that are most intensely felt, or some weighting of number and intensity, can be realized. *De gustibus non est disputandum*—unless, of course, a person's tastes motivate antisocial behavior. Here, too, the shape of morality can be seen as being modeled on that of prudence. A man acts prudently if he strives to give maximum effect to *all* his desires (over the course of a lifetime) but is not judged prudent or imprudent because of the specific natures of the desires he holds. Similarly, moral success or failure is seen as a function of the degree to which harmony of desires among persons obtains rather than in persons having *correct* desires or desire for the *truly worthwhile*.

I must at once admit that the above characterization applies with discomfiting exactitude to the argument of *this* book. The distinctiveness of projects was taken as the starting point for the progression to rights. Individuals are held to have compelling reason to act on the projects that are theirs *because* they are theirs. Personal value was said to be posterior to individual commitment and was left entirely open-ended, not the consequence of any preexistent (impersonal) value out in the world. Whether a project is directed at the noble or the base, is self-absorbed or comprehends the interests of others, aims at the transient or that which endures: these were not allowed to make any difference concerning the rational motivation each person has to act for the sake of his own directive ends. Rights emerged not exactly as a decision procedure for agents to follow, because both doing X and refraining from X will often be consonant with full respect for rights, but as setting interpersonally acceptable bounds for bare permissibility of actions. If the vistas of modern moral philosophy in general are limited to working with the desires that individuals happen to have, then so, too, is the argument of this essay.

I regard this not as an indictment of the procedure followed in the preceding chapters but instead as confirmatory of the limited scope of the theory of rights within moral philosophy. It is not to be supposed that an adequate mapping of who the rights holders are and what rights they have settles anything like all the extant problems of moral philosophy or settles its most important problems. Just as proliferation in public forums of rights claims is to be resisted, so, too, is a conception of moral philosophy in which rights predominate. Rights dictate what one *must* do and refrain from doing; that is all. They leave entirely open what counts as more than barely acceptable conduct and to what projects individuals ought to devote themselves in order to construct a life of maximum value.

Seeking Value

It is the second of these, the question of what projects individuals ought to embrace, that most directly confronts the problem of value. It might be supposed (though wrongly, I believe) that what distinguishes minimally tolerable conduct from that which is pitched at a higher level is the extent to which an agent chooses to go beyond what is strictly obligatory in acting to satisfy the desires of others. A decent person regularly forgoes small pleasures of his own to secure considerably greater satisfactions for others, while a hero or a saint willingly sacrifices almost all of his or her self-absorbed pursuits to bring value to others.[1] Such an analysis, though, takes desires as given and assigns moral rank based on whether the desires one acts to satisfy are one's own or, in the first instance, those of other persons. Whether that which is desired by oneself or anyone else possesses independent value is left out of consideration. It may be reasonable employment of a volitional division of labor to leave to each individual the determination of whether what he aims at has worth, so that to act on behalf of another involves only the attempt to advance the desires that person in fact has. But the question of what has value in its own right cannot be evaded in deliberation over that to which one will devote one's *own* major energies and emotions, or in reflective appraisal of whether one's active life has been well or ill directed. Such fundamental examination of one's life as a pursuer of value may not be common, and properly so if its effect is to divert one for an extended period from action, but when it does occur it is not confined to introspective scrutiny of desires actually held but inquires as to which desires are *worthy* for a being such as oneself.

We can provide a rationale for some of our desires in terms of other, more fundamental desires to which the subsidiary desires are instrumental. A desires X in order to get E: the desire for X is explained by reference to A's desire for E. But what explains the desire for E? Either E is instrumental to the satisfaction of some further desire, say, for E*, or else E is desired for itself. I shall assume that the chain of desires must be finite and noncircular, in which case there are desires unaccounted for by the urge to satisfy other desires. Let us, not very originally, call these "noninstrumental desires." Those noninstrumental desires which are of great moment over long stretches of an individual's life and motivate subsidiary valuations are a person's projects. What is it that can justify a noninstrumental desire for E? Either the desire for E has no justification, is simply a given for A, or else it is justified by something standing ouside of the desires A happens to have.

An appetite is an instance of the former sort of noninstrumental desire. Craving for a kosher dill pickle comes over one, and one either eats a pickle or not. There is no question of it being a good or bad thing to want to eat a pickle (except insofar, of course, as that desire might happen to contribute to or detract from one's other purposes), but for one who comes to have the desire, eating a pickle is a good because eating generates satisfaction. Had the craving instead been for chocolate chip cookies or for sex or for a brisk run around the block, then satisfaction will be achievable along a somewhat different route. One with an appetite for something need not consider whether that for which he has the appetite is intrinsically valuable, only what the costs and benefits of acting to satisfy the appetite are. If the calculation comes out one way, a person acts rationally in attempting to satisfy the appetite; if it comes out the other way, he is best advised to put up with dissatisfaction or, if he can, to extinguish the appetite.

A theory of value that takes all noninstrumental desires as simply given sees even a person's projects as appetites, albeit extraordinarily persistent and consequential appetites. A project pursuer is then one who has an abiding appetite toward the satisfaction of which he directs a major share of his efforts. This is a thoroughly unsatisfactory construal of projects. One devoted to the realization of E cares very deeply that he *achieve* E but also cares that it is *E* he achieves. Should A be made aware that E is difficult of attainment but that some alternative end E* is relatively easily within his grasp, that will not stand as reason for A to transform his commitment to E into a commitment to E* even if such redirection of energies is easily brought about. If it is the dictatorship of the proletariat that commands A's deepest concern, but the proletariat look to be losers in the contest with the generals and the plutocrats, A will not be acting irrationally when he turns down an offer of bargain-basement-priced psychoanalysis guaranteed to turn him into an enthusiastic capitalist tool. That is because A does not value being a success at something or other; what he values is *this* distinctive end. It would be irrational, though, for someone to persist in a forever-to-be-dissatisfied craving for an item if it were within his power to redirect the craving toward something else more readily at hand. If satisfaction is simply satisfaction, one brand as good as another supplied in equal quantity and intensity, then it is immaterial whence satisfaction derives.[2]

One who is overcome with cravings acts rationally to satisfy the cravings, but he also acts rationally if he attempts to *extinguish* them. If desires are extinguished, then they no longer provide an opportunity to achieve satisfaction, but neither do they threaten pangs of dissatisfaction. Optimists will pursue the maximax strategy of entertaining as many appetites as possible so as to maximize chances for satisfaction, but those more pessimistically inclined will prescribe extinction of desire as a prudent maximin strategy for minimizing dissatisfaction. This is the philosophy of the cold shower and also, I believe, of Epicureanism. Extinction of desire is a reasonable exercise of prudence when desire has the character of an appetite, but is inappropriate toward one's projects. One for whom the attainment of E is a directive value cares relatively little for the feeling of satisfaction that will accompany the attainment of E and disvalues only secondarily feelings of dissatisfaction engendered by knowledge that attempts to secure E have failed. What he cares about is E and not his own subjective feelings. Extinguishing desire for E makes no sense because it caters only to the disvalue of the feeling of dissatisfaction and fails to respond to the value that resides in E.

It follows that an ethic proclaiming the centrality of project pursuit cannot assay all desires as appetites of varying intensity and duration. If advancing E is one's project, then extinguishing the desire for E is no good at all. "Better Socrates dissatisfied than a pig satisfied"; that is because Socrates is committed to projects but a pig has none. One cannot take one's commitments to projects as merely psychological quirks, for as such they could not command one's reflective loyalties. One's projects are not instrumental, either in the sense of standing subsidiary to other desires or as value because what one really wants is the feeling of satisfaction their successful completion would bring. Rather, to value one's project is to value that at which the project aims. It is in this way that consideration of rational activity necessarily points beyond itself, to value in the world.

Consider a young man deliberating with full intensity concerning that toward which he will direct himself. Will it be to join the Resistance or to remain with and assist his infirm mother? The Sartrean example is familiar,[3] but I wish to draw a very different moral from it than does its constructor. First, the young man's choice will be radical in one sense, of posing profound implications for the further course of his life, but not in another, of being unconstrained by value in the world. For a choice to partake of the seriousness that makes it a fitting object of intense deliberation, it must be assumed that one is weighing options each of which has value independent of the fact that one is deliberating about them. That is certainly the case in the present example. Both the welfare of the mother and the cause of the Resistance press forcefully upon the chooser as potential claimants on his energies because each is perceived to be *valuable*. That is what makes the choice difficult and also momentous: difficult because the respective values do not present themselves as easily ranked, momentous because the magnitude of value embodied in each is great. Suppose instead that the choice were between the Resistance and blowing up a case of party balloons in preparation for his birthday. It is inconceivable how someone could find those alternatives to call for a *decision*, let alone one demanding intense mental energy. Even an artist as gifted as Sartre would be unable to present this, as it stands, as an episode laden with possibilities for substantial commitment, and not even an Existentialist Hero could conjure up personal value from so arid a foundation. To extract any drama from that pair of alternatives the choice would have to be presented as really being one of whether to fight or to live safely and unadventurously or as revolving around markedly non-standard beliefs about balloons.

A second and closely related point is that the act of commitment does not generate personal value out of thin air. Unless one perceives a course of activity as holding out realizable value (for someone or other), it cannot be viewed as a potential source of personal value for oneself. The cause of the Resistance has value, but so, too, does the welfare of the mother; that is why there is a choice to be made, and that is why it matters to the young man how he chooses. Should neither alternative possess value until given it by the commitment finally undertaken, then there could not be prior deliberation concerning which of several incompatible values is to be advanced through action. That is, if whatever is chosen thereby comes to have value simply in virtue of being chosen, reflection preceding choice will not be deliberation at all but rather will be a curious kind of predictive activity: prediction of what one will eventually choose, and thus of what does not yet but *will* have value-for-oneself! Nothing could be further from our experience of the agonizing appraisals that precede major turning points in our lives. Our efforts then are aimed not at predicting accurately but at choosing wisely, and the question of what one ought to choose does not devolve to the psychological question of what one will be led to choose or even to the question of what is liable to retain one's interest and energies over the long haul. Such introspective examination may be a part of what properly precedes choice, but it is not all of it nor its major component. There is the additional consideration—and it is crucial—of what is *worthy* to command one's allegiance. Unless a man sees himself as poised between two considerable goods, it will seem a slight matter to him which way he jumps.

It follows that there can be no personal value for individuals unless there is impersonal value, no significance to the commitments one undertakes unless there is significance in the world that precedes the act of commitment. Projects deserving of the wholehearted allegiance of an individual must aim at that which has impersonal value. Enrolling in a plan of life is risky, not just because things may not work out according to plan, but because the plan itself may be foolish. Someone who achieves all that he sets out for can yet look back and ask, "Was this all worthwhile?" The answer, tragically, can be no, in which case one's life is seen as vain and empty. If choice, provided only that it were free from the heart, guaranteed its own success, such retrospective appraisal would always have a happy conclusion. Valuational errors, like errors about matters of fact, are possible, and were this not the case there would be no prospect of getting things *right*. What one is either right or wrong about is not what it is that one has aimed at or whether it has been achieved but whether it is *valuable*.

This is not to present an Aristotelian world in which all value is impersonal, prior to acts of commitment, and in which the job of the agent is to recognize where value lies and to plan shrewdly how to realize as great a quantity of it as possible. I have argued that unless there is some objective truth concerning what is valuable and what is not, no one could, at bottom, have reason to direct his activity in one way rather than another. Personal value cannot be conjured out of nothing; it presupposes the existence of impersonal value. However, it has not been claimed that impersonal value provides a decision procedure to which agents rationally must subscribe as setting out for them the projects they are to undertake. That would be at odds with the whole tenor of the previous chapters in which personal value was seen as individuating agents.

It is one thing to say that the possibility of accruing personal value presupposes the existence of impersonal value, quite another to maintain that measures of impersonal value attaching to the various alternatives that present themselves to an individual completely determine for him what he ought to choose. The latter will be true only if each alternative open to an individual possesses a specific value ranking such that the alternative set can be ordinally arrayed from least to most valuable. That may, I suppose, be the case from some cosmic perspective (if there are any cosmic perspectives to be had), but I cannot begin to fathom how beings such as ourselves could ever know what the rankings are. Perhaps a Leibnizian God occupying himself with the diverting task of actualizing the best of all possible worlds will have before him a computer printout of value assignments for each realizable outcome, but value that presents itself for human cognition does not come so neatly packaged in discrete, quantified bundles. There are, though, other modes in which objective value could validly stand behind decisions. At the broadest extreme, value might display itself simply as a binary function: something either has value in itself or lacks value in itself. Of those things that have value, none can be distinguished as having more or less. The significance for practice will be that only that which truly has value in itself is choiceworthy, but it is entirely up to the agent which of several impersonally valuable items he should choose.

An "on/off" model seems too sparsely furnished to fit our apprehensions of value, just as a complete ordering of all possible outcomes is too lavish. Somewhere between these extremes may be found a more recognizable structure of impersonal value, one that displays a partial ordering. There are, on this hypothesis, several ranges of value in which things can fall. That which is "of profound value" stands above "of considerable value," which in turn outranks "of some value." Beneath these categories of positive value are "of no value" and "disvaluable." However, within any particular class no further order presents itself, and the boundaries of each class are themselves fuzzy. An agent engaged in deliberation is to be taken as trying in the first place to determine in which of these broad and vaguely demarcated categories the possibilities that beckon in fact reside. This is a matter for *discovery* and not *decision,* so it is something one might get right or might get wrong. But, in the second place, if confronted with alternatives each of which is at the same value plateau, the agent must *decide* which to pursue. No preestablished value ranking will settle the choice for him.

This is not to be construed as choice among valuationally indistinguishable items like that of Buridan's ass standing equidistant between two inviting piles of hay. Selecting among indistinguishables is trivial, calling for no close scrutiny of opposed merits because there are none to be found no matter how long or how intently one gazes. A flip of a coin will do. But one contemplating the prospects of two very different courses of life, such as joining the Resistance or remaining with one's mother, is not staring at indistinguishables. It is not because these are valuationally equivalent that there is no predetermined ordering along the spectrum of value but because they are *incommensurable.* Each presents the prospect of leading a life of great value; they are, however, lives of extraordinarily different (not greater and lesser) value. To flip a coin labeled "Resistance" and "Mother" is inappropriate in this case, though not because it might give the "wrong" answer. Rather, flipping the coin is abdication of the agent's own responsibility to choose for himself between items each of which is perceived to exert a legitimate claim on him. Allowing a coin to do a job proper to the will is an instance of bad faith. It is to make a show of locating one's decision-making capacity in external circumstances. It is, though, only a show because, whether the coin comes up Resistance or Mother, one must still elect whether to follow its lead. The choice is ultimately between two very different though incommensurable varieties of *value,* and the only relevant basis on which it can be made is careful scrutiny of the value possibilities before one and a deliberate commitment to devote oneself to one or the other.

It may be objected that this leaves the motivation for choosing one way rather than the other floating on air. To say that end E is *different* that E* is not to give a reason for choosing E over E* or vice versa. It is only if the agent perceives E as *better* in some way than E* that he has reason to opt for E. Murky talk about "incommensurables" and "same value plateau" does not begin to explain on what basis an agent could rationally commit himself to E over E*.

It has not been denied that when the young man chooses, he does so on the basis of differences between the disparate paths of life that make one better than the other. Should he elect to join the Resistance, he can rationally do so on the grounds that this course is better than the alternative in expressing loyalty to comrades and in fighting a terrible evil. However, should he choose to remain at home with his mother, he can justify that decision on the grounds that it is the more fitting response to the love and nurturing he has received from her or that it is the most sharply focused acknowledgment he can offer to the value residing in one particular human being whom he loves. Each alternative is better than the other in some respects—and worse in other respects. To say that they are incommensurable, though, is to deny that one of these "betters" is itself clearly and avowedly better than the other "betters." A choice whichever way it goes will have reason behind it, but nothing predetermines which reason ought to prove decisive. Only the individual can determine that for himself. Both E and E* carry impersonal value. It is by deciding between them that the agent generates, in addition, personal value-for himself.

On some mechanistic modelings of choice, a person is presented with alternatives each of which has precisely weighted reasons for and reasons against. He then plays the part of a scale, passively allowing the weights to press on him until one of the alternatives tips the balance and out spews a piece of behavior. It is then easily explained why he acts in the particular way he does—the vector of forces so inclined him—but it seems impossible to offer, without distortion, a sense in which the action can be comprehended as *free*. Mechanisms are passive, they do not act, and so they do not act freely. What I propose instead is a nonmechanistic, nondeterministic understanding of choice. Weights are given, but because they do not all lie along one dimension that allows them to be amalgamated and cumulated, they do not uniquely determine an outcome. They impinge on the agent as reasons, but he then must determine for himself which of the reasons will weigh *decisively*. The outcome is not specified in advance by the universe or churned out by passive reception and processing of impersonal value, but rather is freely *chosen* by the agent in his role as the active arbitrator among values that have presented themselves to him. How the agent chooses in matters where the direction of a life is at stake opens up some valuational possibilities for the future and closes off others. Some physically attainable outcomes then present themselves as motivationally impossible, others as necessary: "I *cannot* choose that; I *must* instead choose this." But impossibility and necessity of that stripe are not inimical to freedom; they rather presuppose a prior episode of uncoerced, freely entered into commitment.

This is, admittedly, speculative. Perhaps it comes to nothing at all. But if it is false or nonsensical, that should be shown by argument and not by putting forth the propositions:

1. All value is well ordered and commensurable such that there is always something to be identified as "the balance of reasons" and
2. Rational choice is the selection of what is, on balance, best

as truths too obvious to merit discussion.

Value and Experience

Philosophical consideration of value pulls in two directions. On the one hand, unless there is value in the world that is ours to grasp, all our planning and scheming and dreaming seems to be in vain. How can it matter to what we devote ourselves if one set of ends is, in itself, as good as any other? If all ends are of equal—that is, no—inherent value, then desire for them is desire for the inherently valueless. One can *say* that desire creates its own value, but not, I think, with much conviction. If it is of value that a desire for the inherently valueless be satisfied, it is because the resultant feeling of satisfaction is itself valuable and not because value has somehow been conferred on the object attained. An ethic in which all value is personal and all desires are appetites seems too shallow to support projects, rights, and a meaningful life of activity.

On the other hand, value that is not generated by the desires of persons but subsists in the world is . . . what? A ghostly normative substance draping itself over some things but not others? A nonempirical quality that jumps out from special blends of ordinary empirical attributes? Positing value as an objective feature of the warp and woof of the world seems metaphysically extravagant. J. L. Mackie writes:

> If there were objective values, then they would be entities or qualities or relations of a very strange sort, utterly different from anything else in the universe. Correspondingly, if we were aware of them, it would have to be by some special faculty of moral perception or intuition, utterly different from our ordinary ways of knowing everything else.[4]

What are not the least bit strange and otherworldly, though, are preferences and desires. We all have them, for this reason or that reason or no special reason at all. Some are common to almost all human beings and others quite idiosyncratic. No special moral sense is required to scrutinize them. One who prefers X to Y typically is introspectively aware that he does so, and through their choices and conversation people reveal their preferences to others. And just as values are *supposed* to do (if they exist and are knowable), preferences provide reason for action. To prefer X to Y is to have reason to select X over Y. For these reasons, it is tempting to maintain that there is no more to ethics or to practical activity in general than choosing efficient means toward the satisfaction of preferences people currently have or will have in the future. There is no independent branch of value theory that illuminates what preferences one ought to have because there are no "oughts" external to actual preference.

If value were, as the charge has it, in an esoteric province of its own, that is, nowhere, and if value cannot be cognized by ordinary means, then it is a chimera. We should give up all thought of devoting ourselves to the truly valuable, in the process constructing lives that are themselves valuable, and instead resign ourselves to the quotidian task of acting on the desires we do have (not by any means an unpleasant task!). The charge, however, is false. It requires no special faculty to discern objective value, and if value in the world did not exist, we could not create it through our desires. It would, I suppose, be surpassingly strange for there to be value subsisting by itself as a Platonic Form, but such self-subsistent value is not something that could be chosen and is of dubious relevance to practical activity. What is of significance to agents is whether there exists value that they can scrutinze and realize through action.

It was said before that a craving that just comes over one presents its object as something that will *satisfy* but not as something inherently *valuable*. When Jones is overcome with desire for a kosher pickle, he has reason to eat one because he will be satisfied if he eats and dissatisfied if he does not eat. Is this a case in which desire creates its own value (or creates *satisfaction* as a surrogate for *value*)? If it does, where would the value lie that has been created? Not simply in the state of affairs: eating a pickle. For if it were eaten and the craving remained, indeed redoubled itself, and if, no matter how many pickles Jones ate, no satisfaction were achieved, we and he would account the act of eating worse than useless. If any value has been engendered, it is value in the state of affairs: achieving satisfaction (through eating a pickle).[5] What, though, gives *having the satisfaction* its value? It will not do to say that it is because Jones desires the feeling of satisfaction, for then the question reemerges one step further along: What gives value to satisfaction of the level-2 desire to have one's level-1 desire satisfied? Should it be maintained that all value is posterior to desire, an infinite regress beckons. One will desire that one's desires be fulfilled, desire the fulfillment of the desire that one's desires be fulfilled, desire the fulfillment of the desire for the fulfillment of the desire that. . . . As regresses go, this one seems especially tiresome because it is so easily avoidable. It is quickly terminated by recognizing that satisfaction is valuable in itself, not of value because it is the object of a prior desire for satisfaction.

This not only avoids the regress but also seems true to experience. The feeling of satisfaction *is* valuable in itself and is perceived as such. We have an interest in achieving satisfaction and avoiding dissatisfaction because of what they are, not because we have a preference for satisfaction over dissatisfaction in the way we might have a preference for baked over mashed potatoes. Is it even intelligible to suppose that someone might change his mind about this and come to prefer dissatisfaction? Suppose he then achieved a record string of one dissatisfaction after another; would this be a good for him or a bad? If it is a good, it is so in spite of the fact that he achieved *satisfaction* of his preference to be dissatisfied! If it is a bad, then preferring dissatisfaction does not render the experience of dissatisfaction valuable no matter how much one prefers dissatisfaction to satisfaction. It may be suggested that the whiff of paradox that presents itself is due to equivocation on 'dissatisfaction'. What is preferred is not that one's desires (including the desire for dissatisfaction) not be satisfied but that one experience the *feeling* that accompanies the nonfulfillment of desire rather than the *feeling* that accompanies desire's fulfillment. This, too, seems incoherent. There is no *feeling of dissatisfaction* separable from the belief that some desire one possesses has not been satisfied. Usually one knows quite well which desire lacks fulfillment, but occasionally there may just be a general apprehension that *something or other* that one wants is lacking. One who believes that there is nothing lacking to him logically cannot feel dissatisfied.

I believe it to be a necessary truth that satisfaction is inherently more valuable than dissatisfaction. If that is correct, then there is at least one value, the value of satisfaction, that is independent of being desired. Of course, if there were no desires at all, there could be no value in the world occasioned by satisfaction of desire. Satisfaction presupposes desire, but the value of satisfaction does not presuppose or in any way rest on antecedent desire for satisfaction. This is not a trick case; there are many other items of experience that directly present themselves as being valuable. They include: pleasure, joy, equanimity, amusement, elation, release of tension, consolation, the experience of beauty. Others directly present themselves as disvalues: intense pain, sorrow, boredom, disgust, horror, fatigue, an itch that won't go away, intense fear. The value quality of each is not a function of its happening to enter into the utility function of an individual as a preference or as opposed to a preference. If value were simply due to preference, the following brief dialogues would not sound distinctly odd:

A: "I had the feeling of the profoundest joy pass over me!"
B: "Oh, really? Is that the sort of thing you go for?"

A: "This book is one of the most boring ever to come my way."
B: "Why don't you just stop reading it?"

A: "I don't happen to mind being bored. As a matter of fact, I rather prefer it to stimulation."

A: "Try one of these smoked clams; they're delicious!"

B: "I suppose they are, but my tastes in food don't happen to run to the delicious. Do yours?"

It is possible to supply a context in which each of these can be given sense, supplying an appropriate instrumental value to boredom and instrumental disvalue to the experience of joy or gastronomic pleasure. That, though, in no way impugns the inherent value/disvalue of the qualities in question. Indeed, it adds yet another sort of value not consequent on being preferred: instrumental value. If E is good and X is maximally conducive to E, then X has instrumental value irrespective of people's desires for X.

Value is not something foreign from ordinary experience but rather suffuses experience. Mackie is wrong when he states that a special cognitive faculty is required for the awareness of value. Mackie is correct to maintain that value is unlike everything else in the universe, but *every* distinctive sort of thing is unlike everything else. Sounds are unlike everything else in the universe; neither smelling roses, thinking a lot about numbers, nor doing somersaults prepare you for sounds. If you've never heard one, nothing else occupies the niche. There's nothing else quite like electrons or like valid arguments or like being a bat. Should one therefore be suspicious of the existence of sounds, electrons, validity, and bats?

It might be objected that the "independence" from desire claimed above for value is limited. At most it has been shown that an entity can possess value independently of that very thing being desired. It does not show that there would be value in a universe lacking conscious, desirous beings. Thus, the independence of value is only independence from particular desire for the valued thing, not independence from the existence of desire as such.

I suspect, but not with any great stock of confidence, that the objection is correct. I do not understand the sort of value that could subsist in a world without consciousness and desire, but neither can I think of any argument to show that there could be none. If all life ceased, will it not yet be of value that the Milky Way continue in existence? I don't know how to begin to approach that question, nor am I confident that I would recognize a fruitful approach should I encounter one. Perhaps it is counterproductive to consider such questions in isolation from a fully developed axiological theory designed to subsume them, and I don't know where to find that theory. However, its absence should not be worrying in the present context. What is under discussion are goods achievable through action, and therefore discussion can be confined to what can be brought about by beings such as ourselves. One may speculate concerning whether the existence of the Milky Way in a lifeless universe would carry value, but no one—I devoutly hope!—will ever be called upon to act accordingly.

It is only when value is conceived as something apart from all other items of experience that it presents itself as something hopelessly mysterious. When conceived instead as a component of all that one experiences (because the having of experience is itself a good), value throws off the metaphysical shroud that would render it inscrutable. That joy is good in itself and that sorrow is bad in itself are facts as evident as any we know. And it was not an act of desire that made them such. Value, rather than always being consequent on desire for a particular thing or experience, is often discovered through serendipity. The man or woman who first ate an oyster could not have desired *that* particular gustatory sensation! There are solidly empirical grounds for affirming that value exists, that some of it is personal value posterior to the undertakings of agents, and that some is impersonal value, prior to particular preferences, desires, and choices.

Value and Projects

For the ancients, unlike their more recent successors, the fundamental question of ethics was, "How shall I live to achieve a life of value?" Subsidiary to it is the question of how the activities of many value-seekers can be harmonized. Because there is impersonal value that can be known to be value, there are better and worse answers to the Life of Value question.

An ethic in which the pursuit of projects is assigned central place is not at liberty to ignore the Life of Value question. If each individual has overriding reason to pursue the projects that are his, that is because they hold out the prospect of attaining value. To have ends to which one is maximally devoted is flatly incompatible with believing that no value resides in that which is sought. I have argued that the fact of commitment itself creates personal value, but such personal value necessarily rests on a foundation of preexistent impersonal value. Deliberation over whether to throw oneself into a radically new way of life and reflection concerning whether one's life achievements have been pure gold or dross both presuppose that acts of commitment are themselves insufficient to construct a life that is truly well aimed at value. A rational agent is not merely someone good at getting what he wants; he is someone who wants what is good to get.

It would require another and longer book to survey more than superficially where value lies. The reader need entertain neither hope nor fear of finding that book ensconced in these final pages. Instead, some tentative passes at the question of where value might lie for beings such as ourselves will be hazarded. Obviously, the suggestions are not put forth as being exhaustive, nor are they systematically developed. There is a tie-in, though, with the theory of basic rights advanced in the preceding eight chapters. Rights arise from the fact of project pursuit. If the projects to which individuals can address themselves have no inherent value, then there is no inherent value to their success or disvalue to their failure. If that were so, individuals might yet *believe* that importance attaches to their efforts, but they will be mistaken. And it will simply not matter whether rights to live as a project pursuer are respected if the projects that rights protect do not matter. Implicit, then, in the theory of basic rights is the proposition that it is possible to construct a life that has meaning and worth.

A systematic and complete practical philosophy will begin with examination of the nature of value as a genus, follow with an account of value *qua* achievable through action, and only at that juncture introduce basic rights as constraints individuals have reason to place on their own action subject to reciprocal constraint on others such that each is afforded moral space to live as a project pursuer. Although I have worked at only the last of these, it was with recognition that the theory of basic rights presupposes the existence of a realm of impersonal value. Value was treated as a black box into which rights can be plugged. That box must exist for rights to have a point, but its precise content need not be specified in advance. I have attempted to construct one module of an integrated system; others can take up the (more difficult) task of constructing the remaining modules. The purpose of this final chapter is to give some reasons for thinking that such construction is possible, not to carry it out.

It was argued above that some conscious states are impersonally valuable, that they have worth for agents not dependent on antecedent desire for those states. Even if that is correct, it is only the barest toehold on impersonal value. Individuals act not only to achieve valuable conscious states but to secure goods external to consciousness. Valuable conscious states are, for the most part, by-products of the achievement of goods in the world. To experience joy is at least usually to be joyful at the existence of some external state of affairs. I doubt that it is possible to have a pure feeling of joy unmediated by a belief that some wonderful event has transpired. Even if possible, it is surely the exception. Similarly, to be amused is to find something amusing, the feeling of disgust takes as its object that which is disgusting, and so on. Valuable experiences go hand in hand with the apprehension of value in the world. Where, in general, is such value to be found?

If agents have reason to commit themselves to their projects, it is because the construction of a coherent and connected life itself has value. The value resident in a coherent life, however, cannot be personal value. For suppose that it were, that coherence among one's efforts has value only for the person who desires coherence and has it in virtue of that desire. Either the desire for coherence overtakes one fitfully and might at any time give way instead to disdain for coherence, or else it persistently shapes one's efforts to be true to a conception of the good around which one's various efforts revolve. If the former, then one's occasional efforts on behalf of the end of leading a coherent life do not themselves amount to action in pursuit of a project. One will have reason to care about coherence only if and when a craving for it happens to overtake one. The sporadic craving for coherence will be on all fours with other appetites. Just as it is of value for a person to eat a kosher dill pickle only when he happens to experience an appetite for a pickle, it will be of value for a person to pursue coherence only when he happens to crave coherence. This, though, is plainly self-defeating. A random desire for coherence will itself lack coherence with the other desires that come to one. Therefore, desire for a coherent life can offer no opportunity for accruing value to one whose craving for coherence is sporadic but only to one who consistently acts on behalf of a coherent conception of the good. This is an *objective* truth. It is simply a fact about value that desire for coherence generates no value for a life that does not already display coherence.

Desire for coherence is a second-order desire. It is the commitment not to coherence as such but to a pattern of activity framed around a particular conception of the good. To have such a conception motivating one's subsidiary valuations and activities is to be a project pursuer. Thus, the impersonal value attaching to the creation of a coherent life just is the value of being a project pursuer, while finding one's good in *this* particular project rather than *that* one is to seek personal value. There is, then, a reciprocity between the impersonal value of being a project pursuer and the personal value carried by particular projects. The value to me of *this* project is consequent upon my commitment to it and not to some other end, but the personal value that accrues to me as I pursue the project that is *mine* presupposes the impersonal value of project pursuit.

If project pursuit as such possesses value that is not conditional on but rather conditions commitment, then beings constituted such that they can undertake projects also are impersonally valuable. I cannot rationally regard my pursuit of projects as good in itself unless I concomitantly regard myself as a being that has worth. Neither, then, can I deny that other project pursuers are valuable. They are exactly like me in the relevant respect: being a project pursuer. For any given person, or even for the whole lot of them, I may have no special affection or regard; I may care not a jot whether their efforts succeed or fail. If so, their existence and their pursuit of value does not constitute personal value for me. However, lack of concern for that which extends beyond the borders of my narrow ego is irrelevant to the question of whether impersonal value resides there. There is project pursuit in the world, whether I care about it or not, and there are project pursuers. Those are facts not of my making, and the value those facts embody is not conferred by me either.

The point is often made that pursuit of one's own ends in total disregard for the interests of others is, on narrow prudential grounds, irrational: the noncooperative outcome of a Prisoner's Dilemma is bad for all participants. What the preceding discussion suggests, though, is that there is deeper reason to count self-absorbed egoism as irrational. The egoist fails to recognize the genuine value that is instantiated in other persons. In not valuing them and their pursuit of projects he makes the error of assigning zero value to that which is truly valuable. We call a man irrational if he neglects to value instrumental means necessary to the attainment of his own ends. They *ought* to be desired because they have (instrumental) value. In just the same sense, one *ought* to value other project pursuers because they too have value. Their value is intrinsic rather than instrumental, but not to respond appropriately to the value that is in other persons is as much a failure of rationality as is inappropriate response to means necessary for the achievement of one's ends. I suspect this is to restate in somewhat different language Kant's dictum that one is always to treat rational beings as ends in themselves. Rational beings/project pursuers have value in themselves, impersonal value, so to regard them merely as means to one's own ends is, irrationally, to act toward them as if their only value was personal value conferred (or denied) through one's own volition.

A being that has value in itself may not be treated as if it were a mere thing, an item that gets whatever value it has by serving as an instrument. It is not optional whether one responds to project pursuers as valuable beings; one *must* do so. However, it is not rationally incumbent on one to value equally all beings that in themselves occupy the same value plateau. It is flatly impossible to act on behalf of all value in the world, let alone to do so with equal intensity and regard for each valuable item. Whether I choose to devote myself to the value in E or in E* is up to me; by making that choice I create personal value where previously there had been only impersonal value. Still, one is not at liberty entirely to disregard the value that is in each project pursuer. At the very least one must respect the interest each has in living as a project pursuer, and that entails forbearance from interference. And because one is oneself a project pursuer with objective value, one may legitimately demand noninterference from all others. In this way we swing back through the arguments of Chapters 2 and 4, but this time explicitly in quest of impersonal value. Some comfort is to be taken in the fact that the earlier discussion, motivated exclusively by a recognition of personal value, is neatly congruent with the present one.

Respect for rights is the minimally acceptable response to value instantiated in project pursuers. However, one who does no more on behalf of others than grudgingly to accord them the moral space that is their due closes off to himself a major avenue along which value can be secured. Self-absorption within the bounds of rights is permissible but unwise. If A cares not only for A's own narrowly defined self-interest but also for the welfare of B, then A accrues value insofar as A's ends are advanced, but also as B prospers. The wider one tosses one's valuational net over the concerns of other project pursuers, the greater the opportunity for securing value through their efforts. The egoist is not, as he might care to think of himself, the shrewd and coolly rational maximizer of value for himself. Rather, he is someone who has confined himself to plowing a narrow furrow whose yield is necessarily scant. To want nothing more than a valuable life for oneself will almost surely prove self-defeating, while to want value for others will, as a side effect, generate value for oneself.

It was noted in the previous chapter that opportunities for securing value are entirely cut off by death for one who is totally self-absorbed. Concern for others renders possible some amelioration of the evil that is death. Because they survive, and because their interests are also one's own, death does not totally extinguish all that is of value to oneself. To devote oneself to goods that outlast the self is a rational response to the fact of one's own mortality. The valuational solipsist in effect refuses to acknowledge the inevitability of his own death. He may ruefully accept as a theoretical proposition that he will die, but he does not frame his projects in a way that responds to this intellective awareness. For all that his activities reveal, he might be acting to secure value for a self that is immortal. Such an individual is, in an extended sense of the term, imprudent. A prudent man, we might say, takes account of prospects for securing value at every stage of his life. Because value and disvalue can accrue to an individual after he is dead, this understanding of prudence does not go far enough. An appropriately modified account recognizes also a prudential interest in value that posthumously accrues to oneself. A person who cares only for himself can have no surviving interests and therefore has no opportunity to secure posthumous value. There is perhaps some irony here. Prudence typically figures in contemporary moral philosophy as just the knack of looking out for Number One, but a person who is maximally prudent in that straitened sense conspicuously falls short of prudence in the broader sense.

If A is devoted to B and B's interests, then A secures value as B does. But among B's concerns may be the prosperity of C. In that case, even if A takes absolutely no interest as such in the affairs of C, C's success redounds directly to the benefit of B and thus indirectly to the benefit of A. Such valuational chains can be indefinitely extended, and the further they reach, the greater the expanse of realizable value open to one so linked to others. That should not be interpreted as holding that the good of C is as valuable to A as is the good of B. C's welfare is, presumably, but one of several components of value-for-B, as is B's welfare a fractional component of value-for-A. The multiplicative product markedly diminishes each further step along the chain; eventually it is negligible. Still, to enroll oneself in the concerns of others is to be a partial beneficiary of the other-regarding ties that they forge. One does better, all else equal, to value persons who in turn value others than to value persons whose concerns are self-directed. Altruism is a more rational policy than egoism, and altruism toward the altruistic is more rational still.[6]

Many projects that present a surface appearance of taking no notice of the interests of others are intelligible only if understood as responsive to the value that is in and generated by persons. Consider, for example, the artist consumed by the urge to create. What he cares about is the creation of beauty and that alone. Artists are notorious for being curtly, even savagely, dismissive of ordinary social niceties. The painting or symphony or novel comes first, family and friends a distant second. The artist gives the appearance of total self-absorption in his own ends. But if the end is to create that which is beautiful, it will also be to create that which will be perceived as beautiful by those competent to evaluate it. A painting is meant to be viewed, a symphony to be heard, a novel to be read—and not by the artist alone. Works of art are vehicles of communication, and communication is possible only within a comprehending community. Art for the artist alone is as problematic as a private language. For a collocation of pigments to be art there must be publicly accessible standards of interpretation that constitute it as such, just as public rules of syntax and semantics are necessary to constitute the emission of a sequence of sounds as the utterance of a sentence. An artist can selfishly withhold his masterwork from others and a speaker can confine himself to soliloquies, but even so they trade on practices that essentially refer to the capacity of others to scrutinize meanings. And, of course, it is rarely the case that an artist will be satisfied perpetually to sequester his creations. The artist who neglects to provide basic courtesies to others nonetheless *hurls* at them his personal vision of the beautiful, He *demands* their wonder and appreciation for what he has wrought. Their acts of valuing the work of art constitute value for the artist. Art that can be valued only by the artist and not by others is a conceptual impossibility; art that in fact is valued only by the artist is a failure.

The scientist who pursues truth, the warrior who lives for honor: they too are to be understood as devoted to ends that would be unintelligible but for the existence of public standards for the recognition and valuation of, respectively, scientific truth and heroic action. The result can be generalized: projects that point out to the world as the arena in which value is to be achieved are projects that aim at creating value that can be valued by beings that are themselves valuable. By way of contrast, a life of involuted fascination with one's own conscious states is solipsistically stunted.

While artists and conquerors may elect to imprint value on the world exclusively through the creation of artifacts and institutions, most individuals will see their clearest path to value as traversing intimate personal relationships. One such relationship, discussed at length in Chapter 7, is that of parent to child. Only a very select few can paint like Leonardo or conquer like Alexander, but intimate association is wonderfully democratic, open to ordinary men and women of all times and places. Because that is so, lives of meaning and value are not the exclusive preserve of aristocrats. To shake the world may be splendid, but to move and be moved by the few people who mean most to one is not a negligible thing either.

Intimate association is always highly *specific*. Love is for the beloved, not for the admirable qualities he or she manifests, and certainly not for whoever happens to possess those qualities in equal or greater degree. Affection for one's native land, for its days of national celebration, its classic foods, landscapes, and the cadences of its language are not reducible to generalized recognition of the utility of ground on which to set one's feet, holidays from work, nutrition, pretty views, and linguistic competence. Familiarity with the subtle nuances that individuate particular persons, places, and ways of life render them candidates for one's sharply focused affections. Such familiarity, though, is not itself chosen by an Autonomous Ego standing above all particularities and weighing each with Olympian detachment. It is rather something one is, in the first instance, born to, and something that ineluctably grows out of the fabric of a life rooted in concrete circumstances. It is, for most individuals, the seedbed of their projects.

No one chooses to be the son or daughter of *this* man and *this* woman, to be formed by the institutions of *this* society, or to bear *this* child. And who one's friends and lovers are is less chosen than discovered: "I *do* love him/her!" Nonetheless, these unchosen relationships are perceived as establishing strong and enduring claims to one's efforts. Individuals find themselves in social situations not of their creation and have reason to value what is presented to them as a given, not just because it is valuable—the world is full of items comparably valuable in themselves—but because it is *theirs*. Devotion to kin and country simply because they are one's own is not chauvinism, is indeed the contrary of chauvinism. The chauvinist insists that his family or his nation is best and that is why he prizes it, indeed why *everyone* should prize it. A nonchauvinistic person's sensibilities are attuned to that with which he is familiar, but he has no need to justify his preferences on alleged grounds of impersonal, universal validity. He prizes the particular and recognizes that others have equivalent reason to find personal value in traditions and relationships which happen to be their own.

There is perhaps no profession the practice of which is more daunting than being an Autonomous Ego, being required to survey the entire domain of impersonal value and to select, without any assistance from focused attachment or a reservoir of familiarity, the endeavors most worthy of one's efforts. For an ordinary man or woman, for even an extraordinary one, the prospect would be paralyzing. When philosophers created the myth of the Autonomous Ego, they borrowed heavily from theology. God is the being who, in keeping with law given to himself by himself, chose to instantiate the actual world out of the infinity of possibilities for creation of value open to him. And a job worthy of a deity it is too! To foist such a model on human beings, though, as the essence of what moral choice is for them can only be accounted an egregious displacement of reality by theory.[7] Persons do not err, do not disown their status as beings with a will, dignity, and value in themselves if they decline to assume the perquisites of God. For beings with a finite purview, nothing can be more appropriate than to attach themselves to the value with which they are familiar.

That is not to denigrate freedom but to recognize the existence of external bounds on its range of application. Within the ambit of one's experience one is faced with incompatible alternatives for realizing value, and one must choose among them without the comforting assurance that possession of a complete ranking of all value would provide. The young man confronted with the choice between the Resistance and his mother sees both as holding out value for him. The woman is his mother and the country subjugated by evil forces is his country. Which course to take is up to him, and in choosing he exercises his freedom. He would be acting with no greater freedom if, instead of taking the alternatives before him as two, he regarded himself as obliged to give proper weight to the value of everyone's mother and every nation's fight for freedom. *Pace* the proponents of autonomy, no one ever has made or could make that sort of free choice.

I have once again given vent to my considerable distrust of philosophical paeans to autonomy, not so much because I believe autonomy to be a bad thing—I believe it to be an *impossible* thing—but because the advocacy of autonomy is typically accompanied by contempt for the actual. If an autonomous being is, like God, to be unconstrained in his choice by anything other than what he takes to be the good-in-itself, then claims rooted in the here and now are at best irrelevancies, at worst pernicious barriers to full realization of the good. It will always be the case that current realities fall short of what would be chosen by someone untrammeled by particular attachments. The institutions of one's polity may be reasonably just, of ancient pedigree, and superior to most of what is visible in the rest of the world, but attachment to those institutions will be reviled as standing in the way of the *truly just society* that might be erected on their ruins. Families, clubs, labor unions, churches, and sodalities provide value to individual lives, but each is easily seen as falling short of ideal human sociality. Not all husbands and wives respect each other's individuality, some children receive much love and others none, leaders and followers are separated by great disparity in power, and so on. Because better can be envisioned, it will seem that there is reason to demolish the old so as to build the new. Of course, not all who fervently preach the doctrine of autonomous choice for individuals and whole societies are madmen willing to destroy present value on the bare chance that better may emerge. There is, I imagine, such a creature as the prudent radical, though I *don't* imagine that there are nearly as many of these as there are madmen. However, while the prospect of failure may be allowed by the proponent of autonomy to count as reason for sticking with the familiar, the *fact of familiarity itself* counts for naught. That *these* are the particular institutions, practices, observances, and customs that we have inherited is not any reason in itself for continuing with them. For to allow what are merely matters of contingent happenstance to constrain one's choice is to forfeit autonomy.

When contempt for the actual is given rein on the macro level of politics, the result is usually massive dislocation, tyranny of the newly empowered elite, and widespread human misery. Effects at the micro level of human relationships are, if less extravagently displayed, no less insidious. To be detached from the familiar is, for many persons, to be thrust into anomie. When the Red Guards pour through, uprooting the landmarks by which persons take their bearings and chart their projects, or when architects of the welfare state impose new patterns on families and neighborhoods at the expense of traditional ways judged by the intelligentsia to be inadequate, opportunities to develop lives of value suffer. The doctrine of autonomy is false to human experience because it simultaneously extols self-direction while systematically uprooting the homey markers that indicate to agents where the value that is accessible to them lies.

Projects need not be created *de novo* to have value. No autonomy that is worth having is forfeited by accepting the given as having legitimate claims on one's efforts. One who is born to a particular family, nation, and religion is not thereby burdened with an anchor restricting his domain of choice but rather is the beneficiary of an inheritance of a manageable number of prospects for fashioning a worthwhile life. Of course, one may have the bad luck to find oneself in a thoroughly corrupt milieu such that no value is to be found close at hand and only escape promises relief. Or one may find oneself unable to be moved by value in the familiar. That truly *is* bad luck, though, not a paradigm of human freedom.

Impersonal Value and Liberal Neutrality

Liberalism recognizes each individual as sovereign with respect to his own ends. One way of expressing this is to say that a liberal regime is *neutral* among the ends to which individuals may commit themselves. Liberal theory is therefore very much at home with a conception of personal value, less so with impersonal value. If there is a realm of value antecedent to choice, then not all ends are created equal. Some simply are better and some are worse. If the world is not neutral among ends, it may seem self-willed ignorance on the part of a regime to exhibit indifference concerning how its citizenry attunes itself.

Of course, no political order can vest in private individuals complete discretion to seek value wherever they choose. There will always be those for whom nothing is more charming than bashing heads, and neutrality toward *that* kind of end would be ludicrous. It is tacitly assumed that liberal neutrality ends where violation of rights begins, and that a hands-off policy is appropriate only toward rightful actions. But once it is admitted that not everything is permitted, why should the line be drawn at rights violations? Why should it not be the business of the state to promote what is *right* rather than merely respect for *rights?*

Several responses suggest themselves. Any political entity possessing power sufficient to impel a citizenry along the path to virtue will also be strong enough to impose on it evils. Private individuals are far more limited in the harms that they can bring about than are public officials. Great concentration of power corrupts, and so power should be spread widely. The state simply cannot know enough about individuals' utility functions and about particular circumstances to make a go of central direction. Individuals will find it demeaning to be instructed in where their good lies and will rebel against even well-intentioned legal moralism. No satisfactory answer has yet been provided to the question: Who will guard the Guardians?

These responses are clichés of liberalism—but no less trustworthy for that. I think that they provide perfectly good support for traditional liberal advocacy of limited government. They do not, however, strike deeply enough. What are pointed to are *technical* problems that beset the politically directed pursuit of virtue. Technical problems admit of solution by technical means. Even if such means have not yet been perfected, even if there is reason to believe they never will be perfected, that does not impugn the value of the end. Objecting on grounds of practicality to direction by Philosopher Kings tacitly admits that such a state would be the best of regimes if only it were attainable and stable, and thus that liberal individualism is no more than a second-best solution to the problem of civility.

To defend liberal neutrality by arguing that the state is likely to do a poorer job of advancing objective value than will individuals acting in their private capacity can enjoy no more than limited success. In contrast, agnosticism concerning the existence of value over and above the preferences of individuals strikes boldly against political and legal moralism. If there is no value other than personal value, or if the only value of which we can have knowledge is value attaching to the satisfaction of individuals' preferences, then there is nothing more for governments to do than to establish and enforce fair procedural rules affording individuals the opportunity to act on the preferences they have. Persons cannot successfully be nudged toward a good that they have not yet learned to desire because there is no such good. The regime of Philosopher Kings is sheer bluff because there are no Philosopher Kings, and if there were, they would have no Form of the Good to guide them. All they have, all any of us has, are personal preferences.

Agnosticism concerning the existence of impersonal value has been a familiar strain within liberal theory since its first noteworthy exposition by Hobbes. Such agnosticism, though, is double-edged. While safeguarding one flank of liberalism it leaves another open. If all value reduces to preference, then there can be no reason at bottom to prefer one thing to another. Deliberation and reflection concerning the ends to which one ought to address oneself become charades. Individuals are construed as peculiar engines for emitting desires, and their rationality is confined to recognizing what is desired and then getting it. Nothing, however, would then undergird the whole desire emission–desire satisfaction process. No meaningful content could even be found in the proposition that satisfying desires is better than not satisfying desires. For if the good for a person just is, definitionally, his getting whatever he happens to desire, then to assert that satisfaction of desires is good (and dissatisfaction of desires is bad) is logically equivalent to saying that getting what one desires is getting what one desires (and not getting what one desires is not getting what one desires). Arid tautologies can do no justificatory work.

If there is no value antecedent to desire, then desire for X is desire for the valueless, and satisfaction for the desire for X is valueless satisfaction. Liberal rights may leave people at liberty to pursue that which they desire, but the whole panoply of desire, rights, and project pursuit becomes empty. Agnosticism toward impersonal value defends liberalism only at the cost of making the conception of practical activity that guides liberalism appear hopelessly shallow. The victory is Pyrrhic. That is why I have attempted to argue that there is impersonal value, not least in project pursuers themselves, that impersonal value is knowable, and that valuing what is in itself valuable engenders personal value for the one who values it. Satisfaction of desire is accounted as good, not because 'good' means getting what one desires, but because the experience of satisfaction is itself impersonally valuable *and* because the object desired is (not always, but sometimes) good in itself. This nonagnostic attitude toward impersonal value avoids shallowness—but is it compatible with liberalism?

Liberal political theory need not and should not fasten itself to a doctrine of neutrality among ends except in one restricted domain: that of state activity. Unlike individuals acting in their private capacity, the state may not commend one rights-respecting mode of life above others.[8] It is only the state that is denied this prerogative. Surely individuals are not illiberal if they make such judgments with regard to their own ends. To have a project is to be very much *partial* concerning ends. One who exhibits neutrality between his own prized project and the strange and ugly designs of someone else is not liberal but a psychopath—or perhaps a utilitarian. Nor does liberalism restrict private individuals from issuing judgments concerning the value of other person's ends. One may shout from the rooftops, hold revival meetings, publish broadsides, advise, remonstrate, and cajole in order to spread the gospel of the superiority of one mode of life and the baseness of another. One may even do so to the point of boorishness, discourtesy, and fanaticism, provided only that rights are not violated in the process.

The state is different. Its possession of title to exercise coercive powers is not justified on grounds of any special ability to discern value but because enforcement of rights is necessary if individuals are to be at liberty to engage in their own pursuit of value. Coercion that goes beyond enforcement of rights goes too far. The function of the state is to protect the rights of agents, not to act as an agent in its own right. Neutrality among the various ends of citizens is not to to be interpreted as the state's assigning equal value to each—how could a presumption of equal value possibly be justified?—but rather as recognition that the state is simply not the sort of entity that is capable of issuing valuations. The state can be depicted as the umpire enforcing the rules of the (meta)game, but not as a player in the game and not even as an arbitrator empowered to settle questions of who should get what and why. The creation of political authority is an agreement to disagree—civilly.

This is recognizable as a picture of the (classically) liberal state. But why that picture rather than some other? It is question-begging to be told that liberalism restricts coercive state activity to the enforcement of rights, and that because the state may do no more than enforce rights it has no title to promote the Truly Good.

If the previous chapters have not provided some answer to that question, what is said in these final pages can hardly do so either. Individuals have reason to pursue what is valuable but additionally have reason to pursue what is *personally* valued. Even if the state were an institution well designed to chart the paths of virtue and worth—and it is not—it cannot announce to individuals what they are to find personally fulfilling. If someone is committed to a good, or even mistakenly believes that what he prizes above all else is valuable, then he does not have reason to abdicate his deepest concerns for others offered in their place. External judges may be in a position to inform A concerning what is valuable but not about what constitutes value-for-A.

Value that one is incapable of valuing or that one is incapable of valuing deeply is not potentially a directive end for oneself. If E* is, by some objective standard, an end of luminous worth and E only a middling valuable end, one who finds himself attracted to E but not E* will do better, in the sense of accruing more value, if he acts on behalf of E. The valuable becomes one's own only to the extent that it is valued: that is a somewhat pretentious way of rephrasing the old adage that no one can be compelled against his will to act virtuously. If one is *made* to advance E* when it is really E that one wants, one's efforts on behalf of E* are not directed by the value that is in E* but instead by the whip or by its civilized equivalent, tax preferences.

To get what one wants is good; to get what one wants when what one wants is good is better; to get what one wants when what one wants is good and one wants it *because* it is good is better still. An external agency might be able to guarantee that one gets what one wants; it might be able to guarantee that one gets what is good; but it cannot guarantee that what one wants is also good, and it cannot make one want what is good *because* it is good. There are some things that persons must do for themselves, and do freely, if they are to be worth doing. This is not a new and radical proposition but one of the oldest verities of moral philosophy. It finds its fullest and most consistent expression in the theory of liberalism.

Epilogue

It is not only contemporary moral philosophy that finds itself more comfortable with discussion of the right than with discussion of value. I too am more comfortable in the former province. This chapter is more experimental and more tentatively offered than the others. (Need I *announce* that fact?) I do not, however, regard it as peripheral to the overall thrust of this essay. The theory of basic rights is but one component of the theory of right, which, in turn, rests on axiology. And that hierarchy collapses under its own weight unless there is a foundation of objective value in the world. If the presentation here has been ungainly, that does not indicate that it is not worth doing but that it should be done better.

Notes

CHAPTER 1

1. The status of fetuses as rights claimants is investigated in Chapter 8.

2. *Anarchy, State, and Utopia* (New York: Basic Books, 1974), pp. 28–35.

3. "Dispensing with Moral Rights," *Political Theory* 6 (February 1978), p. 67.

4. *Reason and Morality* (Chicago: University of Chicago Press, 1978).

5. *Taking Rights Seriously* (Cambridge, Mass.: Harvard University Press, 1977).

6. Cambridge, Mass.: Harvard University Press, 1971.

7. Two helpful extended bibliographical treatments of recent literature on the theory of rights are Rex Martin and James W. Nickel, "A Bibliography on the Nature and Foundations of Rights, 1947–1977," *Political Theory* 6 (1978), pp. 395–413; and Tibor Machan, "Some Recent Work in Human Rights Theory," *American Philosophical Quarterly* 17 (1980), pp. 103–115.

8. As pointedly noted by Thomas Nagel, "Libertarianism Without Foundations," *Yale Law Journal* 85 (1975), pp. 136–149; reprinted in Jeffrey Paul, ed., *Reading Nozick* (Totowa, N.J.: Rowman & Littlefield, 1981), pp. 191–205.

9. "The Nature and Value of Rights," *Journal of Value Inquiry* 4 (1970), p. 252.

10. The thesis that rights claims are replaceable without loss has a long history. Has it been dispensed with too summarily here? Perhaps. If rights discourse is inherently disorderly and incapable of being set on adequate theoretical foundations, then we ought to steel our resolve and put the wounded beast out of its misery. I reject that diagnosis. The theory of basic rights is complex and problematic—but no more so than the remainder of moral theory. It can be put in good order, and this essay is intended as a contribution to that end. So it is the book as a whole which stands as my *extended* argument against the replaceability thesis.

CHAPTER 2

1. *A Theory of Justice* (Cambridge, Mass.: Harvard University Press, 1971), pp. 90–95.

2. I want temporarily to sidestep the fine semantic point of whether it is contradictory to speak of "rights" that may permissibly be violated in uncommon circumstances. If the term 'right' is taken to include inviolability as a part of its definition, then it will be necessary to coin another term—*'prima facie* right', 'quasi-right'— for the less-than-categorical protections of individualism here being contemplated. Since we are still in the preliminary stages of developing an account of basic rights and have not yet endorsed a preferred version, this intrusion of imprecision need not yet concern us.

3. Robert Nozick, *Anarchy, State, and Utopia* (New York: Basic Books, 1974), p. 28.

4. J. J. C. Smart, "Extreme and Restricted Utilitarianism," *Philosophical Quarterly* 6 (1956), p. 349.

5. *Contemplation* of burial at sea may be pleasurable, but to value the future circumstance of one's eventual burial at sea is not the same as, nor reducible to, valuing present pleasurable musing on the prospect.

6. Economists routinely discount over time. That is, the present value of a future good is calculated as a decreasing exponential function of the time periods until that good will be attained and the rate of discount at which current consumption is preferred to future consumption. The grounds underlying time preference as applied in economics are not free from controversy. It is here being assumed that discounting can be entirely explained by the following three factors: (1) assets are productive when invested at a positive real rate of return; (2) greater uncertainty attaches to more distant outcomes, and so, to the extent that one is risk-averse, more certain near-term outcomes will be valued over less certain, because more distant, ones; (3) life spans are finite and not accurately predictable. Some economists, notably those within the Austrian tradition, argue for a time preference that extends beyond these three factors, a *pure* time preference. See Ludwig von Mises, *Human Action* (New Haven: Yale University Press, 1949), pp. 480–485. I find the arguments for pure time preference unconvincing and accordingly adopt an account of rational prudence that rejects valuing the earlier above the later simply because it is earlier. But because I am interested here in prudence only as it can shed some light on theories of moral rationality and not for its own sake, I shall not pursue the issue further.

7. An important nonutilitarian version is constructed by Thomas Nagel in *The Possibility of Altruism* (Oxford: The Clarendon Press, 1970).

8. R. M. Hare, *Moral Thinking* (Oxford: The Clarendon Press, 1981), p. 129.

9. Bernard Williams has consistently emphasized the significance of projects to the moral life. See "A Critique of Utilitarianism," in J. J. C. Smart and Bernard Williams, *Utilitarianism: For and Against* (London: Cambridge University Press, 1973), and the essays in his collection *Moral Luck* (London: Cambridge University Press, 1981). Although the conclusions I draw concerning the theory of basic rights diverge from Williams' own views, I am indebted to him for those discussions.

10. Those who advocate the Foil as being constitutive of morality will say that this entails the rejection of morality as such, but that harsh judgment need not be accepted.

An alternate picture of morality, one compatible with commitment to personal projects, will emerge in this and subsequent chapters.

11. I confess to more than a little disquiet concerning these arguments. The comfortable conclusions that they display often seem to have predetermined the reasoning that ineluctably yields them. It is sometimes tempting to believe that the great charm of utilitarianism is its remarkable flexibility in churning out whatever result happens to be wanted by the particular utilitarian theorist. Perhaps this is too cynical a view. At any rate, one who claims no deep insight into the nature and measurement of utility would be unwise to insist on its truth.

12. See Derek Parfit, "Personal Identity," *Philosophical Review* 80 (1971), pp. 3–27.

13. Compare to this Charles Fried's assertion "that men have [claims] on each other, by virtue of their common humanity, to help maintain and further *their enterprise* as free rational beings pursuing *their life plan*," in *Right and Wrong* (Cambridge, Mass.: Harvard University Press, 1978), p. 124 (emphasis added). Note especially the singular form of 'enterprise' and 'life plan'.

CHAPTER 3

1. A multivalent theory can always be transformed into a univalent theory by forming the disjunctive property being-F_1-or-F_2-or-F_3-or . . . -or-F_n, where each of the F_i are properties conferring moral status. So, in theory, any multivalent account of moral status can be expressed as a univalent theory. However, it is clear that whatever credibility such a univalent theory may possess is parasitic on the warrant of the separate factors adduced in the univalent theory from which it is derived. Also, a multivalent theory can ascribe to different kinds of beings different *degrees* of moral status in virtue of which of the F_i is possessed; these distinctions of degree are lost when the theory is collapsed into its univalent approximation.

2. A notable bullet-biter is Michael Tooley, "Abortion and Infanticide," *Philosophy & Public Affairs* 2 (1972), pp. 37–65.

3. This is a multivalent theory in which one attribute, project pursuit, is the *primary* vehicle by means of which status as a rights holder is achieved. The range of rights holders is broadened by relational properties that tie others to project pursuers. That is, F_1 is a primary property if both F_1 and F_2 confer the status of rights holder, but no being could possess F_2 were there not beings who possessed F_1. An alternate kind of multivalent theory of basic rights would take either of F_1 or F_2 to confer rights, yet without either property being primary. F_1's could exist in the absence of F_2's and F_2's without F_1's. That the world happens to contain both would be a contingent fact that no single unified moral theory could subsume and thereby explain. I see no reason to adopt this picture of irreducible pluralism. There is yet another possible structure that deserves mention: each of F_1, F_2, . . . F_n may presuppose and be presupposed by each of the others. Each would therefore be primary. Further variations on these three structures can be formulated.

4. *On Liberty*, Chapter III, "Of Individuality, as One of the Elements of Well-being,"

in J. M. Robson, ed., *Collected Works of John Stuart Mill*, Vol. XVIII (Toronto: University of Toronto Press, 1977), pp. 260–263.

5. It bears affinity to the conception of a purely autonomous God, acting without constraint, to create the framework of a world that he judges to be ''very good.'' For Kant, it is precisely autonomy that links the moral realm to the theological.

6. This consideration is prompted by G. E. M. Anscombe's essay ''Modern Moral Philosophy,'' *Philosophy* 33 (1958), pp. 1–18.

7. ''On being Conservative,'' in *Rationalism in Politics* (London: Methuen & Co., Ltd., 1962), p. 169. (Emphasis added.)

8. Saul/Paul seems to be an instance of distant stages forming a life with overarching unity. See Krister Stendahl, *Paul Among Jews and Gentiles and Other Essays*, (Philadelphia: Fortress Press, 1976), especially pp. 7–23.

9. See Derek Parfit, ''Later Selves and Moral Principles,'' in Alan Montefiore, ed., *Philosophy and Personal Relations* (London: Routledge and Kegan Paul, 1973), pp. 137–169. Parfit (correctly) notes that there is no necessity that motivational stability characterize a life and therefore concludes (incorrectly) that individualism is unsustainable because it rests on a deficient conception of the self.

10. ''Much is doubtless missing from the *Ethics* of Aristotle. He takes little or no account of the motive of obligation.'' D. J. Allan, *The Philosophy of Aristotle*, 2nd ed. (Oxford: Oxford University Press, 1970), p. 140. But see, in response to Allan, W. F. R. Hardie, *Aristotle's Ethical Theory*, 2nd ed. (Oxford: The Clarendon Press, 1980), p. 335.

11. ''Although some modes of conduct are universally praised, there are others which are regarded as virtues in some societies but not in others. And *the reason in every case for regarding something as a virtue* is that it is believed to be beneficial in the special social and economic conditions of the society concerned.'' P. H. Nowell-Smith, *Ethics* (Harmondsworth: Penguin Books, 1954), p. 250. (Emphasis added.)

12. Henry Veatch, in private correspondence, has challenged this reading. With some trepidation, I stick to it. But see Henry Veatch, *Rational Man* (Bloomington: Indiana University Press, 1962); *Aristotle: A Contemporary Appreciation* (Bloomington: Indiana University Press, 1974).

13. Though not *all* value; see Chapter 9.

14. See, for example, Leo Strauss, *Natural Right and History* (Chicago: University of Chicago Press, 1953), pp. 182–183.

15. In ''Are There any 'Rights' in Aristotle?'' (paper presented to a conference in honor of Father Joseph Owens on Aristotle and Islamic Philosophy, Baruch College, New York, October 29, 1984), Fred D. Miller, Jr., persuasively argues that the notion of rights does have a place within Aristotle's social philosophy. That place, though, appears to be well toward the periphery of Aristotle's concerns.

16. For the distinction between an *enterprise association* and *civil association*, see Michael Oakeshott, *On Human Conduct* (Oxford: The Clarendon Press, 1975), pp. 108–184.

17. See above, Chapter 2, n. 13.

18. See L. Lomasky, "A Refutation of Utilitarianism," *Journal of Value Inquiry* 17 (1983), pp. 259–279.

CHAPTER 4

1. *Nicomachean Ethics,* 1111b26.

2. See Harry Frankfurt, "Freedom of the Will and the Concept of a Person," *Journal of Philosophy* 68 (1971), pp. 5–20.

3. That is one reason why I think that a derivation of rights from the bare fact of agency such as offered by Alan Gewirth in *Reason and Morality* (Chicago: University of Chicago Press, 1978) must fail. It is, however, an instructive failure. If agency is too spare a foundation for the derivation of rights, agency that has more determinant content may get one further along. Project pursuit is here being offered as a candidate for the suitable flesh that ought cover and thereby vivify the bare bones of agency. See my "Gewirth's Generation of Rights," *Philosophical Quarterly* 31 (1981), pp. 248–253.

4. To be more precise, if adequate moral space for project pursuit could be guaranteed by some moral construction other than rights—perhaps through some duties of forbearance imposed on others that are not grounded in correlative rights—then a project pursuer is rationally committed to the disjunctive valuing of *either* rights for himself *or* that alternative protection. I know of no way to demonstrate that *only* the recognition of rights could serve to provide agents adequate moral space. There is, however, no obvious candidate for fulfilling that function not parasitic on a notion of basic rights. So the lack of a uniqueness proof at this and later points of the argument is theoretically unsatisfying but not of great practical concern.

5. Compare this to Mill's general happiness argument in *Utilitarianism.*

6. See Kenneth Minogue, *The Liberal Mind* (London: Methuen & Co., Ltd., 1963), especially pp. 103–112.

7. *The Possibility of Altruism* (Oxford: The Clarendon Press, 1970), especially Chapters XI and XII.

8. It may even be true that one could not understand what it is for *oneself* to have a reason to act unless one had a prior understanding of what it is for *someone or other* to have reason to act. This is a variation on the argument against the possibility of there being a private language. If the case against a private language is strong, it lends weight to the argument being advanced here.

9. One final consideration is that the position being advocated here wins out on grounds of simplicity over a theory that has to introduce some mediating instrumentality to explain how A's recognition that E_2 is B's and provides A any reason at all to advance E_2.

10. See R. D. Luce and Howard Raiffa, *Games and Decisions* (New York: John Wiley and Sons, 1957), Chapter V.

11. A maximax strategy will also lead to the adoption of Active Aggression, but that result is of less relevance. It does not seem plausible that, under the stipulated conditions, it can be rational to pursue a maximax strategy.

12. The considerations adduced in the previous paragraph—indeed, in the entire discussion of Figure 4.1—are eerily similar to those prominent in the current debate over
nuclear weapons policy. Themes of uncertainty, deterrence, cooperation, preemption, and
instability are prominent in both contexts. The similarities are discomfiting.

13. *Leviathan,* Chapters 13–18.

14. The modern economic discipline of public choice theory is an attempt to develop
systematic methods for appraising the likely costs and benefits of alternate forms of sovereignty. For a useful survey of the public choice literature, see Dennis Mueller, *Public
Choice* (New York: Cambridge University Press, 1979).

15. *A Treatise of Human Nature,* Book III, Part II, Section II, "Of the Origin of
Justice and Property."

16. For a more extended treatment of asymmetrical response, see James Buchanan and
Loren Lomasky, "The Matrix of Contractarian Justice," *Social Philosophy & Policy* 2
(1984), pp. 12–32.

17. *Anarchy, State, and Utopia* (New York: Basic Books, 1974), p. 18.

18. *Philosophical Explanations* (Cambridge, Mass.: Harvard University Press, 1981),
p. 4.

19. *Freedom and Reason* (Oxford: The Clarendon Press, 1962), pp. 157–185. It should
be noted that the construal of fanaticism offered in the text differs from Hare's own
depiction of the fanatic.

20. We can define an *extreme fanatic* as one who will not be willing to extend so much
as one unit of deference to others in return for any amount of deference shown to him,
no matter how large that amount may be.

CHAPTER 5

1. Classical liberalism typically does affirm the existence of a few select rights that
entail positive performances on the part of others. These include the right to be defended
against aggression upon one's person or property, the right to participate by voting and
other means in the making of political determinations, and the right to be afforded a fair
trial in the event that criminal charges are lodged. Although these may in toto impose
very limited demands of a positive sort, they are significant as an entering wedge for
those intent to expand the scope of liberalism. If even an austerely classical liberalism
will admit that positive rights have some legitimacy within the overall structure of basic
rights, then the argument between alternative varieties of liberalism becomes one of degree, not of basic principle. Or so it seems. To what extent the positive rights favored by
classical liberals differ in kind from the much more extensive listing of positive rights that
find favor with many contemporary liberals will be discussed in Chapter 6.

2. Richard Dawkins, *The Selfish Gene* (New York: Oxford University Press, 1976).

3. Thomas Nagel, "Brain Bisection and the Unity of Consciousness," in his *Mortal
Questions* (Cambridge: Cambridge University Press, 1979), pp. 147–164.

4. Most energetically explored by Derek Parfit. See his *Reasons and Persons* (Oxford:
Clarendon Press, 1984). This important book crossed my desk while I was preparing final

revisions of *Persons, Rights, and the Moral Community*. It engages many of the themes contained herein and does so with the author's characteristic verve and imagination. I have not been able to take up the challenges presented in *Reasons and Persons* but commend it to the reader as a significant work in the foundations of moral theory.

5. D. D. Raphael, "Human Rights, Old and New," in D. D. Raphael, ed., *Political Theory and the Rights of Man* (Bloomington: Indiana University Press, 1967), p. 64.

6. *A Theory of Justice* (Cambridge, Mass.: Harvard University Press, 1971), p. 440.

7. Ibid. (Emphasis added.)

8. Probably most Americans would deny that they are *morally required* to provide *any amount* of relief to foreign nationals. That claim is more arguable; perhaps intuitions are mixed. However, to the extent that even the minimal welfare right can be rendered persuasive, it would be by way of arguing that a *relatively trivial* sacrifice by Americans would provide *extremely great* benefits to the recipients.

9. It is interesting to consider why we are disinclined to offer a similarly favorable judgment concerning the daughter's consenting to remain indefinitely with her father. It could be maintained that she has a duty to herself to develop an independent life rather than remain in a condition of servility. However, duties to oneself are problematic for several reasons. Alternatively, it could be maintained that the sacrifice is not only extreme but disproportionate: that which the daughter forfeits is of greater value than the gain that accrues to the father. On a purely subjective accounting of value it is difficult to see why that need be so. It may truly be the case that the father's life would be shattered by the daughter leaving. Finally, and perhaps most satisfactorily, it could be held that the ideal for which the daughter sacrifices is itself inherently ignoble such that any degree of contribution to that end is misguided and undeserving of moral commendation. Better that the father be miserable than that he live happily as a tyrant. The plausibility of this last line suggests the insufficiency of a morality based on a purely subjectivistic account of value.

10. For those goods which no one party has the means to produce it will be the case that only a shared obligation could ensure their distribution. Most public goods will be of this sort.

11. With a few exceptions. Lester Thurow, an economist of impeccable welfare liberal credentials, endorses a governmental guaranteed employment program but favors abolishment of minimum wage laws. This represents a more consistent version of welfare liberalism than is usually espoused. See *The Zero-Sum Society* (New York: Basic Books, 1980), p. 145.

12. There are exceptions. If B lacks nothing other than A's noninterference for the attainment of G, then noninterference simply is to bring about the state of affairs: B having G. It can also be the case that noninterference is significantly more costly than provision. If B is a homicidal maniac, allowing B liberty to secure for himself means of subsistence will prove more costly to A than would the feeding and clothing of a suitably incarcerated B. Although many variations on this theme can be devised, they do not touch the central point.

13. By way of contrast, an *ethic of supererogation* need not display a similarly restricted scope. Individuals inclined to pursue a path of heroism or sainthood may be asked

to assume burdens that are almost too heavy for a man to bear. The point, though, is that they are free to *decline* to take this path. If living an extraordinarily good life is perceived to be too difficult a task, then one can choose instead to display no more than minimal goodness. The structure of rights is what provides the standard of minimal goodness.

14. Anthropological findings could be exhibited in support of this modest defense of a place for positive rights. One need not, however, range very far afield to find plausible instances of warranted claims involving more than noninterference. The moral status of *children* is of special interest in this connection. Even staunchly classical liberals will assign to children positive rights of provision, rights held both against private individuals—parents—and against the state. It will not do to condemn as inconsistent this departure from a strict standard of noninterference. Children *are* a special case of non–project pursuers who are engaged in the process of becoming full-fledged project pursuers, and it is not a defect of moral theory but a virtue that special cases be accorded special treatment. The place of children within the moral community is discussed below, in Chapter 7.

15. The formulation is, of course, John Rawls' first principle of justice; *A Theory of Justice*, p. 60.

16. It could be responded that the act does have some adverse *psychological* effect and can therefore be properly proscribed as an act of interference. This, though, will not save the definition but instead opens up even more troublesome problems of specifying what is to count as interference. Suppose that the Russian roulette episode occurred while you were asleep and therefore totally unaffected by it. Would it therefore be a morally innocent diversion of mine—provided, of course, that the chamber with the bullet remained unfired? The conclusion seems unpalatable. Moreover, once psychological effects are admitted, the range over which interference can occur becomes boundless. There is nothing that one can do which someone, somewhere, might find inimical to his equanimity should he find out about it. The realm of the self-regarding would dwindle to that which is done in total secrecy. That is not to say that we should exclude all psychological effects from the moral calculus, only that here too we must *decide* on some reasonable basis which acts that produce unwelcome psychological effects constitute impermissible intrusion and which do not. There is no simple "fact of the matter" that can serve as an unvarying standard.

17. John Locke, *Second Treatise of Government*, Peter Laslett, ed., 2nd ed. (Cambridge: Cambridge University Press, 1967), sect. 242.

18. Of course, philosophically acute natural law theorists avoid this fallacy of misplaced concreteness. For a useful survey and analysis, see Leo Strauss, *Natural Right and History* (Chicago: University of Chicago Press, 1953).

19. See, for example, essays by Robert Holmes, Jeffrey Paul, and Robert Paul Wolff, reprinted in Jeffrey Paul, ed. *Reading Nozick* (Totowa, N.J.: Rowman & Littlefield, 1981), as well as the discussion of compensation in Chapter 6.

20. Or nearly so. If there are some specifiable types of action that no one could reasonably regard as impermissible interference, then whatever one's liberty rights were, they would include the liberty to perform that action.

21. See especially the three volumes of his *Law, Legislation and Liberty* (Chicago: University of Chicago Press, 1973, 1976, 1979).

22. It should be noted that Hayek himself is a classical liberal who emphatically rejects anarchism.

23. There is also the epistemological question of how one knows when a social determination *has been made* as opposed to the social determination being imminent. Also, if persons are to feel free to do A up until the time consensus is achieved, it is problematic whether the spontaneous moral restructuring can occur. A communal understanding that A is perfectly permissible at $t_2, \ldots, t_{n-1}$ will itself be a factor obviating a shared understanding at t_n that A is impermissible.

C H A P T E R   6

1. See James Buchanan and Loren Lomasky, "The Matrix of Contractarian Justice," *Social Philosophy & Policy* 2 (1984), pp. 12–32.

2. It does bear affinity to the theory of ownership expressed by Sir Robert Filmer's *Patriarcha*, a work most notable for spurring the attack of John Locke's *First Treatise of Government*. Also, theological accounts that equate the king with God often take precisely the form of this example, ceding all (ultimate) rights of ownership to one being and nothing to anyone else. The moral, perhaps, is that one man's wildly farfetched construction is another man's sincere philosophical belief.

3. See the splendidly entertaining essay by Samuel C. Wheeler, "Natural Property Rights as Body Rights," *Nous* 14 (1980), pp. 171–194.

4. This argument bears affinity to, but should not be equated with, the different argument to be discussed below, that no one deserves his natural endowments and that, consequently, the fruits of those endowments are open to social redistribution.

5. *Anarchy, State, and Utopia* (New York: Basic Books, 1974), Chapter 7.

6. See Robert M. Adams, "Existence, Self-Interest, and the Problem of Evil," *Nous* 13 (1979), pp. 53–65; Derek Parfit, "On Doing the Best for our Children," in Michael Bayles, ed., *Ethics and Population*, (Cambridge, Mass.: Schenkman, 1976), pp. 100–115; Thomas Schwartz, "Obligations to Posterity," in Richard Sikora and Brian Barry, eds., *Obligations to Future Generations* (Philadelphia: Temple University Press, 1978), pp. 3–13; Gregory Kavka, "The Paradox of Future Individuals," *Philosophy & Public Affairs* 11 (1982), pp. 93–112.

7. Suppose though that my religious preference includes human sacrifice, and I have fixed a hungry eye on you. Won't it then be the case that full freedom of religious expression for me will cast a pall—not to mention pallbearers—on your similar freedom? In a sense that is so, but it entails only a minor reworking of the point. The liberty to follow one's religious beliefs is not unbounded but rather is limited by the moral space of others as constituted by the full system of rights that are in force. This qualification extends to all agents and is perfectly symmetric. Therefore, it does not differentially favor your interest in acting in accord with your religious convictions over my interest. We are called upon equally to respect the same standard of noninterference. Note that this qualification applies to all project pursuit and not merely that involving religious freedom: the

ability to live as a project pursuer is recognized only within a network of moral rights that must be respected however one chooses otherwise to live.

8. Strictly speaking, this holds true for private property. Public goods are, definitionally, those for which consumption is nonrival. The role of public goods within a just order of property rights is discussed below in this chapter.

9. Neither *property* nor *goods* should be equated with *natural resources*.

10. The distinction between the property conception of "Layman" and "Scientific Policymaker" is usefully examined by Bruce Ackerman, *Private Property and the Constitution* (New Haven: Yale University Press, 1977), especially Chapters 5 and 6.

11. See Lawrence C. Becker, *Property Rights* (London: Routledge & Kegan Paul, 1977), for the development of a normative theory of property which includes a critical survey of most historically important attempts to justify or refute claims to property.

12. A persuasive argument to the effect that a social implementation of the ideal of equality will be beset by insuperable conceptual and practical difficulties is offered by H. J. McCloskey, "Egalitarianism, Equality and Justice", *Australasian Journal of Philosophy* 44 (1966), pp. 50–69.

13. Equality can properly enter on the ground floor as a *personal* commitment held by an individual. If A assigns value to equality in holdings, then A is free to give charitably and to urge others to do likewise. The commitment to equality is thus on a par with all other projects persons are at liberty to embrace. As such, it merits no more—nor less— social support than any other project. In particular, the promulgation and enforcement of statutes designed to bring about equality in holdings is a clear violation of basic rights.

14. Nozick, *Anarchy, State, and Utopia*, p. 160.

15. Staunchly classical versions of liberalism have consistently endorsed the right to provision of a fair trial for persons held on criminal charges. In the light of the preceding discussion, this right to provision can be seen as thoroughly consistent with the general primacy of liberty rights. Criminal penalties temporarily or permanently take away from individuals the direction of their own lives. Consequently, an acceptable legal order will make available to accused persons means necessary to prevent the imposition of criminal penalties unless guilt has been thoroughly and fairly established.

16. The phrase is that of Judith Jarvis Thomson in "A Defense of Abortion," *Philosophy & Public Affairs* 1 (1971), p. 62.

17. Nozick, *Anarchy, State, and Utopia*, pp. 174–175.

18. Bruce Ackerman, *Social Justice in the Liberal State* (New Haven: Yale University Press, 1980), p. 31.

19. Variations of that model are relied on by Alan Gibbard, "Natural Property Rights," *Nous* 10 (1976), pp. 77–86; Samuel Scheffler, "Natural Rights, Equality and the Minimal State," *Canadian Journal of Philosophy* 6 (1976), pp. 59–76. See also the discussion of Rawls below.

20. This is, despite some hedging, Ackerman's answer. See *Social Justice in the Liberal State*, pp. 89–95.

21. Cambridge, Mass.: Harvard University Press, 1971. Parenthetical references in this section are to that book.

22. "The Matrix of Contractarian Justice," *Social Philosophy & Policy*.

23. See, for example, John Harsanyi, "Morality and the Theory of Rational Behavior," in Amartya Sen and Bernard Williams, ed., *Utilitarianism and Beyond* (Cambridge, England: Cambridge University Press, 1982), pp. 39–62.

24. See the insightful discussion of Michael Sandel, *Liberalism and the Limits of Justice* (Cambridge, England: Cambridge University Press, 1982), especially pp. 47–59.

25. See his criticism of utilitarianism, pp.22–27.

26. An excellent general treatment of this form of argument is Christopher S. Hill, "Desert and the Moral Arbitrariness of the Natural Lottery," *Philosophical Forum* XVI (1985), pp. 207–222.

27. It is, however, a conception that Charles Beitz persuasively advances in *Political Theory and International Relations* (Princeton: Princeton University Press, 1979). Beitz demonstrates, I believe, that a Rawlsian hypothetical contract restricted to compatriots is theoretically unstable. Either the relevant decision-making unit must be expanded to global dimensions or else the premise of collective control over all morally arbitrary assets must be abandoned. Beitz urges the former course; I have given reasons for selecting the other alternative.

28. See *Anarchy, State, and Utopia,* Chapters 4 and 5, pp. 54–119.

29. That is so on Nozick's own terms. In Chapter 5, I offered a different construal of rights in anarchy and the justification of a state that enforces law. That argument does not rest on dubious considerations of rightful compensation.

30. The classic work on this topic is James Buchanan and Gordon Tullock, *The Calculus of Consent* (Ann Arbor: University of Michigan Press, 1962).

31. See Tibor Machan, "Dissolving the Problem of Public Goods: Financing Government without Coercive Measures," in Tibor Machan, ed., *The Libertarian Reader* (Totowa, N.J.: Rowman & Littlefield, 1982), pp. 201–208.

32. *A Theory of Justice,* p. 112, emphasis added. Rawls expresses indebtedness for this principle to H. L. A. Hart, "Are There Any Natural Rights?" *The Philosophical Review* 64 (1955), pp. 175–191.

33. See Robert Nozick, *Anarchy, State, and Utopia,* pp. 90–95.

34. An extraordinarily insightful analysis of rational precommitment is Jon Elster, *Ulysses and the Sirens* (Cambridge, England: Cambridge University Press, 1979).

35. Analysis of the ways in which governments predictably will fail to allocate resources efficiently is the subject of the relatively new field of *public choice theory.* See especially the many important works of James M. Buchanan.

CHAPTER 7

1. Personal value will enter into relations with non–project pursuers, but only from one side: that of the project pursuers with whom they are in some way associated.

2. An ethic in which not only rights but also all obligations are internal can be constructed. One form of this would be the insistence that one cannot be obligated unless one has *assumed* the obligation. Even though not externally imposed, these are genuine obli-

gations because one is not free subsequently simply to *shed* them. Hobbes holds a view much like this.

3. See Chapter 3, pp. 39–41.

4. It is not difficult to cull examples from the philosophical bestiary. Logical positivism is moored in the unexceptionable proposition that meaningful *judgments about* the world cannot be disconnected from *experience of* the world. Hedonism begins with the recognition of a conceptual link between valuing a state of affairs and taking pleasure in its occurrence. The myopic movement has been completed when these are transmuted, respectively, into the verifiability principle or the universalized dictum that only pleasure is of value. An interesting way to survey the history of philosophy might be to identify for each doctrine its sensible core and then the exclusionary principles that transform it into cant.

5. One well-known assertion to that effect is Michael Tooley, "Abortion and Infanticide," *Philosophy & Public Affairs* 2 (1972), pp. 37–65. I respond to Tooley's argument in "Being a Person—Does It Matter?" *Philosophical Topics* 12 (1982), pp. 139–152.

6. Chapter 8 addresses itself to normative rights theory as applied to beings at the margin of membership in the moral community.

7. I use 'Kantian' as a generic term rather than as a reference specifically to Kant's own writings. The latter pose special difficulties of interpretation. Kant's bifurcation of reality into two disjoint realms, phenomenal and noumenal, and his grounding of morality in free noumenal agency render it undecidable how these cases are to be handled. At the level of phenomena, fetuses and comatose individuals display nothing that can be deemed rational agency. But neither do *we!* Kant seems to be confident that all readers of philosophy books possess a noumenal ego that confers on them moral personality. Do fetuses and the comatose also have a noumenal ago? How can we *know* whether they do? I gladly leave the resolution of these questions to others.

8. Assigning positive value to some event is not the same as being glad that the event occurred. The former concerns judgment, the latter emotion, and no necessary connection obtains between them. One may be perversely glad that a certain event took place even though one recognizes that it would have been better—for oneself, for the world—had the event not taken place. On the other hand, one's emotions may be unengaged by a circumstance that is recognized to be of value. That my parents did not strangle me in my bed is of considerable value to me, but is so routine a forbearance that I am unable to generate much affective energy in response. Very distant events also typically leave one unmoved. Is there anyone, anywhere, who can work himself into joyful appreciation of the fact that the Big Bang took place?

9. However, it may affect one's subsequent treatment as an erstwhile project pursuer. For example, those now infants may be able at some later date to act decisively concerning the interests of one who has entered senile decrepitude or whose interests take in dispositions to be made after his death. The melancholy circumstances that our careers as project pursuers are limited but that we generate interests directed at occurrences postdating our own effective agency is a morally significant datum. Some of its implications are discussed below, in Chapter 8.

10. Suppose, though, that Betty were not merely subject to shifting goals and desires

in response to new information, as we all are to a greater or lesser extent, but that her condition is pathological. New interests do not evolve from old ones but appear out of the blue and disappear just as abruptly; intensity of conviction at one moment might take the opposite direction in the next. We would then be faced with the *Indiscriminate Evaluator* to whom we were introduced in Chapter 2. Personal identity along the dimension of *praxis* would have broken down, and it is questionable whether, for such a being, there could be any interests other than those of the moment.

11. A particularly influential reshaper is quoted as saying, "For I am come to set a man at variance against his father, and the daughter against her mother and the daughter in law against her mother in law. . . . He that loveth father or mother more than me is not worthy of me: and he that loveth son or daughter more than me is not worthy of me." Matthew 10:35–37.

12. A partial exception is Bruce Ackerman's *Social Justice in the Liberal State* (New Haven: Yale University Press, 1980), in which there is an extended treatment of the rights of parents to have children and to favor them in the distribution of parental resources. But Ackerman's primary concern there is to buttress a case for strong egalitarianism in property distribution against the inegalitarian partiality of kin for kin. Familial ties are an obstacle to the achievement of the impersonal ideals of distributive justice that Ackerman endorses, and he bends considerable ingenuity to arguing against the permissibility of acting on partiality toward one's own children. Thus, I take Ackerman's treatment to be not an examination of the role of the family within a liberal order but rather as *opposition* to a liberalism that might fail to generate the pattern of property holding that he believes to be just.

13. Within a *theological* ethic, the justification of a doctrine of human rights can rest on the premises that (1) God creates all and only human beings with souls and (2) having a soul is an internal property that renders one a maximally significant moral being. Obviously, a secular ethic cannot ground itself on these premises. I see no hope at all for making a remotely convincing secularistic case that biological humanity is a necessary and sufficient internalistic condition for having rights.

14. *The Second Treatise of Government,* VI, "Of Paternal Power."

15. A seminal treatment of educational vouchers within a regime of privatized education is Milton Friedman, *Capitalism and Freedom,* Chapter VI, "The Role of Government in Education," (Chicago: University of Chicago Press, 1962), pp. 85–107. The issue of cash grants versus in-kind provision of welfare goods receives an interestingly different treatment in Lester Thurow, "Government Expenditures: Cash or In-Kind Aid?" *Philosophy & Public Affairs* 5 (1976), pp. 361–381.

16. I am grateful to James Buchanan, with whom I have profitably argued these lines. I should add that profit is, in this case, quite distinct from pesuasion.

17. The force of this dilemma was expressed to me in conversation by Jeremy Shearmur.

18. As was argued notably by Ayn Rand in *The Virtue of Selfishness,* (New York: New American Library, 1965), and elsewhere.

19. This theme is skillfully developed in John Elster's "Sour Grapes—Utilitarianism and the Genesis of Wants," in Amartya Sen and Bernard Williams, eds., *Utilitarianism*

and Beyond (Cambridge and New York: Cambridge University Press, 1982), pp. 219–238. See also Elster's *Ulysses and the Sirens* (Cambridge and New York: Cambridge University Press, 1979), where it is interwoven with related explorations of suboptimal rationality.

20. Note that this is significantly different from cases in which one acts on behalf of persons who exhibit weakness of will. The *akratic* is not simply counterposed to what he could have been, but to what he *was* and what he *will be*. In acting to keep the *akratic* from jeopardizing his own best-considered ends, we are appealing to (some of) the expressed intentions of the individual, and we take those values as negating the personal value for him of morally weak action. This is not to deny that the phenomenon of moral weakness poses many vexing problems. Again, see Elster's *Ulysses and the Sirens* for a rich analysis.

21. See John Plamenatz, *Consent, Freedom and Political Obligation* (Oxford: Oxford University Press, 1968), especially Chapters II and V.

22. A recent attempt of heroic proportions is Richard Brandt, *A Theory of the Good and the Right* (Oxford: Oxford University Press, 1979).

23. See Thomas Szasz, *The Myth of Mental Illness* (New York: Harper & Row, 1974).

CHAPTER 8

1. The last of these is from Judith Jarvis Thomson, "A Defense of Abortion," *Philosophy & Public Affairs* 1 (1971), pp. 47–66.

2. Metaphysics and epistemology reside somewhere between mathematics or logic, on the one hand, and moral philosophy, on the other, along the universality/particularity continuum. It can be expected that metaphysical and epistemological judgments will support a relatively wider range of counterfactual hypotheses, but it does not follow that the range is unlimited. For example, the question of what constitutes the identity of a person over time is often explored by imagining the fissioning and fusing of persons and asking what we would say about identity then. It is not altogether clear, though, that an acceptable account of the identity of persons *as they are* must be able to answer such questions, and it is yet more doubtful that any interesting consequences can be drawn for moral theory. But see Derek Parfit, "Personal Identity," *Philosophical Review* 80 (1971), pp. 3–27; "On 'The Importance of Self-Identity,' " *Journal of Philosophy* 68 (1972), pp. 683–690; "Later Selves and Moral Principles," in Alan Montefiore, ed., *Philosophy and Personal Relations* (London: Routledge and Kegan Paul, 1973).

3. This section is built on and somewhat modifies my "Being a Person: Does it Matter?" *Philosophical Topics* 12 (1982), pp. 139–152.

4. It is difficult to date the onset of new trends in a discipline with a 2500-year history. But a visible indicator of the new dispensation was the appearance in 1971 of the journal *Philosophy & Public Affairs*. It has subsequently been joined by a handful of other philosophy journals devoted to applied ethics. In the first issue of *Philosophy & Public Affairs*, two of its five essays addressed the abortion issue: Thomson's "A Defense of

Abortion'' and Roger Wertheimer, ''Understanding the Abortion Argument,'' pp. 67–95.

5. 410 U.S. 113, 93 S.Ct. 705 (1973).

6. As only a few pages back I issued strictures against reliance in moral philosophy on the use of thought experiments, readers will be forgiven if they take the previous paragraph to be a particularly blatant example of methodological inconsistency. Recall, though, that internalist theories profess to ground rights ascriptions in properties that do moral work across all possible worlds, or at least those recognizably close to the actual world. The preceding remarks are intended as an *ad hominem* counter to one variety of internalism.

7. See the discussion of reflective equilibrium in John Rawls' *A Theory of Justice*, (Cambridge, Mass.: Harvard University Press, 1971), especially pp. 48–51, on which I heavily rely.

8. See Michael Tooley, ''Abortion and Infanticide,'' *Philosophy & Public Affairs* 2 (1972), pp. 37–65.

9. It is not being claimed that *ontological* individuation is marked by birth. Rather, the claim is *epistemological;* recognizability of the individuating characteristics of particular human beings crosses the critical hump when they are born. It is the epistemic factor that is crucial for moral motivation.

10. See David Lyons, *Forms and Limits of Utilitarianism* (Oxford: The Clarendon Press, 1965).

11. For a more fully developed argument along these lines, see R. M. Hare, *Moral Thinking* (Oxford: The Clarendon Press, 1981), especially Chapter 3, ''The Archangel and the Prole.''

12. Similar considerations apply to those whose project pursuit is cut short by death. They are discussed in the next section.

13. One who gambles on his own future self-sufficiency and loses thereby imposes costs on others. It is unpleasant to be faced with the suffering of others and remains so even if they largely brought that suffering upon themselves. It is understandable, then, that individuals will seek to create institutions that shield them from the dilemma of either providing aid (at a cost) or being confronted with misery (also a cost). Social Security provision of old-age pensions and health care can be viewed as a means for avoiding this dilemma, and thus as not *purely* paternalistic in motivation. Is a mandatory social insurance program of this sort justifiable on the ground that it eliminates the incentive to free ride on the beneficent sentiments of others? The issue is too involved to be satisfactorily addressed here, but one comment is in order. It is one thing to require persons to divert current income to insurance protection, quite another for the state to erect a monopolistic insurance program mandatorily imposed on everyone. Considerations congruent with those advanced in the previous chapter concerning state provision of primary education apply. See also my ''Medical Progress and National Health Care,'' *Philosophy & Public Affairs* 10 (1981), pp. 65–88.

14. Obviously this will not hold for performances that specifically presume A's capacity to act as a project pursuer. For example, one can neither respect nor violate the liberty rights of A at time *t* if A is not able to act at *t*. However, the rightful exercise of a liberty

by A at $t-1$ to bring about some event at t logically *can* be violated by B's performance at t.

15. This will be true, strictly speaking, only if it is *being dead* that will advance the person's interests rather than *performing the act of causing* one's own death. If one lives for honor and honor alone but honor requires that one kill oneself rather than live in ignominy or shamefully die at the hand of another, then there may be much personal value in killing oneself but no value or even disvalue in the fact of ceasing to live.

16. See, for example, James Rachels, "Active and Passive Euthanasia," *New England Journal of Medicine* 292 (January 9, 1975), pp. 78–80.

17. See Thomas Nagel, "Death," in his *Mortal Questions* (Cambridge: Cambridge University Press, 1979), pp. 1–10.

18. *Nicomachean Ethics,* 1100a10–22, trans. by W. D. Ross.

19. A macro-level equivalent to the micro-level injury done through violation of a deathbed promise is the injury done by the state when it imposes confiscatory inheritance taxes. That is to adopt the policy of taking the dead to be nullities having no further claim on the living concerning the disposition of their rightfully acquired assets once they have taken their last breath. Confiscatory inheritance taxation runs roughshod over the deceased's interest in the ends his property will serve, substituting instead politically sanctioned ends to be advanced regardless of individual interest. It is an especially cruel injury because it deprives the dead of one of their last opportunities for securing the goods that they value. The dead can no longer offer loved ones their advice, their encouragement, sympathy in times of hardship, and joy when things go well; all they can do is pass on worldly goods to intended beneficiaries. To be robbed of that opportunity is to have one's ability to exercise agency sharply curtailed. If it is wrong while an individual lives to commandeer his goods as collective property subject to the collective will, it is equally wrong to do so after he has died.

20. The term is George Pitcher's in "The Misfortunes of the Dead," *American Philosophical Quarterly* 21 (1984), pp. 183–188.

21. *Harm to Others* (New York: Oxford University Press, 1984), p. 91.

22. The literature has become vast. Two representative animal rights tracts are Tom Regan, *All that Dwell Therein: Essays on Animal Rights and Environmental Ethics* (Berkeley: University of California Press, 1982); and Peter Singer, *Animal Liberation* (London: Jonathan Cape, 1976). See also Michael Tooley, "Abortion and Infanticide."

23. It may violate the rights of a person, though. If I torture your pet poodle, I wrong it and you as well: it as a sentient being for whom pain is an evil and you as a rights holder entitled to the full use and enjoyment of your property.

CHAPTER 9

1. That is not equivalent to asserting that the saint or hero sacrifices his or her own *good* for the good of others. That would not be admirable but crazy. Sacrifice for others is rational only if motivated by location of one's own good in the welfare of others. Otherwise it is masochistic abnegation.

2. Suppose, though, that someone able to bring about redirection of his cravings when such redirection promises increased satisfaction nonetheless quite deliberately and thoughtfully resists doing so. Jones, recently transplanted from Manhattan to Fiji, finds the kosher dill pickles he craves unavailable but refuses to do anything to eliminate those cravings. He turns down psychoanalysis, passes up opportunities to acquire instead a fondness for betel nuts, will not discard the Lower East Side Pickle Company catalogs he longingly leafs through each day. Should we say that Jones is acting irrationally? Yes— if Jones' recurrent desires for pickles are merely cravings. But if they instead express his conception of what the good life for him necessarily involves, then he does not act irrationally to conserve desires that he realizes in advance will bring him a train of dissatisfaction. Admittedly, it is hard to see how anyone could subscribe to that particular conception of the good—"The life without kosher dill pickles is not worth living!" is a slogan not apt to inspire—so charitable observers will tend to ascribe some deeper purpose: fidelity to his roots perhaps, or the conviction that one should not give in to circumstances. In any case, the point of the example is that an amalgamation of all desires to appetites is awkward.

3. "The Humanism of Existentialism" trans. by Bernard Frechtman (1947), in Jean-Paul Sartre, *Essays in Existentialism* (New York: Citadel Press, 1965), pp. 31–62.

4. *Ethics: Inventing Right and Wrong* (New York: Penguin Books, 1977), p. 38.

5. The parentheses are inserted to indicate that the source of satisfaction is, in the given case, irrelevant. Equivalent satisfaction, whatever the appetite that occasioned it, will hold out equivalent value.

6. The achievement of sociality presupposes the existence of networks of interlocking regard among persons who live in contiguity. Were such networks absent, a rights-respecting moral community would be impossible. But relations of affection and concern do more than undergird respect for rights; they make possible direct and indirect reception of value from the project pursuit of others. Living in a polity, then, is more than convenient; it is a prerequisite for realizing maximum value.

7. Kant, unlike latter-day champions of autonomy, at least had the good grace to house Autonomous Egos outside of the phenomenal world. They, like God, reside in a noumenal realm beyond space, time, and the categories of possible experience. In the absence of such distractions, autonomy is, I suppose, easier.

8. I must confess to some uneasiness concerning how this point should be put. It seems straightforward to classify as impermissible the state's coercive prohibition of an activity that, though not in violation of rights, is deemed to be immoral: for example, tossing pornographers into jail because what they publish is wicked. Only slightly less clean-cut are state impositions of differential treatment that fall short of outright prohibition: so-called sin taxes. Requiring pornographers to purchase a license for $10,000 before going into business or taxing bourbon and vodka drinkers many times more heavily than those whose tastes run to milk and Coca-Cola are examples. State activity that does not involve the imposition of harms on those pursuing disfavored activities is more difficult. Is it permissible for the president to proclaim the third Tuesday in April "Anti-Smut Day"? May the surgeon general (whose salary comes from coercively extracted taxes) take to the airways to issue dire warnings about the evils of tobacco? If even these err against neu-

trality, what of the award of public honors? If someone who has fought bravely against the nation's enemies is awarded the Congressional Medal of Honor, does that invidiously discriminate against one who has opted instead to sit safely in his study and write philosophy books? That would represent a *very* austere insistence on state neutrality. Is it permissible for the state to sanction marriage between a man and a woman but not between a man and a man or a woman and a woman? Suppose that a homosexual couple were at liberty to *do* whatever they wished with each other and to *contract* in whatever manner was agreeable to them—only that what they do and how they contract will not receive official recognition as constituting *being married*. Is nonconferral of this benefit an illegitimate *non*exercise of state powers? I find these and similar questions about the proper bounds of noncoercive state activity exceedingly puzzling.

Bibliography

Ackerman, Bruce, *Private Property and the Constitution* (New Haven: Yale University Press, 1977).
———. *Social Justice in the Liberal State* (New Haven: Yale University Press, 1980).
Adams, Robert M., "Existence, Self-Interest, and the Problem of Evil," *Nous* 13 (1979), 53–63.
Allan, D. J., *The Philosophy of Aristotle*, 2nd ed. (Oxford: Oxford University Press, 1970).
Anscombe, G. E. M., "Modern Moral Philosophy," *Philosophy* 33 (1959), 1–18.
Aristotle, *Nicomachean Ethics*.
Becker, Lawrence C., *Property Rights: Philosophic Foundations* (London: Routledge & Kegan Paul, 1977).
Beitz, Charles, *Political Theory and International Relations* (Princeton: Princeton University Press, 1979).
Brandt, Richard, *A Theory of the Good and the Right* (Oxford: Oxford University Press, 1979).
Buchanan, James, and Tullock, Gordon, *The Calculus of Consent* (Ann Arbor: University of Michigan Press, 1962).
Buchanan, James, and Lomasky, Loren, "The Matrix of Contractarian Justice," *Social Philosophy & Policy* 2 (1984), 12–32.
Dawkins, Richard, *The Selfish Gene* (New York: Oxford University Press, 1976).
Dworkin, Ronald, *Taking Rights Seriously* (Cambridge: Harvard University Press, 1977).
Elster, Jon, "Sour Grapes—Utilitarianism and the Genesis of Wants," in *Utilitarianism and Beyond*, eds. Amartya Sen and Bernard Williams (Cambridge: Cambridge University Press, 1982), 219–238.
———. *Ulysses and the Sirens* (Cambridge: Cambridge University Press, 1979).
Feinberg, Joel, "The Nature and Value of Rights," *Journal of Value Inquiry* 4 (1970), 243–257.
———. *Harm to Others* (New York: Oxford University Press, 1984).
Filmer, Robert, *Patriarcha*.

Frankfurt, Harry, "Freedom of the Will and the Concept of a Person," *Journal of Philosophy* 68 (1971), 5–20.

Fried, Charles, *Right and Wrong* (Cambridge: Harvard University Press, 1978).

Friedman, Milton, *Capitalism and Freedom* (Chicago: University of Chicago Press, 1962).

Gewirth, Alan, *Reason and Morality* (Chicago: University of Chicago Press, 1978).

Gibbard, Alan, "Natural Property Rights," *Nous* 10 (1976), 77–86.

Hardie, W. F. R., *Aristotle's Ethical Theory*, 2nd ed. (Oxford: The Clarendon Press, 1980).

Hare, R. M., *Freedom and Reason* (Oxford: The Clarendon Press, 1962).

————. *Moral Thinking* (Oxford: The Clarendon Press, 1981).

Harsanyi, John, "Morality and the Theory of Rational Behavior" in *Utilitarianism and Beyond*, eds. Amartya Sen and Bernard Williams (Cambridge: Cambridge University Press, 1982), 39–62.

Hart, H. L. A., "Are There Any Natural Rights?" *The Philosophical Review* 64 (1955), 175–191.

Hayek, F. A., *Law, Legislation and Liberty*, 3 vols. (Chicago: University of Chicago Press, 1973–1979).

Hill, Christopher S., "Desert and Moral Arbitrariness of the Natural Lottery," *Philosophical Forum* XVI (1985), 207–222.

Hobbes, Thomas, *Leviathan*.

Hume, David, *A Treatise of Human Nature*.

Kavka, Gregory, "The Paradox of Future Individuals," *Philosophy and Public Affairs* 11 (1982), 93–112.

Locke, John, *First Treatise of Government*.

————. *Second Treatise of Government*.

Lomasky, Loren E., "A Refutation of Utilitarianism," *Journal of Value Inquiry* 17 (1983), 259–279.

————. "Being A Person—Does It Matter?" *Philosophical Topics* 12 (1982), 139–152.

————. "Gewirth's Generation of Rights," *Philosophical Quarterly* 31 (1981), 248–253.

————. "Medical Progress and National Health Care," *Philosophy and Public Affairs* 10 (1981), 65–88.

Luce, R. D., and Raffia, Howard, *Games and Decisions* (New York: John Wiley and Sons, 1957).

Lyons, David, *Forms and Limits of Utilitarianism* (Oxford: The Clarendon Press, 1965).

Machan, Tibor, "Dissolving the Problem of Public Goods: Financing Government Without Coercive Measures" in *The Libertarian Reader*, ed. Tibor Machan (Totowa, N.J.: Rowman & Littlefield, 1982), 201–208.

————. "Some Recent Work in Human Rights Theory," *American Philosophical Quarterly* 17 (1980), 103–115.

Mackie, J. L., *Ethics: Inventing Right and Wrong* (New York: Penguin Books, 1977).

Martin, Rex, and Nickel, James W., "A Bibliography on the Nature and Foundations of Rights, 1947–1977, *Political Theory* 6 (Feb. 1978), 385–413.

McCloskey, H. J., "Egalitarianism, Equality and Justice," *Australasian Journal of Philosophy* 44 (1966), 50–69.

Mill, J. S., *On Liberty*.

Miller, Fred D., "Are There Any 'Rights' in Aristotle?" Conference in Honor of Father Joseph Owens on Aristotle and Islamic Philosophy, Baruch College, New York, October 29, 1984.

Minogue, Kenneth, *The Liberal Mind* (London: Methuen & Co., 1963).

Mises, Ludwig von, *Human Action* (New Haven: Yale University Press, 1949).

Mueller, Dennis, *Public Choice* (New York: Cambridge University Press, 1979).

Nagel, Thomas, "Brain Bisection and the Unity of Consciousness," in Thomas Nagel, *Mortal Questions* (Cambridge: Cambridge University Press, 1979), 147–164.

———. "Death," in Thomas Nagel, *Mortal Questions* (Cambridge: Cambridge University Press, 1979), 1–10.

———. "Libertarianism Without Foundations," *Yale Law Journal* 85 (1975), 136–149. Rpt. in *Reading Nozick*, ed. Jeffrey Paul (Totowa, N.J.: Rowman & Littlefield, 1981), 103–115.

———. *The Possibility of Altruism* (Oxford: The Clarendon Press, 1970).

Nowell-Smith, P. H., *Ethics* (Harmondsworth: Penguin Books, 1954).

Nozick, Robert, *Anarchy, State, and Utopia* (New York: Basic Books, 1974).

———. *Philosophical Explanations* (Cambridge: Harvard University Press, 1981).

Oakeshott, Michael, "On Being Conservative," in *Rationalism in Politics* (London: Methuen & Co., 1962).

———. *On Human Conduct* (Oxford: The Clarendon Press, 1975).

Parfit, Derek, "Later Selves and Moral Principals" in *Philosophy and Personal Relations*, ed. Alan Montefiore (London: Routledge and Kegan Paul, 1973), 137–169.

———. "On 'The Importance of Self-Identity,' " *Journal of Philosophy* 68 (1972), 683–690.

———. "On Doing the Best for our Children," in *Ethics and Population*, ed. Michael Bayles (Cambridge, Mass.: Schenkman, 1976), 100–115.

———. "Personal Identity, *Philosophical Review* 80 (1971), 3–27.

———. *Reasons and Persons* (Oxford: The Clarendon Press, 1984).

Paul, Jeffrey, ed., *Reading Nozick* (Totowa, N.J.: Rowman & Littlefield, 1981).

Pitcher, George, "The Misfortunes of the Dead," *American Philosophical Quarterly* 21 (1984), 183–188.

Plamenatz, John, *Consent, Freedom and Political Obligation* (Oxford: Oxford University Press, 1968).

Rachels, James, "Active and Passive Euthanasia," *New England Journal of Medicine* 292 (Jan. 9, 1975), 78–80.

Rand, Ayn, *The Virtue of Selfishness* (New York: New American Library, 1965).

Raphael, D. D., "Human Rights Old and New," in *Political Theory and the Rights of Man*, ed. D. D. Raphael (Bloomington: Indiana University Press, 1967).

Rawls, John, *A Theory of Justice* (Cambridge: Harvard University Press, 1971).

Regan, Tom, *All that Dwell Therein: Essays on Animal Rights and Environmental Ethics* (Berkeley: University of California Press, 1982).

Sandel, Michael, *Liberalism and the Limits of Justice* (Cambridge: Cambridge University Press, 1982).

Sartre, Jean-Paul, "The Humanism of Existentialism," in *Essays in Existentialism*, trans. Bernard Fretchman (New York: Citadel Press, 1965), 31–62.

Scheffler, Samuel, "Natural Rights, Equality and the Minimal State," *Canadian Journal of Philosophy* 6 (1976), 59–75.

Schwartz, Thomas, "Obligations to Posterity" in *Obligations to Future Generations*, eds. Richard Sikora and Brian Barry (Philadelphia: Temple University Press, 1978), 3–13.

Singer, Peter, *Animal Liberation* (London: Jonathan Cape, 1976).

Smart, J. J. C., "Extreme and Restricted Utilitarianism," *Philosophical Quarterly* 6 (1956).

Stendahl, Krister, *Paul among the Jews and Gentiles and Other Essays* (Philadelphia: Fortress Press, 1976).

Strauss, Leo, *Natural Right and History* (Chicago: University of Chicago Press, 1953).

Szasz, Thomas, *The Myth of Mental Illness* (New York: Harper and Row, 1974).

Thomson, Judith Jarvis, "A Defense of Abortion," *Philosophy and Public Affairs* 1 (1971), 47–66.

Thurow, Lester, "Government Expenditures: Cash or In-Kind Aid?" *Philosophy and Public Affairs* 5 (1976), 361–381.

———. *The Zero Sum Society* (New York: Basic Books, 1980).

Tooley, Michael, "Abortion and Infanticide," *Philosophy and Public Affairs* 2 (1972), 37–65.

Veatch, Henry, *Aristotle: A Contemporary Appreciation* (Bloomington: Indiana University Press, 1974).

———. *Rational Man* (Bloomington: Indiana University Press, 1962).

Wertheimer, Roger, "Understanding the Abortion Argument," *Philosophy and Public Affairs* 1 (1971), 67–95.

Wheeler, Samuel C., "Natural Property Rights as Body Rights," *Nous* 14 (1980), 171–194.

Williams, Bernard, "A Critique of Utilitarianism," in *Utilitarianism: For and Against*, eds. J. J. C. Smart and Bernard Williams (London: Cambridge University Press, 1973).

———. *Moral Luck* (London: Cambridge University Press, 1981).

Young, Robert, "Dispensing With Moral Rights," *Political Theory* 6 (Feb. 1978), 63–74.

Index

Printed in the United States
135353LV00002B/236/A

Made in the USA
Lexington, KY
10 January 2011